2

The Khyber Pass

The Khyber Pass

A History of Empire and Invasion

PADDY DOCHERTY

UNION SQUARE PRESS
An imprint of Sterling Publishing Co., Inc.

New York / London
www.sterlingpublishing.com

STERLING and the distinctive Sterling logo are
registered trademarks of Sterling Publishing Co., Inc.

Library of Congress Cataloging-in-Publication Data

Docherty, Paddy.
  The Khyber Pass : a history of empire and invasion / Paddy Docherty.
    p. cm.
  Originally published: London : Faber and Faber, 2007.
  Includes bibliographical references and index.
  ISBN-13: 978-1-4027-5696-2
  ISBN-10: 1-4027-5696-8
  1. Khyber Pass (Afghanistan and Pakistan)--History. 2. Docherty, Paddy--Travel--
Khyber Pass (Afghanistan and Pakistan) I. Title.
  DS374.K5D63 2008
  954.91'23--dc22

                                            2007040534

10 9 8 7 6 5 4 3 2 1

Published in 2008 by Sterling Publishing Co., Inc.
387 Park Avenue South, New York, NY 10016
© 2007 by Paddy Docherty
Maps © 2007 by Andras Bereznay
First published in 2007 in Great Britain by Faber and Faber Limited

Sterling ISBN-13: 978-1-4027-5696-2
         ISBN-10: 1-4027-5696-8

For information about custom editions, special sales, premium and
corporate purchases, please contact Sterling Special Sales
Department at 800-805-5489 or specialsales@sterlingpublishing.com.

This book is dedicated to my parents,
Margaret and Bob, with thanks

Contents

List of Illustrations

Acknowledgments

I would like to thank all the people in Pakistan and Afghanistan who welcomed me so warmly in the winter of 2003. Among these, I would especially like to thank Naveed Butt for the tea and biscuits at Lahore Junction and Iftikhar Hussain for sharing his excellent supper on the Khyber Mail. I am most grateful to Crispin Thorold and Bilal Sarwary of the BBC in Kabul for their very generous hospitality. Thank you to Ambassador Rainer Eberle, formerly of the German Embassy in Kabul, for the Christmas Day champagne.

Closer to home, I owe a tremendous debt of thanks to my editors Julian Loose and Henry Volans at Faber and Faber and my agent Robert Caskie, without whom this book would not have come into being. I would also like to thank Katherine Armstrong and everyone else at Faber for being such a pleasure to work with, and Paula Turner for her crucial contribution. Many other people have helped in various ways, and I thank Marcelle Adamson, Krassimira Olah, Stefka Regelous, Mitra Sharafi, Sophie Green and William Govan. I am grateful to Sobia Quazi for so stylishly putting up with me during the writing of this book and to Dr. John Darwin for his continued patience over my perpetually delayed doctorate. I thank the Oppenheim–John Downes Memorial Trust for their generous assistance. Special thanks go to Clare Owen and to Elham Chegini. Most of all, I would like to thank my parents, Margaret and Bob, without whose support this book could not have been written.

Illustration Credits

The author and publishers are grateful to the following for permission to reproduce illustrations:

Plate section 10: British Library Board. All Rights Reserved. (Or.2780.f.49v); 11: British Library Board. All Rights Reserved. (OR.3714.f.368); 13: British Library Board. All Rights Reserved. (Maps 51900.1.); 4: Araldo de Luca/Corbis; 6: Mary Evans Picture Library; 14: Courtesy of the Council of the National Army Museum, London; 7: National Geographic, v.177, no. 3; 3 and 5: The Trustees of the British Museum.

Illustrations in the text pp. 21, 43, 59, 77, 109, 141, 158, 163, 217, 225, 229: Bob Docherty; pp. 70, 103, 173: Mary Evans Picture Library.

Maps

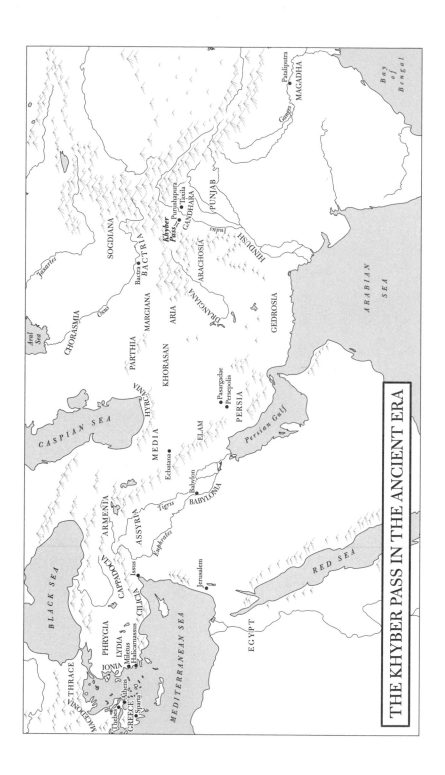

THE KHYBER PASS IN THE ANCIENT ERA

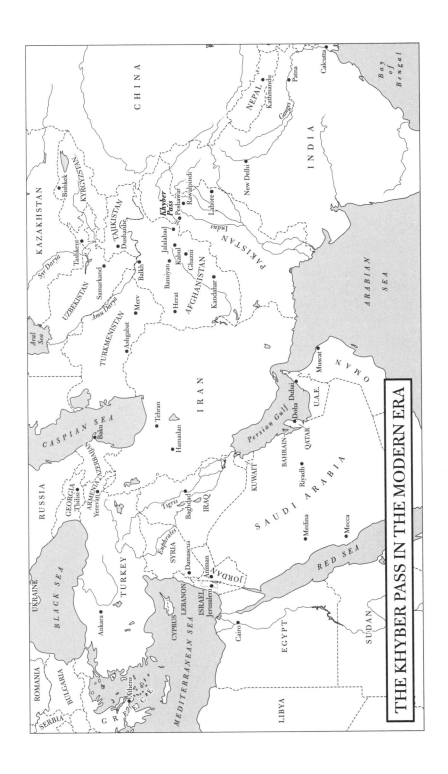

THE KHYBER PASS IN THE MODERN ERA

Prologue

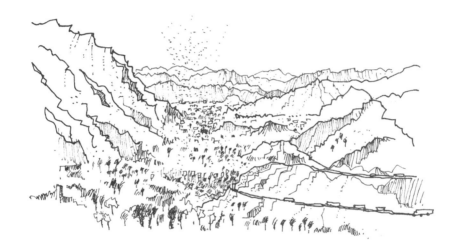

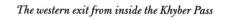

The western exit from inside the Khyber Pass

It was the bitter endgame of the disastrous First Afghan War. John Nicholson was riding through the Khyber Pass toward India, heading for the frontier and safety. A young junior officer in the army of British India, his regiment had been sent to Afghanistan following the invasion of 1839, and had remained while British fortunes in the country declined and then collapsed. As the main British army marched to its complete destruction on the terrible retreat from Kabul in January 1842, Nicholson and a handful of other British officers had been captured in Ghazni and endured several months of cruel captivity in Afghan hands. Then a new British force—known as the "Army of Retribution"—had mounted a second invasion, taking their vicious revenge on the Afghan population and leaving Kabul in flames. Nicholson had been freed, and on the morning of November 4, 1842, the journey through the Khyber Pass—the legendary passage into India—was all that lay between him and allied territory.

The march from Kabul had been grim and dangerous. The dead of January still littered the roadside all the way from the Afghan capital to the city of Jalalabad, halfway to the Khyber: an army of over 16,000 soldiers and camp followers had been destroyed in just a few days as they struggled to quit Afghanistan along the difficult, mountainous route to India. Countless skeletons lay scattered about as a testament to the lethal thoroughness of both the Afghan tribesmen and the severe winter weather. Now these two killers had returned to harass the homeward journey of the Army of Retribution; though proclaimed by the British as the triumphant return of a conquering force, the withdrawal risked becoming a second costly retreat.

Despite the dangers of ambush and icy weather, Nicholson and his unit had arrived safely at the western entrance of the Khyber Pass on November 1. Here he enjoyed some consolation for his sufferings of the last few months: he was reunited with his younger brother, Alexander, after a separation of almost four years. Having followed John into a military career, Alexander had sailed out to India earlier that year and had just arrived on the frontier with his regiment to cover the withdrawal of the army from Afghanistan. Given their youth—John Nicholson was nineteen, Alexander just seventeen—and the anxious circumstances in which they found themselves, it must have been an emotional meeting, but neither man left a written account. After two days together, the Nicholson brothers were again split up: John remained with the rear guard, while Alexander set off into the Khyber Pass on November 3, his regiment providing escort for an army division on its journey to India. John followed a day later.

Thus John Nicholson came to be riding through the Khyber Pass on a November day in 1842 amid the hurried, anxious withdrawal of a vulnerable army. Once through the thirty miles of this famous mountain route, he would be clear of Afghan territory and could rest at last after two years of war and captivity. Though short in distance, the narrow width and rocky heights of the Khyber Pass made it—especially in a time of war—the most precarious stretch of the road to India. The Pathan tribesmen of the Khyber were especially renowned for their ferocity, even in a country of fighting men, and were feared for their ability to close the road to unwelcome armies, or at least to make them pay the price. Hilltop forts kept watch over the full length of the Pass, simple strongholds that were manned by tribesmen in times of crisis, giving them a clear shot over most of this crucial passage. Set above cliffs and reached only by an arduous climb, they gave warning of intruders in the Khyber and allowed tribesmen to fire on the road at their leisure. In the most constricted stretches, where tan-colored rock confines the road tightly, these tiny citadels commanded the passage with particular power (see color plate 1). Elsewhere, still under the gaze of these boxlike forts, lengths of the Pass widen out, the grand walls of rock drawing back from the road to stand a mile apart. Here the scattered houses and sentinel towers must have seemed less forbidding as Nicholson rode by with his regiment, the claustrophobia of the straits perhaps diminished by the broader sky, and the rugged scenery even acquiring a fleeting beauty. Such openness was deceptive, a momentary relief before the Pass closed up suddenly once again, like a muscle contracting.

Nicholson and his men would surely have felt at their most vulnerable at Ali Masjid, near the middle of the Pass: sheer cliffs rise up dramatically to some 500 feet, allowing the road just a few feet to squeeze through. The narrow heights of the Ali Masjid gap make it the most easily defended point in the Pass, a bastion from which a few sniping tribesmen can delay an entire army with ease.

On this occasion, no such obstacle was encountered, but after the force had squeezed its way through the straits of Ali Masjid, Nicholson and a companion, Ensign Julius Dennys, spotted the pale flesh of a European corpse some way off. Ignoring strict instructions not to leave the main path, the two officers rode over: it was clear that a British unit had been ambushed and overwhelmed. On reaching the body, they saw that it had been horribly mutilated and left dead and naked on the ground. By a dreadful chance, it was Alexander. His genitals had been hacked from his body and stuffed into his mouth in the Afghan custom. John Nicholson left no account of his emotions on finding his brother—Victorian soldiers not normally being given to such expression—but we can imagine it to be the worst shock possible. His companions wrote of his being overcome with grief as they buried the body inside the Khyber. John Nicholson would go on to rise to the rank of general before dying gloriously during the Indian Mutiny in 1857; his brother would have no such chance.

Over 150 years later, I stood by Ali Masjid, close to the place where Alexander Nicholson was killed, with the savage reputation of the Khyber Pass running through my mind; many such incidents in this hostile landscape left the British with a respectful fear of the Khyber throughout the years of the Raj. Moreover, its importance as the historic gateway to their valuable Indian empire gave them a sharp awareness that the Khyber Pass was a strategic possession without equal. The long and anxious experience of guarding the frontier came to raise the Khyber into a special category of imperial iconography, its very name conjuring images of mountains that were rugged, forbidding and—as the crucial line in the defense of India—matchless in their consequence. The Khyber Pass stood alongside the Straits of Gibraltar and the Suez Canal as one of the strategic keys that locked up the world before the age of flight, and thus became a critical focus for imperial anxiety and military planners. The Khyber Pass entered the British popular imagination as a romantic, legendary prize to be defended at all costs.

The Pass stretches for thirty miles through the Sefid Koh—the "White Mountains"—from Afghanistan at the western end to the plains of Peshawar at the eastern. Its complete length now lies in the Northwest Frontier Province of Pakistan, the legendary Northwest Frontier not just of Pakistan but of the entire Subcontinent. This was the front line in the defense of India, and the cause of concern through the centuries about the threat from Afghanistan and lands beyond it. Today it remains a turbulent frontier, as American and British soldiers—along with those of many other western nations—fight in Afghanistan against a resurgent Taliban and their Al Qaida allies. To gain a sight of this scene of conflict I continued west from Ali Masjid and stood by the neatly tended Khyber Rifles camp at Michni, looking down upon the border (see color plate 2). Taking in a magnificent view of the western entrance to the Pass—a grand vista of rock and sky—I thought of the concentration of incident and activity that had passed through this slim mountain defile across the years. Sitting in the gap a tantalizing mile or so ahead of me, the border town of Torkham marked the beginning of the Khyber with an assortment of small buildings clustered around the crossing point. The modest town seemed like debris from a rock fall, strewn at the base of the mountain and scattering into the evergreen trees that lay cast across the floor of the Pass. A mucky haze from kitchen fires drifted above the town, merging into the mist over the mountains beyond.

Hard up against the southern edge of the town, the dark brown rock rises in a sudden curve, forming a jagged ridge that stretches deep into the mountains. Beneath this madly serrated blade, a steep escarpment descends into the valley, the stone dusted with red. During the harsh winters, these heights gain a covering of snow. To the right, across the way, the north side of the Pass climbs more gently but to the same intractable peaks, the mountainside scarred with dual lines of road that cut sandy grey slashes in the greenish rock. Higher up is the railway, burrowing so frequently into the mountain that barely any of the track can be seen. An enduring relic of the British era but not currently in use, it terminates at the border. Below these roads and rails, the floor of the Pass widens once inside the entrance; between the great stony walls, trees and hillocks dot the stretch of dun earth. Michni perches above this scene, looking out upon the two huge flanks of mountain lunging in toward the narrow Torkham gap. Past the town I could see Afghanistan, visible as a succession of mountain ridges undulating beyond the border into the distance, gaining in height as they disappear, like waves cresting higher as they get further out to sea.

The Khyber Pass marks more than just a border, more than a line on a map staffed by officials manning a barrier and browsing through passports. It is truly a frontier, an ancient zone of contested ground, long disputed and never entirely at peace, incorporated intermittently into empires and states but remaining unmastered by even the most powerful. Inside the Khyber I saw long files of Pakistani soldiers marching to their mountain maneuvers and felt the tension of a frontier, an uneasiness evident everywhere and manifested in the tribesman by the roadside with an AK 47 slung across his back. Continuing intratribal rivalries amplify this air of violence; the guns are not merely for show. This sense of perpetual foreboding, of life on the edge of things, is most evident in the few villages inside the Khyber: houses here are small forts, walled and defended, often for several families of close relatives. Low, angular constructions built of baked mud, they have rifle embrasures in place of windows. Among these earthen keeps, I saw no children playing, nor villagers pausing on their way to pass words with their neighbors. In the Khyber, life is shut up behind defenses.

As I traveled through the Pass, I imagined this tense Khyber atmosphere to have gone unchanged since young Alexander Nicholson was killed, and to have stretched back much further in time to the very earliest days. In a powerful way, it is a consequence of the centuries of volatility and exchange that define this frontier region, a fertile liaison between armies and ideas that has been crucial to the formation of empires and the spread of religions across the mountain barrier. Through a slim chance of geography, the Khyber Pass has been witness to a remarkably intense military and cultural interaction that forms the essence of the story of the regions that it joins together. No other mountain pass, strategic road or vital waterway in the world has seen such a rich concentration of history pass through. Besides the British and their nervous watch on the Indian frontier, other peoples have dominated the region too, from the Mauryans and Parthians of ancient days to the Sikhs and Pathans of more recent times. Moreover, the Khyber Pass has been the essential route for the armies of Persians, Greeks, Scythians, Kushans, White Huns, Turks, Mongols, Mughals and Afghans, who have passed through to invade India at different times across the centuries, creating empires and seeding cultures in their wake. At once familiar and little known, the Khyber Pass provides a valuable lens for observing history in a world where empires continue to rise and fall, allowing us to look upon the invaders that marched through it to create kingdoms or to destroy them. By telling the story of the Khyber from the earliest times, I will hope to show how military and cultural exchange along its narrow width created the world we recognize today in the surrounding regions. I will, moreover, aim to chart the rich global connections across thousands of years that show that globalization is a phenomenon much older than the modern day.

Toward the end of my own first visit to the Khyber, I began to return to Peshawar as the sky darkened into evening, and paused to look down upon the final mile of the legendary road to India. I saw jumbled low hills lying in the foreground, crumbling with gravelly scree, through which the road wound back and forth upon itself, meandering crazily toward the slim opening ahead, a tarmac river wending its way to the plains. The ground was an earthy, mossy brown, sprinkled with scrub and flashes of bright green from a few trees on the floor of the Pass. Ahead, two ridges north and south stretched in toward each other, gracefully declining. They did not meet. The small gap left between the curving mountain arcs is the eastern end of the Khyber Pass: beyond this lie the plains, rivers, peoples and civilizations of the Subcontinent. I stood looking out on this sight, the tantalizing glimpse of the grand objective that every passing monarch, soldier and migrant will have enjoyed across the centuries. After a difficult passage through hostile mountains peopled with unforgiving tribesmen, the flat plains ahead offered ease and bounty, the luxury and wealth of India being near to hand at last. The violent, creative and lasting consequences of many such journeys form the story of the Khyber Pass.

Our tale begins over 2,500 years ago, with the early days of the Persians and their rise to imperial might.

CHAPTER ONE

The First Persians

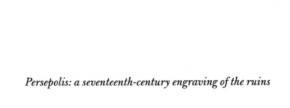

Persepolis: a seventeenth-century engraving of the ruins

I am Darius the Great King
King of Kings
King of Persia
King of Lands

BISITUN INSCRIPTION

The Khyber Pass emerges from myth into history with the rise of the Persians and the legendary founder of their first empire. When Cyrus the Great was born in the sixth century BC, so the Greek historian Herodotus tells us, the Persians were a subject people, living under the sway of the Medes, a cousin tribe of Iranian stock. King Astyages ruled Media from his capital at Ecbatana (modern Hamadan) to the northwest of Persia, and had made himself hated for his cruelty. The Medes had only recently established their kingdom in a revolt against Scythian invaders and through making war against the Assyrians; now they had extended their realm to encompass their neighbors in Persia.

In the rich account given by Herodotus, Astyages once had a troubling dream in which his daughter Mandane urinated continuously, so copiously that Ecbatana was flooded, then the whole of Media, then the rest of Asia. Seeking an interpretation from his priest, Astyages was alarmed to hear that his dream presaged that his daughter's child would rule all of Asia. When Mandane was old enough to marry, Astyages—still worried about the dream—declined to wed her to a Mede of suitable rank, and chose instead Cambyses, a Persian nobleman. Although of good family and character, as a Persian he was considered to rank below a Mede even of modest standing: his children could not be kings.

Mandane and Cambyses had not been married a year when Astyages had another dream, in which a vine grew from Mandane's crotch and spread over Asia, covering every part of the known world with rapidly growing creepers. The priest declared that it once again foretold that her child would be king of Asia. As Mandane was then pregnant, Astyages decided to put an end to his fears for his throne by killing the child as soon as it was born. He ordered a trusted kinsman, Harpagus, to remove the baby on the day of its birth, kill it and dispose of the body however he pleased. On the day, the newborn child was torn from the arms of its mother, dressed in a funerary shroud and secretly carried from the palace by Harpagus. Perhaps moved by the injustice, or perhaps out of fear of having royal blood on his hands, Harpagus decided not to murder the baby himself, but summoned a servant of Astyages, a herdsman named Mitradates, who lived in the hill country outside Ecbatana. Harpagus instructed Mitradates to take the child into the mountains, expose the cradle and watch over it until the baby was dead.

It happened that the wife of Mitradates was also pregnant, and on the very day that Harpagus summoned Mitradates, she bore a stillborn child. Returning to his cottage with the high-born baby in his arms, and finding his own child dead, Mitradates told his wife of his terrible task. In tears, she begged the herdsman not to kill the royal baby but to exchange it with their dead child and raise it as their own. Thus the stillborn infant was dressed in the royal funeral clothes, and the royal boy dressed in swaddling rags. The next day, Mitradates carried his own dead son to Harpagus and the deception was complete.

Ten years later, however, this child—Cyrus, though not yet called by that name—was revealed as the grandson of the king. As the son of Mitradates the herdsman, Cyrus was playing with the other boys of the village when one day they elected him their king in a game. The young Cyrus set about giving tasks to his new subjects, making one his minister, another his bodyguard and so on, but the game ended when he thrashed one boy—the son of a nobleman—for disobedience. This boy ran home to his father, who then went to the king to ask for redress against the low-born son of a herdsman, and Mitradates and Cyrus were summoned to the palace.

When Astyages took the young boy to task for his rough handling of the nobleman's son, Cyrus gave a dignified defense of his actions, but said that he was ready for his punishment if the king so willed. His regal bearing and proud speech, but most especially the boy's resemblance to himself, suggested to the king his real identity. Struggling to contain his rising anger and fear, Astyages had Cyrus sent into another room, and threatened Mitradates with torture if he did not speak the truth about the boy; the herdsman could do nothing but tell all. With his silent fury then focused on his kinsman Harpagus, Astyages ordered him to the palace. Seeing the herdsman present and judging honesty to be his best defense , Harpagus also told the truth of his side of the story, explaining how he had sought to avoid for himself the offence of murdering a royal grandson by transferring the deed to Mitradates, and how he had given careful instructions for the carrying out of the murder.

Astyages gave Harpagus the full tale of Mitradates' compassionate adaptation of the scheme. Affecting great relief at the infant's survival, and joy at no longer having the murder of his daughter's child on his conscience, Astyages bade Harpagus join him for a feast that night, to celebrate the happy deliverance. The king told Harpagus to send his own son, a boy of thirteen, to visit the newly returned royal child. Harpagus went home in high spirits, happy to have escaped so lightly from a king known for malice, sending his son—his only child—to play with the prince as the king had bidden.

When the son of Harpagus arrived at the palace, he was not taken to see the young Cyrus but to the slaughterhouse of the palace kitchens, where he was killed and butchered, rendered into an array of joints and cuts, properly prepared for the table. His head, hands and feet were placed on a separate platter covered with a lid. Variously roasted or boiled, this meat of his own son was put before Harpagus that evening at the banquet. All the other guests, Astyages included, were served mutton cooked in a similar way.

Harpagus ate his fill with relish, and when he could eat no more Astyages asked if he had enjoyed his dinner. When assured that the food had been excellent, Astyages ordered the covered dish containing the boy's feet, hands and head to be placed before Harpagus, who was invited to try a little more of that which he had enjoyed so much. On raising the lid, and seeing the fragmentary remains of his son, Harpagus did not break down as might be expected, but feigned acceptance of the king's punishment. Gathering the last pieces of his child, he carried them home for burial. Herodotus does not record his feelings, but we can only imagine the sickening horror and the wild, angry sense of violation that Harpagus suppressed as he calmly left the palace to polish his plans for revenge.

So Astyages punished Harpagus. To decide the fate of the young prince, he once again consulted his priest, who advised that the royal dreams of Mandane had been fulfilled: the boy had been a king—to his playmates—and was no longer a danger to Astyages. The priest suggested that Cyrus be sent away to his paternal lands of Persia as a precaution and, having done so, Astyages considered the matter resolved.

Patience was clearly a characteristic of the wronged Harpagus, for he waited years for an opportunity of taking revenge on the king. During this time, Cyrus was becoming famed throughout Persia. Known for his bravery and wisdom even in his youth, he was gaining a good reputation, and the power that accompanies it. When reports of him reached Harpagus, he saw in the prince the perfect vehicle for his vengeance: having also been misused by Astyages, Cyrus too might harbor ideas of revenge. To draw the prince into his schemes, Harpagus began courting him with presents and charming letters; the harsh rule of Astyages also assisted Harpagus in recruiting leading nobles into his plot. Eventually, he was able to gain their backing to replace Astyages with the Persian prince.

When alerted by Harpagus, Cyrus managed to raise the Persian army and put himself at its head, whereupon he marched on Ecbatana. Astyages placed Harpagus in charge of the Median army, forgetting—in his panic— the wrong that he had done to him. When the two forces met, therefore, there was barely a battle: the few Medes who were not in the plot had little chance of victory when their comrades all around were deserting to the Persians. Astyages found the time to summon his priest—the one who had advised him to send Cyrus to Persia to blunt his potential danger—and have him impaled, before he himself was captured by the Persians and the Median rebels.

Thus Herodotus tells us how Cyrus the Great came to rule over the Medes. It is impossible to corroborate this rich tale of righted wrongs and convenient coincidence, since Herodotus was lighting a new way by making a rare written record in an age with an oral tradition. Truth, opinion, rumor, myth and legend were all intermingled: fact and imagination were inseparable.

Herodotus does not tell us, but other sources, such as the Nabonidus Chronicle, record that when the revolt against Astyages broke out, Cyrus was on the throne of the vassal kingdom of Persia, having succeeded his father Cambyses in 559 BC. While Cyrus was building a new capital city at Pasargadae, the nobility in Media was indeed becoming restless, along with the population. The revolt against the king broke out in 553 BC, and the rule of Astyages was ended finally when Cyrus captured Ecbatana in 550 BC. In an age not known for treating captured kings with compassion, Cyrus showed signs of his quality of mercy, merely imprisoning his defeated rival, not slaying him in some creative and sanguinary manner. Nor did he raze Ecbatana (the customary treatment for a city seized in war) but made it joint capital with Pasargadae. This munificence was to become characteristic of his rule, and to leave him with an enduring reputation for clemency and tolerance.

In defeating Astyages, Cyrus had made himself the master of two realms and united two Iranian peoples to found what we know as the Achaemenian Empire, named by later ages for his dynastic predecessor Achaemenes. What next for an ambitious and skilful young monarch? His new kingdom sat astride important trade routes that linked Asia Minor, the Mediterranean and Egypt in the west with India and Central Asia in the east, giving it advantages of strategic geography and significant wealth. Well placed and profitable it was, but still modest in extent; Cyrus was, however, well supplied with the appetite and self-confidence to rectify this territorial deficit, and followed a boldly expansionist strategy from the very beginning of his energetic rule as emperor.

His first intention was to capture the Mediterranean coast and seize control of its great seaports, the western termini of the trade routes over which he already held considerable sway. Perhaps not yet feeling strong enough to tackle his powerful neighbor, Babylon, immediately to the west, Cyrus turned his attention to the wealthy state of Lydia (in the west of modern Turkey). This kingdom had been ruled since 561 BC by Croesus, he of the legendary riches. Cyrus secured his flank through an unopposed occupation of Cilicia, and then, in 547 BC, marched on Lydia and conquered it quickly, again sparing the life of its king; Lydia became a satrapy of the empire under a Persian governor.

To achieve complete domination of Asia Minor and a good outlet to the Mediterranean, Cyrus had next to conquer the Greek trading colonies on the Ionian coast, offspring of the Greek mainland states across the Aegean Sea. These were attractive possessions, wealthy commercial cities with navies of their own. It seems that these Greek settlements had accepted Croesus as overlord; after his victory over Lydia, Cyrus demanded their capitulation to him as their new ruler. All but one refused to submit, and they were reduced separately, by force or treachery: Persian wealth, used to bribe Greek officials and generals, was a powerful ally of Persian arms. Lack of unity between the Greek cities, and the advantage that one element of the population—the merchants—saw in joining the rich and expanding Persian realm, ensured that Cyrus faced only piecemeal resistance. The annexation of these Greek settlements by Cyrus the Great in the 540s BC began the long history of Persian–Greek tension that would reach its climax over two centuries later with the savage invasion of Persia by Alexander the Great.

Having substantially enhanced his power on his western flank, Cyrus next turned to his east, where the goal was security. The steppes of Central Asia had long been a source of instability because of its multitudinous nomadic tribes—horsemen who would appear suddenly, and devastatingly, to raid the settlements of civilized areas. Sometimes they would return home with their booty, but sometimes they would stay and make themselves rulers. The Scythians, an Iranian nomadic people distantly related to the Persians, had done just this in the seventh century BC, sweeping into Asia Minor, Syria and Palestine. They pillaged as they went and had remained to bring the kingdom of Media under their subjection for decades, until it was freed by Cyaxares, the father of Astyages.

An equestrian and thus highly mobile people, the Scythians—in their different tribal incarnations—had come to dominate a wide stretch of land from the Oxus river in the east to the Crimea and southern Russia in the west. The horsemen that raided the Middle East in the seventh century BC had swarmed south through the Caucasus Mountains to harass the old civilizations; others in the east troubled Khorasan, the northeast of modern Iran. Their range and speed of movement gave them mastery of wide swathes of country, and the ability to deliver shocking assaults on their sedentary targets.

There is a tendency for many people educated in a tradition inherited from the Greeks and Romans to treat nomadic peoples such as the Scythians as mere barbarians. Yet they had lessons for the settled societies that they encountered, certainly in the realm of warfare: during the period of Scythian domination of the Medes, Cyaxares is said to have profited from the Scythian military example, and learnt effective tactics for mounted combat, which he later turned upon his unwitting teachers.

Besides their impressive cavalry skills, the Scythians had a vibrant culture of decorative metalwork: numerous burial mounds found around the Black Sea coast in the Ukraine have provided archaeologists with evidence of their customs, mode of life, dress and weapons, especially because they sent their dead into the afterlife with the arms and accoutrements of the living. A warrior was usually buried with a bow, arrows and spear; a king went to his grave with armor, helmet, swords, bow, arrows, spears and sometimes even his horse. These graves have yielded many finely crafted pieces of metalwork in which panthers, lions, deer and other animals are rendered artfully in precious materials, including gold, decorating swords, shields and armor. Such finds have demonstrated the sophistication of Scythian craftsmen and the the depth and richness of their imagination.

From burial mounds like these we can imagine a detailed picture of the Scythian fighting men—aggressive horsemen descending the passes of the Caucasus, or pressing home attacks on the plains of Khorasan. The mounted warrior rides, hair and beard uncut, his only armor a girdle of leather with iron scales to cover his abdomen. From his belt swing an iron sword and a battle-axe, short-handled with a long and narrow blade for cutting deeply into opposing limbs. In one hand he carries a spear armed with an extended, elegant point; in the other a shield made of bone strips fixed to a wooden backing. His saddlecloth is perhaps made from the flayed skin of a captured foe: leathered hands and feet, deprived of their flesh and bone, dangle dispiritedly about the flanks of his horse. Scalps of the defeated, taken as a measure of martial prowess, decorate the bridle.

The Scythian king is mounted for battle in a full cuirass of tiny iron plates sewn to a leather tunic and a close-fitting helmet of bronze, an iron-coated chin strap gripping it firmly to him. This is a headdress designed for protection not for show. His battle-axe and the scabbard of his iron sword are finely chased in gold, with scenes of fantastical animals—griffins shooting arrows and giant fish leaping over them. He holds a circular shield of iron, perhaps bearing a gold boss of a panther or a lioness. Gold is liberally used to decorate the bridle and chest strap of his horse, and plates his quiver and bow case.

Tribesmen such as these were the threat that Cyrus faced on his north-eastern frontier. In meeting this menace, he came to the Khyber Pass, conquering Hyrcania, Parthia, Drangiana, Aria, Arachosia, Sogdiana and Chorasmia in turn, taking his border to the Jaxartes river (the modern Syr Darya). This amounts to several years of campaigning, from the region south of the Caspian Sea, through modern Khorasan and Seistan to western and southern Afghanistan and Uzbekistan. On his return, Cyrus brought Margiana (part of modern Turkmenistan) into his fold. Finally, he subjected Bactria and its great city of Bactra (modern Balkh) in northern Afghanistan. His territory now included the mountain routes into India.

After several years of campaigning on his eastern borders, Cyrus was able to turn his attention toward Babylon in 539 BC. The time was auspicious: its king, Nabonidus, was growing in unpopularity over his increasing obsession with the cultish practices of ancient religions, and many elements of the population were favorable toward the Persian king. Defensive measures were neglected, and when Cyrus advanced on the city, it fell to him without resistance. Although the royal citadel held out for several days, Nabonidus was captured. As was his custom, Cyrus did not harm the imprisoned king, and Nabonidus died naturally a year later, the new king decreeing a period of mourning in which he himself took part.

The benevolent and enlightened policy with which Cyrus treated Babylon and its people reflects the wider Achaemenian approach to their conquered lands. Captured countries were not forced into the Persian frame, either in governance or culture. Institutions of religion and rule were, for the most part, left unchanged: new Persian officials took up posts alongside their local counterparts, and native beliefs were honored. Cyrus and his successors generally took care to rule in the name of the local god, and were generous in both laws and taxes, giving substance to their claim of legitimate succession. Cities were not sacked and massacres not employed as a tool of domination. In Babylon, Cyrus restored to the temples many idols that had been seized by Nabonidus, and instituted religious freedom. Above all other acts, he is celebrated for liberating the exiled Jews who had been held in captivity in Babylon for almost fifty years since the days of Nebuchadnezzar. Cyrus provided for their return to

Jerusalem, where he ordered a temple to be built for them. For this, he is remembered with honor in the Old Testament.

To a degree, this liberal tendency was an admission of the cultural superiority of many of the nations that the early Achaemenians brought under their rule. The Persians were still relative newcomers in the community of civilizations, and when they gained possession of the advanced cultures of Babylon, Egypt, the Greek cities of Asia Minor and parts of India, it would have been regressive to destroy those civilizations to impose their own. The Persians would gain far more by leaving intact societies of valuable cultural achievement; the civilization of the Persians themselves, a culture that would come to be wonderfully rich and enduring, was in its infancy.

The cultural and political autonomy the Achaemenians granted also had a practical dimension: given the vast and rapidly increasing size of the Persian realm, close management of the lives of people from the Aegean Sea to the Indus river would have been impossible. Yet this practical policy was hardly ruthlessly pragmatic. The preservation of other cultures, and the extent of determination left in local hands, may explain why the death of Cyrus was followed by the near collapse of the empire. A *laissez-faire* government led to an unstable state, which underwent convulsions of unrest in the decade after the founder of the empire died. As a confederation of subject kingdoms, with their own centers of authority and with ambitious local rulers still in place, the Achaemenian hold over their realm was superficial. As we will see, it was only the forceful brilliance of Darius that reconstructed the empire.

Cyrus the Great died on the frontier in 529 BC, fighting the Massagetae, a Scythian tribe, while trying to shore up his frontiers. Under Queen Tomyris, the Massagetae had gathered in great numbers and soundly beat the Persian army just north of the Jaxartes river, the first and only significant defeat suffered by the emperor. Classical authors give differing accounts of his end. Ctesias has him dying in camp after a mortal battle wound, having nominated his son Cambyses as successor. Diodorus makes him a prisoner of the Scythian queen, who has him crucified. Herodotus has him dead in battle and posthumously beheaded by Tomyris, who fulfils her vow to give the Persian king his fill of blood by placing his severed head in a wineskin full of it. In contrast to these violent deaths, Xenophon has him dying at home, abed, surrounded by his family. Which of these accounts is closest to the truth is impossible to know, but we can safely say that he died on the frontier, fighting his distant kin to reinforce the borders of the empire that he had created.

Cyrus was succeeded by his son Cambyses, who has a less noble reputation. His short and cruel reign came to an end in 522 BC amid an attempted coup, when he died from a self-inflicted wound. It was through leading a group of Persian noblemen in a rebellion against the usurper, Gaumata, that Darius the Great came to the fore. A member of a cadet branch of the Achaemenian family, Darius ensured that the pretender was killed—in some accounts wielding the dagger himself—and was proclaimed king just two months after the death of Cambyses.

The end of Gaumata was the beginning of two years of rebellions, which saw Darius fight in every part of the empire to restore Achaemenian rule. Even in the heartlands of Persia itself and Media, the new king had to enforce his rule violently. Throughout the empire—right up to the Khyber Pass—unrest had to be suppressed, and Darius fought nineteen battles against nine rebel kings. It is this time of violence that Darius celebrated in 519 BC by cutting a bold inscription into a cliff face at Behistun (now Bisitun), in what is now northwest Iran, on the Royal Road between Babylon and Ecbatana. An ardent Zoroastrian, follower of the venerable Iranian faith in which truth and deceit—light and darkness—battle for supremacy, he invoked the name of the Wise Lord, Ahura Mazda, many times in support of his rule. In three languages—Old Persian, Elamite and Babylonian—the King of Kings made his claim to dominion over the Earth, listing his lands and peoples, a register of most of the known world:

> Darius the king says: "These are the countries which belong to me. By the favor of Ahura Mazda I was their king: Persia, Elam, Babylon, Assyria, Arabia, Egypt, the People-by-the-Sea, Lydia, Ionia, Media, Armenia, Cappadocia, Parthia, Drangiana, Aria, Chorasmia, Bactria, Sogdiana, Gandhara, Scythia, Sattagydia, Arachosia and Maka, altogether twenty-three countries. . . . These are the countries which belong to me. By the favor of Ahura Mazda they are my subjects; they brought tribute to me. What I said to them, either by night or by day, that they did."

These names mean little in the modern world: they are the ancient terms

Henry Rawlinson's own drawing of Bisitun

for his vast empire covering Iran, Iraq, Jordan, Israel, Egypt, Syria, Turkey, Armenia, Afghanistan, parts of northwest India and much of Central Asia. Darius leaves no doubt about who should be considered master of this enormous realm.

Mount Bisitun is a sharp point rising suddenly and grandly out of the plain; the inscription is carved into a smoothed face of the hard brown rock 300 feet up, measuring about 70 feet wide by 20 feet high. In several panels, hewn flat by Achaemenian craftsmen, the word of the emperor is recorded in cuneiform script, made up of many thousands of tiny chiseled triangles. These texts surround a relief showing several figures: Darius himself is the dominating character, standing in profile with one bare foot on the body of the usurper Gaumata, whom he had slain to gain the throne. In his left hand, the emperor holds his bow, symbol of his military prowess and of the violence he was prepared to use to maintain his grip on power; it rests on the carcass of the pretender.

His right hand is raised toward Ahura Mazda. A pious gesture, it is also an acknowledgment of submission: before him stand the nine rebel kings, bound by their necks, their heads low but their faces raised as they await judgment. These mutinous monarchs, under-kings of the Achaemenians, dared question the right of the emperor to rule them and paid for their temerity: the inscriptions tell in gruesome detail how Darius slew them. The number—and varied dress—of these rebel kings suggests the widespread discontent with which the new king of kings had to deal when he came to power. Darius himself is dressed in a simple tunic that covers his shoulders and reaches down to his sturdy calves. He wears a skullcap and has his full beard plaited in the Persian style. His long hair is dressed similarly, braided and gathered into a heavy mass at the base of his neck.

Above this scene hovers the symbol of the Zoroastrian faith, the winged *faravahar*, casting a holy light upon the king. Its prominence tells us of the importance attached by Darius to divine sanction. Moreover, that the inscription is out of reach, high up in the rocks, and cannot be read from the ground, suggests that the intended audience was heavenly. The effort of scaling the cliff to view the work would involve such a risk that only the suicidally curious among his subjects would undertake it. Darius was playing to the sole audience of the Wise Lord, Ahura Mazda.

 Written material from Achaemenian Persia is rare; the Bisitun inscription is thus very valuable as a historical document, giving later ages crucial knowledge of the Achaemenian period. Since the inscriptions are in three languages, it has also played an important role in deciphering ancient writings. In the 1830s, Henry Rawlinson, an enterprising young officer of the British East India Company, managed to scale the cliff and made copies of the great inscription. Using knowledge of ancient Persian derived from Zoroastrian texts, Rawlinson was able by 1839 to decode the Persian cuneiform writing system. With the accompanying texts in Elamite and Babylonian now decipherable, Rawlinson could unlock understanding of such scripts found throughout the ancient Middle East. The Bisitun inscription performed the same role for cuneiform scripts that the Rosetta Stone had for the decoding of hieroglyphics after its discovery in Egypt in 1799.

That Darius had to fight to maintain the Achaemenian lands gives a special gravity to the words cut in stone, and to the picture of the emperor in triumph over his enemies. It was for his quelling of these rebellions across most of the known world, thus restoring the fortunes of the Persian rulers and setting them on the path to a glorious future, that the king became known as Darius the Great. Under his rule, the Achaemenian realm expanded further, into Europe and into India.

To build such an empire, Darius needed to improve on the ad hoc imperial system that he inherited, and began by reorganizing his satraps—powerful provincial governors, usually Persian noblemen, often an Achaemenian prince. Cyrus occasionally installed them in parts of his empire but had not done so systematically; Darius divided the empire into twenty satrapies, placing a royal governor in each of these provinces to enhance central control. In an age when communication was largely dependent on the horse, there must have been a temptation for these powerful figures, even those loyal to the center, to break away and declare independence from a faraway king. This was a feature of the decline of many empires in the coming centuries, when satraps or vassal kings sensed weakness and sought their own advantage. Darius was aware of this possibility—Cyrus the Great had, after all, been a vassal king himself—and, to counter it, set up a network of military commanders alongside the satraps, also answerable directly to the king. These generals had responsibility for the forces of four or five satrapies each, reducing the likelihood of treacherous collusion between satrap and soldier.

Another innovation designed to weld the empire together was the establishment of a road system. Royal roads were built that connected Persia with the Aegean coast, and Ecbatana with Egypt via Babylon, allowing great distances to be covered rapidly. While trade caravans took three months to travel from Persia to Ephesus in Ionia, royal messengers could travel this distance in a week, using fresh horses provided by relay stations along the 1,677-mile route. This road system was extended into the Kabul valley, and on into India when the Achaemenians advanced beyond their foothold in Gandhara. Essential for efficient government, the roads proved crucial to the development of commerce across the empire as well. Darius also introduced a regulated coinage, an organized tax system and official weights and measures. Indeed, such was his concern for the commercial and fiscal aspects of his realm that Herodotus reports the Persians saying that Cyrus was a father, Cambyses a tyrant and Darius a tradesman.

The abandoned skeleton of the great palace of Persepolis remains as evidence of another bold imperial venture. As soon as Darius had finished building one palace, at Susa, he began the construction of another, a grand new capital city known to us—through the Greeks—as Persepolis, the City of Persia. Standing alone by a mountainside just over thirty miles from the city of Shiraz, a stately terrace cuts into the rock to provide a broad platform—over thirty acres—for several separate palaces, along with treasuries, stables and barracks. Begun by Darius and continued by his son Xerxes and his successors, it is now ruined, but gives a clear picture of the home of the Achaemenian court.

The main terrace is reached by an impressive staircase. Hard by the stairway is the Xerxes Gate, guarded by winged bulls in stone, human-headed, inspired by those that protected the palaces of Assyria. Ahead, up another magnificent staircase, is the Apadana, the throne room or audience hall, the focus of the public business of this seat of government. Seventy-two great fluted columns, the height of twelve men and surmounted by carved lions and bulls, held aloft a cedar-wood ceiling of which, sadly, nothing remains. Many of the pillars, however, still stand. To one side of the Apadana is the Hall of a Hundred Columns, initiated by Xerxes but unfinished in his lifetime.

The Apadana stairway bears a line of stone soldiers carved into its front face, standing ready to protect the king (see color plate 3). These are the royal guard, the Immortals, so called because their number was never allowed to fall below 10,000; a passing soldier or bystander was recruited immediately if ever one should die. Carved into the stone next to them is a row of courtiers—Persians and Medes—waiting to do the bidding of the king. Then comes a procession of men of the subject nations, rising up the stairs, bringing gifts from their own lands to the emperor—rare animals, jewelry, fine cloth.

Religious art also plays its part. The *faravahar*, seen at Bisitun, is used here too, demonstrating the royal attachment to Zoroastrianism and the imperial claim to divine sanction. The royal faith was already ancient when Persepolis was being built: its prophet was Zarathustra—to the Greeks, Zoroaster—who lived around 1200 BC. He was a priest in the polytheistic sacrificial cult of the early Bronze Age Iranian tribes, in which water and fire were venerated above all. At the age of thirty, Zarathustra received a revelation and proclaimed Ahura Mazda as the one true god; in opposition was Angra Mainyu, the Hostile Spirit who had chosen to promote evil. Zarathustra declared that Ahura Mazda had created the world as a battleground upon which to fight Angra Mainyu and hasten the inevitable triumph of good: every man had therefore to make a choice between good and evil and take part in the great struggle. Zoroastrians hold fire to be especially sacred as the giver of energy and light to this fight against evil, and fire temples are found in many Achaemenian sites. Through his employment of the symbolizm of Zoroastrianism, Darius sought to use religion as an ally to his rule.

Persepolis is valuable for the historical evidence of its inscriptions, dating toward the end of the reign of Darius. These texts are crucial for our understanding of the Persian relationship with India, for there is an important difference between them and the earlier inscription at Bisitun. In the list of lands subject to the empire, a new province has been added: Hindush, or as we would say, India.

Herodotus mentions the Persian incursion into India but gives little away. We know that Darius ordered the building of a fleet of boats in his province of Gandhara, at a town called Caspatyrus (perhaps modern Peshawar). Under the command of a Greek navigator, Scylax of Caryanda, this fleet set off to explore the Indus river to the sea, then sail home to Persia, with the intention of opening a sea route to link the eastern provinces of the empire to the central lands. This ambitious exploration took thirty months but added greatly to Persian knowledge of geography.

The details of the subsequent Persian annexation of the northwest of India are unknown ("Hindush" here means western India and the Indus valley to its exit into the Arabian Sea, and does not imply mastery of most of the Subcontinent). Herodotus tells us that Darius subdued the Indians: at some time between the cutting of the cliff face at Bisitun and the carving of the inscriptions at Persepolis, a Persian army traveled through the Khyber Pass and secured Hindush for the empire. Imagine the Immortals passing through the Khyber, carrying their bows and quivers and their broad-bladed spears with pomegranate butt-spikes. With their hair and beards braided, and wearing thick circlets of twisted cord on their heads, think of them marching through the mountains on to the plains of India with the proud posture of the loyal troops of the royal household, not knowing what they would find ahead, but certain of their imperial power.

There were many good reasons to absorb Indian lands into the empire, especially for a king as fond of money as Darius; through long-established trading links, and means such as the Scylax expedition, the Persians were doubtless aware of the great wealth India offered. Darius made Hindush the twentieth satrapy of the empire, and it paid huge amounts in tax. The annual tribute from the Indian lands was 360 talents of gold, equivalent to 4,680 talents of silver. By contrast, the next richest satrapy, Babylon, paid 1,000 silver talents; some paid much less, such as Gandhara, which paid just 170. It is extremely difficult to translate ancient money into modern equivalents, but, as a guide, one silver talent would have paid the wages of an artisan for at least sixteen years. India was clearly a very desirable addition to the Achaemenian realm.

The Persians may have extended their lands deeper into India in pursuit of profit, but the impact of their annexation was much greater and longer lasting than a temporary rise in Achaemenian income. It was the beginning of an enduring cultural interaction between the Persian and Indian worlds that saw a rich exchange of material and intellectual culture for many hundreds of years under successive empires and dynasties. The Khyber Pass was traversed in both directions by poets, craftsmen, adventurers and office-seekers, scholars and holy men, all hoping to participate in this fruitful transaction. Taxila, the principal city of Gandhara and close to the Khyber Pass, was a natural meeting point of cultures: the city became an intellectual center of some repute, and a destination for itinerant scholars and holy men. That Persian is, even now, a common language for much of the region is eloquent testimony to the impact of the Achaemenian advance into India.

In a sense, this new intercourse between the Persian and Indian peoples was a reunion. The coming together of two cultures with common Aryan roots, after a separation of several centuries, perhaps explains the ease with which they intermingled, and the longevity and depth of the re-established connection. Remaining cultural similarities must have been evident. It is most likely that by the turn of the fifth century BC, a Persian in India *was* considered a foreigner, and, as someone ignorant of the Rig Veda—the ancient Sanskrit hymns that form one of the bases of Indian culture and Hindu belief—probably a barbarian too. However, the Persian language was recognizable as being close to Sanskrit and Prakrit, the dominant languages in northern India, all being of the Indo-European language family. Further, the Brahmins of India would recognize vestiges of the old

Aryan fire cults (which had a place in Vedic Brahminism) in the Zoroastrianism of the Persians.

The practical manifestations of the annexation of Hindush were varied and appeared quickly. Besides tribute in gold, Indian soldiers fought in the army of Xerxes in his Greek campaign. Thousands of miles to the west of Hindush—a distance probably traveled on foot—Indians were playing a part in the fate of the great classical civilizations of the Mediterranean.

This early conjunction was just the beginning. India gave Iran her music, the sciences of mathematics and logic, its tradition of romantic literature, ivory carving and silk weaving. Iran gave India many political and administrative ideas, a corpus of important literature, expertise in metalwork and architecture, along with techniques for building in stone. In later years, stimuli from the sophisticated urban culture of Iran—more cosmopolitan than its Hindu neighbor—were essential fillips to Indian development; the Khyber Pass was the essential means of transmission. That the exchange was freely welcomed by both sides is undoubted: Persian was to become the language of government and the elite under the Muslim rulers of India from AD 1000, who quite naturally embraced whatever came from Iran. It is a compelling thought that the body of literature written in India in the Persian language during the medieval and early modern period vastly outweighs that composed in Iran itself.

The influence and impact of the Great Kings Cyrus and Darius thus lives on into the modern age, but after 200 years of existence both glorious and troubled, the Achaemenian Empire itself was to suffer terribly at the hands of one of the most famous conquerors of all.

CHAPTER TWO

Alexander the Great

The British Museum bust of Alexander

> Asia and Europe are now one and the same kingdom.
>
> Alexander the Great in *The History of Alexander*
>
> by QUINTUS CURTIUS RUFUS

One day in 326 BC, an Indian king named Porus stood on the eastern bank of the Hydaspes river, in what is now Pakistan. Across the water he would have seen many thousands of soldiers gathering, preparing to cross the river and invade his kingdom. There was a strong force from the neighboring principality of Taxila, whose ruler was long a rival of Porus and now sought his final defeat. There were cavalrymen from faraway Central Asia—from Arachosia, Bactria and Sogdiana. There were Scythian mercenary horsemen from across the Jaxartes. Among all these massed warriors, however, the strangest sight—and undoubtedly the most troubling—would have been the Greek and Macedonian veterans led by their king and commander, Alexander the Great. The Indian king faced the prospect of meeting in battle with the belligerent young conqueror who had marched his soldiers across Asia in a rapid succession of brilliant victories.

Alexander had reinforced his army from each one of his conquered lands over several years of campaigning, and had before him on the Hydaspes a vast force, said by Arrian to number as many as 120,000 men, though this looks like an exaggeration. Porus had a considerably smaller army at his disposal, perhaps 30,000 infantry, up to 4,000 cavalry and 300 chariots. His greatest strength lay in his elephants, feared by the Greeks for their size and horrendous trumpeting—and awful smell. Given the disparity in numbers, however, it seems that Porus aimed to use the river as his principal defense: if he could prevent Alexander effecting a crossing in force, and thus avoid a pitched battle against superior numbers, Porus might have a chance of retaining his kingdom. In this he would be assisted by the rising waters of the Hydaspes: the weather was growing warmer as summer approached, melting the Himalayan snows that fed the river, and already causing it to swell dangerously. The longer he contested a crossing, the harder it would be for Alexander to get an army across.

Pitching camp on the west bank of the river, Alexander set about stretching the defenders, sending decoys up and down the river banks to feint crossings and cause alarms. At the same time, he made a show of storing huge amounts of grain to suggest that he was settling in to await the diminished waters of autumn and an easier passage over the river. Alexander had brought boats used previously for crossing the Indus river, dismantled and carted the 200 miles to this new riverine obstacle; these were reassembled while Alexander scouted the river banks.

When the crossing did come, it was under cover of a morning thunderstorm. Alexander had chosen a river headland some miles from camp, and had hidden most of his boats there, quietly gathering his battalions under cover. Craterus, a senior Macedonian general, was left in charge of the main camp, with a force ready to make a crossing once the Indian army was thrown into disorder by the news of the principal landing. During the night, Alexander had taken a strong division—around 11,000 men—to the prepared crossing point, and as dawn broke they set off across the river.

Arrian tells us that a single boat carried the king and his generals, the men who would later fight each other for Alexander's legacy—Perdiccas would become regent for the king's infant son; Ptolemy made himself king of Egypt; Lysimachus was to become king of Thrace; Seleucus would inherit the Asian parts of the empire. This was a rare concentration of historical potential; had the vessel foundered in the swelling waters and its passengers perished, the world ahead would have played out very differently. There would have been no Cleopatra, no Seleucid realm to embed Greek culture in Asia, and the corpse of Alexander's empire would have been dismembered into very different fragments.

The invaders made their landing, only to discover themselves on an island: the swollen river had opened a new channel, separating them from the main east bank. With the sun rising and the Indian scouts patrolling the river, time was pressing. Finding a safe ford across this obstacle was essential to success. Several attempts were made, but each time the water proved too deep. Eventually, a way was found, though the foot soldiers had to wade across in water up to their necks.

When news of this landing reached Porus, he had a difficult choice to make. Was this crossing the main attack, or another diversion? The Macedonian camp could be seen across the river, still with everything in place and still busy with soldiers. How much of his force could he risk detaching to meet the landed threat? Porus dispatched around 2,000 men and 120 chariots under the command of his son. Racing to the landing site, they found a strong force of invaders already drawn up for fighting; as the Indians approached, Alexander sent forward horse archers—Sogdians or Bactrians—to engage the Indian cavalry, then committed his own heavy cavalry. The Indian chariots struggled in the mud caused by the storm, and were a hindrance to their fellows; the Indians were beaten off, losing perhaps 400 of their number, including the young prince.

The returning remnants of his mauled squadron told Porus that the main force of invaders was across the river; he had failed to prevent a crossing in force and the reckoning was now upon him. He decided to move virtually his entire army against Alexander's division, leaving only a small body of soldiers to defend the camp against a possible crossing by Craterus. As Alexander marched to engage him, Porus had time to deploy his forces into battle positions, the elephants being arranged like mobile forts in his front line, the cavalry on his flanks. Porus himself was an unusually large man and wore armor embellished with gold and silver. Known to be courageous and to possess skills of command, the test before him must surely have been the greatest he had faced, as he surveyed the oncoming aggressors from the back of his huge war elephant, the largest in his army.

Alexander began the action with his Central Asian horse archers, a rapid rolling wave of arrows advancing against the enemy cavalry. The Indians attempted a wheeling maneuver in counter, but were then engaged by the heavy companion cavalry, led by Alexander himself, which beat the Indians back. Some of the Indian horsemen repaired in confusion to their own lines where they caused a crush among their soldiers. Then the infantry engagement began, wherein Porus had his main hope of victory through the triumph of his elephants, but the Macedonians coped with them admirably. According to Arrian, the phalanx advanced to press the elephants and threw missiles at the beasts, no doubt also using their *sarisae* (long two-handed spears or pikes) to dislodge the soldiers mounted on top. The Macedonian spearmen pressed forward relentlessly, and the cavalry enveloped the Indian flanks. The battle turned into a general slaughter; those Indians who escaped back to their camp found Craterus and his men, now across the river, waiting ready to cut them down.

Porus himself fought on, still mounted on his elephant, until all was beyond lost. With difficulty, he was wounded and forced to surrender, then taken before Alexander. Accounts of their conversation differ, but it seems that the king was impressed by the bravery of his captive, for Porus was restored to his kingly status—under the suzerainty of Alexander—and given further lands to add to his principality.

So Alexander added more territory to his empire and another vassal ruler to his retinue, but how did this European king come to be so far from home, fighting battles in India? How had he brought his soldiers to the edge of the known world, marching them from Greece all the way to the Hydaspes? To understand the appearance of Alexander and his army in India, we must go back to his pursuit of the destruction of the Achaemenian Empire of Persia, the great rivals of the Greeks. After the aggressive young conqueror launched his invasion of Asia in 334 BC, the grand realm of unrivaled reach and riches fell to him in a scant few years, and he marched his Macedonian veterans to the furthest reaches of the empire, beyond the Khyber Pass.

That a small kingdom on the fringes of the Greek world could marshal her neighbors and deal such a blow to the hegemon speaks of serious decline in the Persian state; it also speaks of the violent skill that Alexander brought to his pursuit of conquest. If the gradual decline of Achaemenian power was the means for his belligerent thrust into Asia, the motive was provided, in part, by the Achaemenian victories against the Greeks generations before. Alexander was the climactic resolution to over two centuries of tension in which Greeks and Persians played an intricate game of diplomacy and war. This is not to imply Greek unity—alliances were made with gold and broken with gold, often joining Greek and Persian against Greek. The triangle of Athens, Sparta and Persia dominated this era of armed politicking, other city states being drawn in as ballast in the weighty struggles of the principal players, who played not for a Greek national principle but for their own gain. Persia was the first resort of many a disgraced or disadvantaged Greek general or statesman, and the provider of the means to rejoin the fight, provoking many shifts of allegiance and lengthening many wars. The Peloponnesian War of the late fifth century BC, famously recorded by the historian Thucydides, was the epitome of these bitter and ruinous struggles.

The Greeks remained disunited against the Persians until Macedonia, a Hellenized state of little consequence on the edge of the Greek world, rose to power under Philip II, the father of Alexander. Philip built an army of unrivaled professionalism and used it to forge Macedonia into the paramount power of the Greek peninsula; this was Alexander's inheritance: a state organized for war around the person of the king, with a hardened army and regional power. These Macedonian outsiders, non-Greek by descent but culturally Hellenized, injected a semi-barbarian vigor into a sophisticated but tired Greece, and were to take Greek culture across the world in a military effervescence of startling speed.

When Philip became its ruler in 359 BC, Macedonia was not a powerful kingdom. It faced rowdy tribes of barbarians to the north, and the risk of being overwhelmed by the advanced Greek states to the south. Philip recognized that military strength was essential to ensuring the survival and success of his new realm, and set about improving his modest forces, expanding his territory as they grew more capable. He began by arming his infantry of peasant levies with long and heavy spears—the famous *sarisae*—and clothed them in light armor. Toughened through long marches in the hot sun, and drilled and disciplined by mercenary generals, these troops secured his northern frontiers against the primitively equipped and untrained tribesmen. To face the Greek threat, however, heavier forces were required, and Philip expanded the prestigious Companion Cavalry, the elite close comrades of the king himself. Non-Macedonians from the Greek states were settled on new fiefs in conquered lands, providing the king with a larger aristocracy from which to draw these cavalrymen.

The hoplite—a heavy infantry soldier—had been the mainstay of Greek armies for centuries. Armored in bronze breastplates and wearing grandly crested helmets, they carried broad circular shields that they used in tight defensive formations, each shield protecting the bearer and the soldier to his left. Armed with long spears and short swords, and harshly trained as professional soldiers, they were an essential part of the state apparatus of every city in Greece. The Spartans at Thermopylae had demonstrated the determined resistance that disciplined units of such soldiers could offer. By the time of the rise of Macedonia, however, hoplites throughout Greece were becoming more lightly armed—perhaps reflecting a desire for greater speed and ease of movement, or perhaps indicating the reduced finances available for such expensive equipment after decades of war. When Philip tightened his grip on the silver mines of Thrace, he acquired the means to develop his own force of heavy infantry, and he began to outdo the Greek states to the south in the weight of forces—individually and collectively—that he could bring to bear.

Through judicious territorial gains and cunning husbanding of resources, Philip had made himself the richest ruler among the Hellenes, unmatched in treasure except by the emperor of Persia. This wealth allowed Philip to do more than just equip his armies. He could now buy friends in the Greek cities, and recruit mercenaries to bolster his already commanding military advantage; ambitious for hegemony over a united Greece, Philip wanted to lead it to war against the Persians. While there were voices in Greece arguing for federation and an attack on Persia, there were others who feared Macedonian strength, calling for resistance to the evident aspirations of the newly powerful king in the north. With Philip increasing his purchase over the Greek states and tension growing between the principal players, a reckoning was unavoidable. It came in 338 BC, in battle at Chaeronea. The armies of Athens and Thebes broke themselves against the unmoving lines of the Macedonian hoplites, superior now to those whose former glories they imitated. With Thebes and Athens beaten and Sparta suborned, Philip was supreme in Greece. After formalizing his leadership by the creation of the League of Corinth, a coalition firmly in his grip, Philip declared war against Persia on behalf of his reluctant new allies in the following year. Greece had been united by force, and Philip had achieved his aim of making war on the Great King. An advance party of 10,000 soldiers crossed into Asia in the spring of 336 BC to prepare positions for the main force that would follow. It was to be a different king who led the awaited invasion.

As the culmination of his Asian ambitions approached, Philip II was assassinated during his daughter's wedding celebrations in 336 BC. Alexander's succession was not untroubled: an infant son of a new wife of the polygamous Philip provided a potential focus for mutiny, and some members of the League of Corinth tried to take advantage of the king's youth to free themselves from Macedonian dominance. The first problem was solved when Olympias, Alexander's mother, murdered the rival royal baby along with its mother; the second matter was dealt with when Alexander burnt Thebes to the ground and enslaved its population. The League of Corinth fell into line, chastened.

Although Alexander was only twenty years old when he came to the throne, it should not be thought that he was naïve or inexperienced. At the age of sixteen he had conducted royal business as regent when Philip was away on campaign, and he had joined his father in the north on several fighting seasons. At the battle of Chaeronea, Alexander had commanded the Macedonian left and had broken the Theban line with his cavalry charges, an essential contribution to Philip's triumph. The young prince had also been to Athens as part of the diplomatic mission that imposed the new order. Alexander was already hardened in war and had been exposed to the subtleties of statecraft.

It took two years for the young king to secure his hold over Macedonia and Greece, and to make certain that the tribal peoples to the north were under submission. In 334 BC, Alexander was ready to seize the grand plans of his father with angry enthusiasm, and prepared to invade Asia to make war on Darius III, the new Persian king. In the spring, he crossed the Hellespont with a large army: around 30,000 foot soldiers and 5,000 cavalry. Joined to the advance forces sent to Asia by Philip, this gave Alexander an army of almost 50,000, the largest expedition ever to set foot outside Greece; a force of 12,000 phalanx soldiers was left to defend his interests at home. As his vessel made landfall on the Asian shore of the Hellespont, Alexander leapt to the beach in full armor. In a clear gesture of intent, he cast his spear firmly into the sand.

A stone bust originally from Alexandria—the city he founded in Egypt—and now in the British Museum provides a good picture of the young invader. A shock of unruly hair, curls tumbling down his neck. Heavy lips with a suggestive cast under a straight, immodest nose running directly into a prominent brow, his head set in its characteristic leftward tilt. In coins the languid eroticism of the British Museum bust becomes sterner, perhaps catching a visual likeness of the harsh manner and strident voice reported by Plutarch, the Greek biographer, in his *Parallel Lives*. This was the young man setting out to conquer Asia.

The Persians appeared to be relatively untroubled by this development; they had, after all, held at bay the advance force of Macedonians for two years. Superior in cavalry, they were, however, deficient in infantry and were dependent upon Greek mercenaries. Memnon of Rhodes, a Greek general in Persian service, saw the danger and argued for withdrawal into Asia Minor, leaving scorched earth behind them to weaken the invaders before meeting in battle in the interior. However, the Persian satrap Arsites wished to avoid the despoliation of his territories and wanted a quick resolution, so the Persian forces took up positions on the Granicus river, only thirty miles or so from the Hellespont where Alexander was marshaling his forces for the march inland. Advancing to engage, and overcoming the difficulty of attacking up the steep banks of the river, Alexander led his cavalry into thick fighting in which he himself nearly died: his helmet was shattered, and he was saved from the *coup de grâce* by Cleitus the Black, who severed the hand bearing the sword about to fall on the king. With Alexander safe, the quality of the Macedonians told. The Persians were routed, numerous commanders falling among the dead. Most of the Greek mercenaries fighting for Darius were massacred, the few survivors being enslaved and sent to Macedonia to work the fields.

That Greeks were in the army opposing Alexander denies his invasion the status of the pan-Hellenic crusade against the Achaemenians for which he wished. Although his army did contain units contributed by his forcibly united allies in the League of Corinth, their numbers were small; Sparta, for one, contributed none at all. It was, therefore, the Macedonians themselves, the Royal Army, who carried the burden of the fighting, from the Granicus all the way to India. The elite of this army was the *hetairoi,* or companion cavalry, trained to charge home with long spears, *xysta,* of cornel wood. During his pitched battles, Alexander himself fought among them. Of equal tactical importance but much greater numbers was the foot phalanx, or *pezhetairoi* and *asthetairoi,* who formed a deep battle line. Armed with the *sarisa,* they carried a medium-size shield of wood covered in bronze that gave them their other name, *chalkaspides,* or "bronze shields."

Alexander also relied on an elite unit that usually formed the junction between companions and the foot phalanx, the *hypaspistai* (later renamed the *argyraspides* from their silver shields). In pitched battle they carried the same arms as the foot companions, but could fight with swords and javelins on the special missions with which Alexander frequently entrusted them. All these Macedonian soldiers wore bronze helmets, often formed like Phrygian caps, and body armor either of linen or bronze. Besides their spears, they carried the forward-curved Macedonian sword, the *kopis* or *machaira*, that Curtius tells us was used to great effect against the trunks of the elephants at the Hydaspes. In the ensuing years, Alexander's army was to include growing quantities of foreign auxiliaries, but these Macedonian units were its core, and in their scarlet, purple and blue tunics, they presented an immediately identifiable and impressive array.

This early victory at the Granicus left Asia Minor open to Alexander. Arsites escaped the battle only to commit suicide, aware of his responsibility for the defeat; Memnon of Rhodes also fled, later to lead the resistance along the Aegean coast. There was, however, little that the Persians could place in the way of Alexander as he advanced from his first success in Asia, striking south into Lydia and toward the Greek cities of the coast. Ephesus surrendered to him willingly; Miletus resisted and Alexander's siege engines made short work of its fortifications. The defending forces were slaughtered, but the city left whole. Halicarnassus— home town of Herodotus—also resisted, under the command of Memnon. After a siege that proved expensive to the invader, Memnon withdrew his forces to the citadel and fired the city, leaving its ruin to Alexander. Judging the capture of the citadel too difficult, Alexander left a force to contain its defenders and continued on his occupation of Asia Minor. The impatience with which the king dealt with such obstacles suggests his determined focus on grander objectives, goals that exceeded the mere reduction of a resisting city. The speed of his progress, and the superficial grasp he took over the lands through which he passed at this time left swathes of Asia Minor unpacified and barely in Alexander's orbit, as he pushed on in an effort to bring his Persian opposite to a reckoning. Alexander took as many risks with his strategy as he did with his own life in battle.

By the time Alexander diverted himself from Halicarnassus, it was the autumn of 334 BC. For the winter season, he divided his forces, sending Parmenion—a senior Macedonian general later to rile Alexander with his *lèse majesté*—to subdue the interior, while Alexander continued south, reached the Mediterranean coast and then swung back north to plunge into the heart of Asia Minor. In early 333 BC, he was in Phrygia, at the old capital of Gordium. His rapid strides across Anatolia left much unconquered behind him, and many peoples unsubdued. Even at the end of Alexander's reign, ten years later, inaccessible areas of Asia Minor had still not been induced to accept the Alexandrine embrace.

In the early summer of 333 BC, Alexander marched south across Asia Minor to Cilicia, the fertile province bordering the corner of the Mediterranean where Anatolia turns south into Syria and the Holy Land. Darius was gathering forces at Babylon in preparation for a decisive battle to end Alexander's ambitions in Asia. For the next months, Alexander based himself in Cilicia—partly due to an illness of several weeks—as the Persian army made its gradual approach. When the king had recovered fully, he set off east to meet Darius and his army. For a time, the two armies were within striking distance, just south of the town of Issus, but there was a pause. Both forces stood firm on their chosen ground, waiting for the enemy to leave his favored territory to fight at a disadvantage. Alexander kept to the coast, aiming to employ the sea to guard one flank and the mountains the other. Darius wanted to entice the Macedonians inland on to the plains where the superior Persian numbers could deploy effectively and overwhelm the invaders.

After a few days of tension, it was Darius who quit his preferred field to seek a resolution, making an encircling march to take Alexander in the rear. Despite this maneuver, which caught Alexander off his guard, the resulting battle of Issus was a disaster for the Persians. Their army had still to squeeze itself into the slight coastal strip, ceding their advantage in numbers before the fight began, and making tactical movement difficult. Alexander himself led the cavalry charge that began the battle, and his horsemen forced their way toward the Persian king. While the Macedonian flanks came under pressure, the spearhead of companion cavalry fought their way closer to Darius, who was fighting in the thick.

This scene is thought to be recorded in the famous Alexander Mosaic from Pompeii, a later copy of a painting by a Greek master contemporary to the battle (see color plate 4). It shows Alexander, his horse rearing among the violence, just feet away from Darius in his grand chariot, spears lowered menacingly about him and horses thrashing in the carnage. The Macedonian king wears the uniform of the companion cavalry: a white linen cuirass, with the green cord of the Royal Squadron, shoulder pieces made fast with red bindings. A thick band of small metal plates mails his waist, and fringed strips of whitened linen hang to his thighs to complete his armor. He wears a cloak of purple bordered with golden yellow, clasped at the throat with bronze, and sits upon a saddlecloth of panther skin. In his right hand, Alexander wields a long spear, a short sword hanging to his left.

Darius, in danger of being captured, withdrew from the battlefield. As the news spread through his army, a general retreat began in which the Persian superiority in numbers became a terrible handicap in their constrained positions. The chaotic withdrawal proved more costly than the battle proper, there being too great a crush to allow easy escape, and the Macedonians continued to press forward ruthlessly. Although the numbers are exaggerated for propaganda effect, the classical sources tell of 500 Macedonian dead to 100,000 Persian. The true figures are not known with certainty, but there was undoubtedly a brutal imbalance.

So Alexander had defeated the Great King, and was poised to march into the center of the empire. However, putting the integrity of his grand strategy ahead of his zeal, the Macedonian did not plunge intemperately into Babylonia and the Achaemenian heartlands of Persia. It was to be another two years before Alexander and Darius met again in battle. In the interval, Alexander occupied Syria, the Mediterranean coast and Egypt, to secure his flank and divest Darius of resources. During this period, the Achaemenian offered terms three times, and three times they were rejected, his increasing generosity with lands and hands-in-marriage irrelevant to Alexander's concept of universal monarchy: the world would be united under him by conquest, and not divided by negotiation. By 331 BC, when the two kings again clashed, at Gaugamela—near what is now Mosul in the Kurdish part of Iraq—Alexander had halved the empire. Deprived of his western lands, Darius had to look to his east for the means to defend his core Iranian provinces. At the battle of Gaugamela, therefore, Darius fielded soldiers from India, Bactria and Sogdiana, and Scythians from beyond the frontier, in such numbers that it was with difficulty that all were armed and armored. His force was even larger than the powerful army that Alexander had beaten at Issus, but numbers again failed to prevail and he was again defeated, once more fleeing the field. This was the end for Darius, now a disgraced monarch: he escaped east—only to be seized and later murdered by Bessus, the satrap of Bactria—while Alexander marched south and entered Babylon in triumph. In an echo of the magnanimity of Cyrus the Great—whose tomb he was later to venerate—Alexander ordered that the temple of Bel, destroyed by Xerxes, should be rebuilt.

With the Great King in flight, there was no organized resistance in Persia, and Alexander moved east with relative ease to take possession of the imperial center and its capitals; Persepolis, the grand glory of Achaemenian art and power, was in the hands of the conquerors. The great palace complex was burnt, and the city surrounding it was sacked by Alexander's army. Perhaps the palace was set alight by accident amid one of the drunken revels that featured regularly in Alexander's court life. More likely, it was fired in revenge for the destruction of Athens by Xerxes in 480 BC, making it a symbolic act of state vandalism: the young representative of a resurgent Hellenic world destroying the culture that had sought to rule it.

Besides lighting fires to burn Persepolis, Alexander is remembered for putting them out. To the Zoroastrians, fire is especially sacred as the supplier of energy and light to the fight against evil, and temples are built to house flames that may have been kept burning continuously for hundreds of years. Thus it is especially damning to Alexander that he is remembered in Zoroastrian tradition as having *extinguished many fires*. There is no suggestion that this was a deliberate policy—the invasion did not have a religious character—and it no doubt happened during the looting of temples. These depredations had a serious impact on the faith, however, by killing priests who were essential to the transmission of a precious oral body of hymns and liturgy. In Zoroastrian scripture, Alexander alone shares the epithet *Guzastag*, "the Accursed," with the evil spirit Angra Mainyu.

While the occupation and annexation of Iran proper was achieved without serious hindrance, it took Alexander a great deal longer to subdue the northeast of the Iranian world, the frontier provinces of the Achaemenian Empire that included the Khyber Pass. After murdering Darius, Bessus revealed his own ambitions on the crown and repaired to his satrapy of Bactria to raise its forces against Alexander. In his typical fashion, the Macedonian king responded by immediately marching on Bactria, and found Aria, Arachosia, Drangiana and Sogdiana also in the Bessus camp. By the spring of 329 BC, Alexander had subdued Drangiana and Aria, and was able to march through Arachosia with little resistance. He halted in the valley of the Kabul river to found another Alexandria—now Bagram, near the modern city of Kabul—before advancing north into Bactria. Bessus fled into Sogdiana, and, with his forces deserting him ahead of the conquering king, was surrendered to Alexander by Sogdian noblemen keen to make their peace with the new power. Bessus was humiliated and his nose and ears mutilated before he was executed, Alexander claiming to avenge the death of Darius. The end of Bessus did not end the revolts, however, and trouble continued in Bactria and Sogdiana, spreading beyond the Jaxartes, the Achaemenian frontier. Once again echoing Cyrus the Great, Alexander had to fight the tribes beyond the frontier—including the Massagetae—to shore up the borders of his empire. In all, these efforts took two years of hard campaigning.

In the spring of 327 BC, he married Roxane, a princess of Bactria, said by the contemporary sources to be the most beautiful woman in the world bar Statira, the wife of Darius III, no doubt an intentionally mischievous slight. That the first wife of the king came from a conquered people of Iranian stock, and not from the nobility of Macedonia—or Greece at the least—was further evidence of Alexander's increasing orientalization, already suggested by his growing fondness for wearing Persian dress. It may be that Alexander felt that, at the age of twenty-nine, he should provide an heir without waiting until his return to Europe, but there was also a deeper reason for marrying an Asian bride. In *The History of Alexander*, Quintus Curtius Rufus, a Roman historian basing his work on Greek accounts from the time, has Alexander explaining his thinking, saying that he has united Europe and Asia into one kingdom, and that he sought to "erase all distinction between conquered and conqueror." Amid other signs of Alexander's vision of a lasting *imperium* over Asia—not least seven continuous years of campaigning to conquer it—his choice of wife implies a desire to cement the union with an offspring of both continents.

This vision, and Alexander's claim to the Achaemenian Empire in its entirety, made necessary the conquest of India. Fired by his astonishing success in every land he had ventured to so far, it seems that Alexander was coming to view the world as one monarchy with him at its head. Having conquered the hegemonic Persian power and made it his own, absorbing along with it the ancient civilizations of Egypt and Babylonia, and having mastered all resisters and rebels from Thebes to the Jaxartes, Alexander saw no obstacle to extending his rule over all mankind. The Hellenic conception of geography at the time had the Ocean—the great sea at the end of the world—not much beyond the Indus river: Alexander seems to have believed that a short campaign in India would complete his global conquest. Quintus Curtius Rufus has him explaining his urgent desire to continue east:

> We are coming to where the sun rises, to the Ocean. Unless cowardice stands in our way, we shall return home from there in triumph, after bringing the ends of the earth into subjection!

With the rebel provinces of Sogdiana and Bactria finally subdued, Alexander was ready to march into India to place his armies at the end of the world and make himself supreme among rulers of every era. Once again putting strategic soundness ahead of tempting prospects, Alexander took half the army along the valley of the Kabul river, striking into the mountains north of the route to India, securing this important road by a campaigning season of terrorism against the tribes that might threaten it. While he scoured the hill country for potential adversaries, in what are now the Kunar and Swat valleys, Alexander sent ahead the other half of the army, under Hephaestion and Perdiccas, to secure a crossing over the Indus and await his arrival.

So it was that in early 327 BC one-half of Alexander's army marched through the Khyber Pass without the king at its head. As the bright weather of spring defeated the snow of winter, the veterans of Macedon, reinforced by men of the conquered nations, set out on another chapter of their long war. We can imagine them in marching order, now with their tight breastplates removed and slung across their backs. They balance their *sarisae* on their shoulders, the long points swaying without order as they tramp over the rough paths into the Subcontinent, for the moment lacking the unmoving discipline of their battle formation. At the narrow confine by Ali Masjid, where the Khyber closes to just feet in width, the army would have squeezed through, two or three abreast, looking up warily at the steep heights immediately above them; unknown creatures might inhabit these mountains, for assuredly India was full of wonders. Perhaps the squadrons of cavalry from Bactria and Sogdiana followed behind the hoplites, dust thrown up by the hooves of their horses as they sauntered loose-reined into India. These thousands of men, vanquishers of half of Asia, tramped down the curving trail as the Khyber Pass opens out on to the plains of the Subcontinent. As the chilly mountain sun glinted off their spearheads and sword blades, imagine the fear rising within a distant onlooker at the approach of this unknown army.

The two generals reached the Indus river without great incident and set about building a bridge over the river—probably near Ohind—to carry the reunited army into what is known in the modern world as the Punjab. This Land of Five Rivers (named from the Persian *panj*, meaning five, and *ab*, water) was cut through by the Jhelum, Chenab, Ravi, Beas and Sutlej rivers, running south and uniting in the Indus itself, a riverine blessing that provided for fertile agriculture after irrigation in later centuries. To invaders, the rivers were obstacles that could hinder armies but Hephaestion and Perdiccas had time for their task, for it was not until the spring of 326 BC that Alexander joined them, having harassed the mountain peoples to his satisfaction. When the king arrived, they celebrated with athletic games and sacrifices, and the army crossed the mighty river.

They were in friendly territory, for this was the principality of Ambhi, the raja of Taxila, who had approached Alexander during his campaign in Sogdiana. At this meeting, Ambhi had offered his submission to the Macedonian king and invited him to invade India; Ambhi was locked in rivalry with his neighbor, Porus, and sought to use the army of foreign invaders to defeat him. Being confirmed in his rule by Alexander, Ambhi had provisioned Hephaestion and Perdiccas while they fashioned their bridge, and now welcomed Alexander into his principality as his overlord. Alexander did not need such persuasion to attempt the conquest of India, but certainly the Subcontinent was not united against outsiders.

The Achaemenian hold over their former possessions in northwest India had certainly withered by this time. It is possible that the Persian grip continued until the end of Darius at Gaugamela, for Indians fought for him at that battle, and the ready submission to Alexander by the raja of Taxila may indicate that he accepted him as the legitimate successor of the Achaemenians: Ambhi may have ruled Gandhara as a vassal king of the Persian emperor. However, it is not known with certainty; perhaps the Achaemenian collapse under the Macedonian onslaught freed the Indians of Gandhara and Hindush from what had anyway become only a nominal Persian suzerainty.

As Alexander and his reunited army approached Taxila, there was an anxious moment when a force sent by Ambhi to greet his new master was mistaken for a hostile defense , there being elephants interspersed between the files of soldiers. The Macedonians began to form their combat ranks, but Ambhi himself sped his horse forward to offer assurance, Alexander riding out to meet him between their advancing armies; without a language in common, the two rulers smiled their way to an understanding, and the Macedonian army entered the great city in peace. The generosity with which Ambhi bestowed gifts upon Alexander suggests that his attachment to him was not merely a scheme to gain use of his army: besides fifty-six fighting elephants, flocks of sheep and 3,000 highly prized bulls, Ambhi made a present of eighty talents of silver coin. Pleased with this show of fealty, Alexander returned all these offerings to Ambhi, adding 1,000 silver talents from his baggage train, much gold and silver plate, Persian cloth and thirty horses from the royal stables along with their golden trappings. We can imagine that Ambhi was pleased with the results of his early affiliation to Alexander; the Macedonian officers were not, feeling that their greater devotion to the king's cause was ill-recognized.

There is no account of what the people of Taxila thought of the Macedonians (or Yavanas, as they called them—a corruption of "Ionian" that became a general term for Europeans and was used until as late as the nineteenth century). Since the city had already been a center of fused cultures for centuries, and a destination for peoples from far afield, it may be that the veteran soldiery of Macedon attracted casual glances only. Certainly, there were unusual sights for the invaders, long distant from home: one such of special interest to Alexander was the famous ascetics of the city, wise men of strange habits and great learning. The king could not go to them with dignity, and they declined invitations to attend the king, so Alexander—showing remarkable restraint for a ruler of rapidly expanding egotism—sent an officer, Onesicritus, himself formerly a student of the cynic philosopher Diogenes, to see them. Finding over a dozen of these philosophic recluses sitting naked in the hot sun outside the city, Onesicritus explained the king's desire to speak with them; they replied that the king must come in person and sit naked on the baking stones in order to acquire their wisdom. On hearing of the Greek philosophers, the Indian ascetics replied that they were pleased that the Yavana had learned men but said it was unfortunate that they insisted on maintaining a habit as unnecessary as wearing clothes. Eventually, the raja of Taxila persuaded— no doubt with difficulty—one of their number, Calanus, to accompany Alexander, and he joined the royal camp. Journeying all the way to Persia with the army over the next few years, Calanus fell ill and committed suicide on a funeral pyre in 324 BC, amid a farewell from the entire army and athletic games held in honor of his passing.

There was some reciprocal exchange of learning: among Alexander's expedition was Pyrrho, the skeptic philosopher, who is said to have conversed with Indian wise men, perhaps these very ascetics in Taxila. It is quite remarkable that Pyrrho had journeyed as far as India since his skeptical ideas were based on apathy: all action is founded on belief, all belief is delusion, and delusion brings pain. Therefore, absence of activity is ideal; happiness comes through a freedom from delusion, and thus through inactivity. If Pyrrho had ever tried to convert Alexander to his way of thinking, we can suppose that he failed.

Alexander did not stay long in Taxila. After a few days in the city, he had received the submission of other rulers of the region, but also had word that Porus, the rival of Ambhi, had refused to submit: famed as a warrior, and with his enemy in Alexander's camp, he would trust to arms to defend his sovereignty. Such a challenge to his imperium was impossible for Alexander to resist, and he marched immediately to subdue Porus with violence. Thus it was that the king of Macedonia came to fight on the banks of the Hydaspes to enforce his arbitrary claim on Indian lands thousands of miles from home. Through defeating Porus and then absorbing him into his regime as a vassal king, Alexander expanded his domain and a Hellenic king ruled the Punjab.

The irresistible machine of victory continued its progress around the world, and Alexander seems to have had no intention of bringing it to a halt. He pressed on, crossing the Acesines river (modern Chenab) and then the Ravi, annexing the territory to Porus, now his friend, being drawn—perhaps unwittingly—into Indian power politics. The army marched on eastward and came to the Beas river, known to them as the Hyphasis. Eighty miles distant was the Sutlej, the last river in the Indus system of the Punjab, and beyond that lay the Ganges, the famous and fabled river, the heart of India. At the time, the power in the Ganges plain was a kingdom called Magadha, centered on the great riparian city of Pataliputra, and Alexander had been hearing tempting reports of its wealth. The ancient accounts are clear that he meant to continue his thrust deep into India to conquer this new target.

In the May of 326 BC on the banks of the Beas, however, his Macedonian soldiery would go no further. The seemingly endless grind of campaigning, this war that was extended every time another potential conquest appeared on the horizon, had taken its weary toll on Macedonian morale. Alexander had often used his forceful charm in urging his army to continue, but it was no longer enough; they wanted to return home to enjoy the spoils of war. In a gathering with the king, a senior commander named Coenus voiced the opinion of the soldiers, to great royal anger. A second meeting with his officers on the following day left Alexander still without support, and he withdrew to his tent for three days, hoping to shame his veterans into agreement. No softening came, so Alexander ordered the performance of the sacrifices usually made before a river crossing; when the auguries of the gods proved unfavorable—no doubt with priestly assistance—the king was able to present his decision to turn back as a response to a divine verdict, not the refusal of his soldiers. Alexander never forgave his veterans for their failure to sustain his wild ambitions. In the three years that he had left alive, the non-Macedonian element of his court and army grew in power, and his fellow countrymen were increasingly placed on the margin. More immediately, Coenus suddenly fell dead from a mysterious disease just a few days after his displeasing advocacy at the Beas river; suspicions were raised that his death was not a natural one.

The invasion force then returned to the Hydaspes. Alexander dealt only superficially with the necessary business of the conquered areas before leaving for home: a satrap was not appointed over the lands of Porus, leaving the Indian prince freedom to rule as he pleased. This gives us the impression that Alexander had lost interest in India, and, having been thwarted here, was keen to move on to grand schemes in other places. Certainly he would not retrace his steps: a large fleet of boats—perhaps a thousand, or even two—was built on the Hydaspes to carry the bulk of the army down the Indus to the Arabian Sea, an amplified echo of the voyage of Scylax two centuries before.

After great celebrations of music and more athletic games, the fleet set off in November 326 BC. On the banks, Hephaestion and Craterus marched with a column of soldiers each, and it was surely with some relief that the army set off home. This was to be no simple return journey, however: battles were fought the length of the river to bring every last tribe and village into submission to the departing king. No rest was afforded the fatigued soldiers; in one city siege, Alexander nearly died on the battlements with an arrow in the chest, such was his determination to inspire his men to continued military glory.

It took nine months for the fleet and army to travel down the Indus, fighting whoever they could find. Many towns and cities were razed and their populations slaughtered until Alexander came to the coast in July 325 BC. Here he divided his forces, sending the fleet under Nearchus to sail home along the coast of Gedrosia—Baluchistan in modern Iran and Pakistan—and thence into the Persian Gulf. Having already sent Craterus with half the army to travel home through Arachosia, Alexander took the remainder and set off on a difficult and costly crossing of the inhospitable Gedrosian desert. The sources disagree on the casualties caused by this risky crossing, but the hardship was undoubtedly substantial and starvation a constant threat. Following this daring but expensive feat, Alexander's share of the army reunited with Craterus, traveled through Persia and by the spring of 324 BC the king was in Babylon.

Alexander had just a year to live. It was in Babylon that he died, in June 323 BC, after developing a fever following a riotous banquet during which he is said to have drained a twelve-pint bumper of wine. At the time, Alexander was again planning to expand his frontiers by an invasion of

Arabia, and an eventual conquest of North Africa. His restless ambition vaulted over geography: perhaps only the Macedonian veterans—upon whom he relied for the realization of such dreams—could check his unbounded desire for conquests. Throughout history, few rulers can rival Alexander in his assumption of mastery over the world.

For all the convulsive violence of Alexander's two-year visitation upon India, his impact on the Subcontinent was slight—a sharp smack from which it quickly recovered without any lasting damage being done. Memories of the west thereafter were largely of the Achaemenian Empire—a lasting presence that impressed itself upon northwest India through two centuries of rule—while not a single surviving early Indian source mentions Alexander. The layer of government that he added was very superficial, comprising the installation of a few satraps and the recognition of a few kings as vassals, and did not long survive him. He founded cities in India, as he did all over his conquered lands, but none lasted to flower. By his conquest of Bactria, he had sown the seeds of a Hellenic culture that would later flourish and revisit India, but this was over a century after Alexander returned west. The vigorous exertion that he demanded of himself and his soldiers, the subduing of everybody they could find, seems wasted when the final measure is taken.

The real function that Alexander served in his Indian adventure was as an enabler for those who came afterward. By finally demolishing Achaemenian authority, and by disrupting the existing states and principalities without establishing a lasting successor, he introduced chaos into the governance of northwest India. Such a situation demanded reforming and rebuilding, and new states and principalities rose on the ruins of the old, making chances for ambitious men and opportunists. One such aspiring ruler was to use the confusion that Alexander left behind to fashion himself a new empire.

CHAPTER THREE

The Mauryan Empire

Detail of the Ashokan pillar at Vaishali

A man is not a great man because he is a warrior and kills other men; but because he hurts not any living being, he in truth is called a great man.

THE DHAMMAPADA

You must realize this: that a prince, and especially a new prince, cannot observe all those things which give men a reputation for virtue, because in order to maintain his state he is often forced to act in defiance of good faith, of charity, of kindness, of religion.

The Prince by MACHIAVELLI

Before Alexander quit India, leaving the Punjab in chaos, he is said to have met with a man of great talent and purpose, an ambitious youth seeking a kingdom for himself. His name was Chandragupta Maurya, and he would exploit the disorder to make himself founder of one of the greatest dynasties in Indian history.

Chandragupta seems to have been self-possessed, even cocksure, and undaunted by his audience with the famous conqueror. We have no account of their conversation, but Plutarch tells us that Chandragupta would afterward often criticize Alexander for his failure to march on Magadha and make himself king on the Ganges. Where the Macedonian missed the opportunity, Chandragupta took the chance, launching a campaign against the Nanda dynasty of Magadha not long after his meeting with Alexander.

The founder of the house, Mahapadma Nanda, had been an able king, successfully husbanding wealth and power to develop and consolidate a kingdom on the Gangetic plains. He died in 329 BC, on the eve of Alexander's incursion into India, and was succeeded by his seven sons who ruled jointly, an unusual arrangement full of the potential for discord and disaster. There are also signs that the sons were less skilled and popular than their father, and indications that the kingdom began to disintegrate: the conquered territory of Kalinga, for example, very likely regained its independence. When Alexander was conquering the Punjab, therefore, powerful Magadha was showing signs of decay. It was through his astute exploitation of Magadhan weakness, and of the northwestern confusion left in the wake of Alexander, that Chandragupta Maurya was able to make himself emperor.

According to one of the most engaging accounts of his early years, Chandragupta was of princely birth and cheeky wit, a bright young man being marked out for future success. He is said to have been living at the court of the Nanda kings when a neighboring ruler sent them a gift, a grand cage containing a lion made of wax, rendered so artfully that it seemed to be real. The accompanying letter declared that anyone who could make the lion run without opening the cage should be acknowledged to be an exceptionally talented man, and destined for great things. The kings and courtiers, failing to understand the double meaning in the challenge, had few ideas about solving the riddle, so Chandragupta—still yet a boy—came forward. On being given permission to attempt a solution, he took an iron rod and heated it to redness, then thrust it through the bars of the cage, deep into the lion. The wax ran, the lion disappeared and Chandragupta had solved the riddle.

Perhaps it was through one such display of his precocious abilities that he offended his hosts, for the sources suggest that Chandragupta was forced to flee the court. An alternative is that he was maltreated by the Nandas and reacted to his handling with such firmness that flight became a necessity. It may have been shortly after he became an outcast that the youthful adventurer came to the attention of Chanakya, a fateful meeting that would propel them both to prominence. Chanakya was an experienced figure from the Brahmin priestly caste—perhaps formerly a royal official—and had been insulted by one of the Nanda kings. Harboring designs of vengeance, he was busy assembling the means of obtaining it, and became interested in the potential of this youthful prodigy to help him in his scheme. Together, Chandragupta and Chanakya would go on to create an empire: Chandragupta provided suitable royal qualities of intelligence, vision and charisma, while Chanakya brought a merciless experience of human affairs and a sophisticated philosophy of government that found practical expression in the Mauryan imperial system.

The Buddhist traditions maintain that Chanakya had also recruited another youth, a prince named Pabbato, as a useful element in his project of vengeance. Both young men lived with Chanakya for a time, while he taught them every accomplishment that would be useful to a pretender to the crown, a period in which the Brahmin could also assess each boy for his kingly qualities. As a mark of future royal distinction, he placed around the neck of each one a woolen cord woven with gold thread, a valuable gift in promise of riches ahead. After some time, Chanakya had made his choice; he knew which of his protégés would attain royalty. However, he decided to put his opinion to the test. One day, Chandragupta was lying sleeping under a tree, and Chanakya handed a sword to Pabbato, telling him to return with Chandragupta's golden cord, but without cutting it or untying it. Shortly afterward, Pabbato returned without the cord, declaring the task to be impossible. On the following day, Chanakya repeated the test, with the actors reversed: Chandragupta approached the sleeping Pabbato, and pondered the task. Deciding that the instruction could only be fulfilled by cutting off Pabbato's head, he wielded the sword, recovered the cord and returned it to Chanakya. Chandragupta had ably demonstrated the ruthless ambition that overcomes obstacles, and Chanakya was vindicated in his selection.

After several years of training for his royal prospects, Chandragupta had become a man, and Chanakya judged him capable of commanding an army. The time for revenge had come, and the conspirators put their scheme into violent action, raising a revolt against the Nandas in the heart of Magadha. Despite their extensive preparations and Chandragupta's heightened qualities, they were unable to overcome the military superiority of the Nanda kings, and the rebellion failed. Chandragupta's nascent army was destroyed, but the plotters escaped. Tutor and pupil thus began to wander the plains and forests seeking a means of recovering their fortunes and an easier arena in which to fight the Nandas. Accordingly, they made their way to the northwest provinces, on the fringes of Nanda influence; it is likely that this was when Chandragupta met Alexander the Great in the Punjab, and the occasion would be around 326 or 325 BC.

The establishment of a following in this fresh field and the accrual of resources sufficient for a second bid for power will have taken Chandragupta some years. In the meantime, Philip, Alexander's representative in the Punjab, was murdered in 324 BC by his mercenary soldiers, and Eudemos was installed to replace him. The region was under a superficial Greek government only, for their resources were sparse and can only have declined after Alexander's death in 323 BC as many Greeks sought to return home. The Indian conquests, far to the east of the centers of Macedonian maneuvering, were not the prime concern during the succession struggles that racked the Alexandrine empire, and turbulence was a characteristic of the region in these years, with competing powers emerging to contest for rule. This was all to the advantage of Chandragupta. As the Punjab became restive, he increased his influence and waited for the right time.

It came in 317 BC when Eudemos treacherously murdered Porus, Alexander's appointed vassal king of much of the Punjab. The consequent revolt against Greek rule was led by Chandragupta, and Eudemos was forced from the country, taking a significant force with him to fight against Antigonus in Syria; those Greek soldiers and officers who remained in India were put to the sword. Chandragupta had made himself master of the Punjab and the Indus valley, amplifying his forces and transforming himself at once into a king with extensive lands and subjects. With his powers augmented, he launched a war on Magadha. Provinces were captured one by one, from the frontier to Pataliputra itself. All seven of the Nanda kings were killed in the fighting, and Chandragupta Maurya became undisputed ruler of Magadha, a new emperor and founder of a dynasty: he was crowned at Pataliputra in 313 BC. Chanakya, who had schooled the king to his throne, became his chief minister.

In this office, Chanakya became the prime mover in the organization of an efficient state, with an advanced and carefully designed administration. Such a system was essential to provide the capacity for growth, and the Mauryan realm was aggressively expansionary: Chandragupta is the first ruler that can be considered emperor of all India in a meaningful sense, and he continued his conquests immediately after obtaining security in the Ganges region. Kashmir was captured, adding considerably to the imperial domain in the north. Mauryan forces campaigned into southern India: Saurashtra (modern Gujarat) was annexed, and Chandragupta conquered a sizeable measure of the Deccan, the plateau forming the north of the Indian peninsula. Inscriptions in Mysore, a country far to the south of his center of power on the northern rivers, attest to his domination. Alongside the emperor, Chanakya was essential to effecting these gains, and he became associated with piercing ruthlessness in his pursuit of imperial ends.

One of the legends that transmit this reputation to us surrounds Chanakya and the birth of Bindusara, the son and heir of Chandragupta. It shows the frightening clarity that Chanakya brought to bear on matters concerning the empire, and the mercilessness with which he could execute his decisions. Early in the reign, the emperor was in need of a son to secure the dynasty, and Chanakya would let no scruple deter him from this end. As a shrewd minister, full of foresight in turbulent times, he had sought to render Chandragupta immune to poison through a gradual inoculation, putting tiny but increasing amounts of toxin in his every meal. One day, at the royal table, Chanakya saw the queen—then bearing inside her the emperor's first child—take a morsel of food from the plate of Chandragupta, and raise it to her mouth. Not having time to prevent her placing the poisonous scrap between her lips, Chanakya made a rapid and ruthless calculation that the only way to save the life of the unborn child was to cut off the queen's head before she could swallow the noxious food. He seized a sword and, without hesitation, severed the queen's neck. Then he had the baby cut from the queen's dead body and placed in the womb of a goat, from where it later emerged, alive and well except for blemished skin (hence the name, Bindusara meaning, roughly, "covered in spots"). Although this story can only be a myth, it is a powerful indicator of the reputation that Chanakya had, in his own time and in later ages, as an unfeeling statesman of vision.

He is renowned for his association with a famous literary work also: the *Arthashastra,* a handbook of advice on the essential matters of rule—royal duties, justice, administration, war, diplomacy and espionage. Traditionally, the author is identified with Chanakya, writing under the name of Kautilya, though this is not certain. It is possible that he supplied only a fraction of the content of the book, which was later amplified and developed by adherents and scholars.

The Sanskrit manuscript of Kautilya's *Arthashastra* was discovered in 1905 by a librarian in Mysore. It set out a system of government of some complexity. The king was assisted by an assembly of counselors, forming a parliament of sorts, and a class of high officials supervized all the branches of administration. The sophisticated organization of the army was in the hands of a war department of six boards, each headed by a senior official. The civil administration was organized similarly, and carried out functions of surprising modernity, such as setting wage rates for artisans, collecting statistics, recording births and deaths, and supervising weights and measures; there is much borrowing from the

Achaemenian model of imperial government, far to the west. It may be that the *Arthashastra* describes the actual system that Kautilya—or Chanakya—put in place, perhaps recorded by loyal servants or followers who made inferences from the practice to divine his likely theory. Certainly, it can be read as evidence that there was a recognized need to recover after the shock of Alexander's invasion of Indian lands, a pressing requirement for a united and solid state system to provide a stronger defense against turbulence in the future. It is also evidence that Kautilya saw opportunity in the chaos, a chance to construct afresh a state ordered along lines of rationality and efficiency.

For all the importance of Kautilya's administrative innovations and bureaucratic developments, it is his philosophy of government that is remarkable for its depth and power, and for its advanced ideas. Contained in a series of maxims in the *Arthashastra*, it is most likely that this element is the work of Kautilya himself. He abandons the tradition of the divine origin of kings and establishes that the condition and future of society is in the hands of man, not fate. Through *udyama* (a life of activity) a king can determine the nature of existence in his kingdom and become the creator of an era. A rationalist, Kautilya took a secular approach to society and government, but was prepared to use religion and religious institutions in the service of the state where necessary. The *Arthashastra* has been condemned as a handbook of *realpolitik*; it was certainly a controversial work, and it was for its thread of pragmatism—exaggerated by elaborate myths—that Kautilya is often compared to Machiavelli. He successfully employed this realism in extending the realm in every direction.

Besides illuminating the philosophy of the rulers and the government they organized, the *Arthashastra* is useful to us for its material about daily life in the Mauryan Empire. Agriculture was rich and varied, and of great importance for government revenues: Kautilya tells of rice, barley, wheat, sesame, linseed, mustard, pulses, sugar cane and cotton being grown and, inevitably, taxed. Wool, silk and hemp were worn. Precious stones, gold, iron and copper were mined by the state, and many other metals—silver, bronze, lead, tin, brass—were widely used. This productivity supported networks of trade with regions as far away as China and Babylon, and maritime trade was active. The Mauryans also built a major road from Pataliputra to Taxila, a close forerunner of the Grand Trunk Road built by the British two thousand years later. Besides constructing roads to accommodate trade and armies, public works of the government included the building of caravanserais, the development of wells, irrigation schemes and dams, and the planting of orchards.

The Mauryan capital was at Pataliputra on the Ganges, a city encircled by a great palisade of timber with 570 towers and 64 gates. Many of the buildings were also made of wood and brick; the royal palace was stone-built, with impressive masonry in its carved pillars and capital stones, inspired by those of Persepolis. The quality of this work reminds us that the *Arthashastra* provides for the vigorous protection of artisans, as essential servants of the state: anyone causing a craftsman to lose the use of his hands or eyes was punished by death. Such attention to material culture seems to have created a flourishing environment: excavations reveal a sophisticated style of living in the city and some degree of popular art—terracotta statuettes of fertility symbols and painted tableware, for example. Women had important roles in the cultural life of the city, as entertainers, dancing girls, and—given Chanakya's practical approach to governance—spies. Indeed, his pragmatism extends to prostitutes—they were given a measure of legal privilege, and taxed on their earnings.

One of the more unusual roles fulfilled by women was the protection of the emperor: Chandragupta maintained a female bodyguard of archers—regarded as unassailably loyal—who accompanied him while hunting and served him in his chambers. When traveling, the emperor would sit atop a great elephant or ride on horseback, clad in fine muslin embroidered with purple and gold. His palace was said to be of remarkable beauty, exceeding those of the Persian emperors in its loveliness, and to abound with gilded pillars embellished with vines of gold, and birds rendered in silver. Peacocks and pheasants wandered through the elegant gardens and orchards, and large pools bore fish that only the royal children might catch. On occasion, the emperor would order that animals be brought to fight for his amusement: Chandragupta would watch elephants in combat, or bulls, rhinoceroses or rams.

The chaos that Alexander had left in the Punjab had made this cultured kingdom possible. Soon it was itself threatened in the very same way, again by Greeks: in 305 BC, Emperor Seleucus, one of Alexander's successors, marched his army through the Khyber Pass in an effort to reclaim the Punjab from Chandragupta.

Alexander had died in 323 BC without an heir, though his Bactrian bride Roxane was pregnant. His generals gathered in Babylon and decided to await the birth, postponing rivalries that were surely already in their minds. During this pause, the infantry mutinied in favor of Arrhidaeus, a mentally deficient elder brother of Alexander who had lived quietly without royal function until this time. When Roxane's child proved to be a boy (given the name of Alexander), a compromise was reached in which the two claimants would reign as joint kings, an unlikely pairing of infant and idiot in which both were necessarily the tools of their guardians. Perdiccas, the general who had led the army through the Khyber Pass just four years before, became regent, succeeded by Antipater, Alexander's senior diplomat. In 317 BC, the wife of Arrhidaeus attempted to throw off the guiding hand that pressed upon her husband so heavily; both were murdered in reply. By 311 BC Cassander, the son of Antipater, had become supreme over the Macedonian lands and felt secure enough to do away with Roxane and her child.

The division of the empire was well advanced by this time, the fractious generals letting no mere puppet kings prevent them from exercising their ambitions and fighting each other for the spoils of Alexander's victories. One grand and sweeping empire had been carved into five parts: Cassander held Macedonia, and Lysimachus made himself king of Thrace; Ptolemy, the forebear of Cleopatra, had undisputed rule of Egypt after defeating an invasion by Perdiccas; Asia Minor and western Asia to the Euphrates river was in the hands of Antigonus, and the Iranian lands up to the Indian and Central Asian frontiers was the domain of Seleucus.

These rivalries over the imperial corpse had occupied the energies of Alexander's successors for almost two decades. Finally, Seleucus was ready to attempt the recovery of the Indian lands that Alexander had fought hard to conquer but had never properly absorbed into the empire. Thus, in 305 BC, he advanced through the Khyber Pass, a Macedonian general once again marching an army into India. Sadly, we know little of the details of the campaign, but in the peace treaty that concluded the war Seleucus ceded an enormous share of his eastern lands to the new power in India, including Aria, Arachosia, Gandhara and Gedrosia, in return for marriage bonds and a valuable 500 elephants. Each general formally recognized the other's empire, and the treaty seems to have been regarded as a settlement marking permanent friendship. Along with much of modern Afghanistan and Baluchistan, the crucial Khyber Pass was now in the hands of the Mauryan Empire.

It is not known whether Chandragupta himself took a daughter of Seleucus as his wife, but sources do refer to one of his queens by the name of Durdhara, possibly a corruption of the Greek name Diodora. Since Seleucus had himself married an Iranian noblewoman named Apama, it is an intriguing possibility that future emperors of the Mauryan line may have mingled Greek and Iranian blood with Indian. There was also a diplomatic exchange, for the Greek envoy Megasthenes was sent to Pataliputra and recorded his experiences of Indian life in his *Indica*, a lost writing transmitted to us in fragments by other writers.

The treaty added greatly to the lands of Chandragupta and augmented his powers through control of the northwestern trade routes. Seleucus failed to regain the Indian territories of Alexander, but ultimately the treaty worked to his advantage too. The wars of the Alexandrine successors were to continue in western Asia; with his eastern marches secured by the new friendship with Chandragupta, Seleucus could turn back to his western frontier with confidence. Most importantly, the 500 elephants from the Indian king were to be essential to victory in the battle that formed the climactic end of the long dissolution of Alexander's conquests. In 301 BC, the successor kings met in a final reckoning at Ipsus in Asia Minor. These elephants resulted in the victory of Seleucus and the death of Antigonus in the battle; his kingdom was divided between the victors. Five successor kingdoms had become four and the struggle between Alexander's generals was over. Thus did the Indian elephant help decide the shape of the west.

Chandragupta's settlement with Seleucus was the culmination of his career. He had made himself emperor and had conquered much of the Subcontinent of India, establishing a sophisticated imperial system as he went. For all his grand achievements, however, he is little enough known twenty-three centuries later, at least in the West, and the name of Chandra-gupta does not resonate as it should. Perhaps this is because of his retreat in later years: the Jains (the highly ascetic sect that grew out of Hinduism) claimed that Chandragupta joined them, abdicated his throne and repaired to Mysore to end his life through gradual starvation in the Jain fashion, in around 289 BC.

Besides the gruesome myth of his beginning, very little is known about the reign of Bindusara, the son and heir of Chandragupta; it was his grandson Ashoka who was to achieve greater fame, becoming renowned even into the modern day as a monk-king, seen by some as tantamount to a saint for the way he drew together religion and government. We have an intriguing source for his reign, a rare supply of royal words inscribed in stone: the Edicts of Ashoka are an essential means of reconstructing his reign. Perhaps inspired by the Achaemenian use of rock inscriptions, Ashoka caused his words to be displayed around the empire, cut into suitable rocks or on to pillars of sandstone erected for public display. Both the content and location of these Edicts tell us much about the extent of the Mauryan realm, and—especially—Ashoka's religious concerns and policy.

Buddhist sources imply that Ashoka was an unattractive person who was disliked by his father. Nonetheless, it seems that Bindusara had uses for him in government, and Ashoka apparently spent time in Taxila, probably putting down a revolt: it may be that Gandharan distance from the Ganges—and the old links to the Iranian world—fuelled separatist ambitions. Though he was not the crown prince, Ashoka made a bid for the throne following the death of his father, and a four-year succession struggle followed in which a number of his brothers were killed. The Buddhist sources say that ninety-nine siblings died, an exaggeration that nonetheless suggests considerable bloodshed. Ashoka emerged from this violent interregnum as the new emperor.

At this stage in his life, Ashoka was known for his callous nature. He is said to have gained the sobriquet Chandashoka—Ashoka the Cruel—by burning dead all 500 of his harem women after one of them had teased him about his ugliness. This aspect of the royal character found expression in the most significant event of his reign: his conquest of Kalinga. Now comprising the modern Indian province of Orissa on the eastern coast of the Indian peninsula, Kalinga had remained unconquered under Chandragupta and Bindusara, perhaps because of its military stoutness, for Ashoka had to fight hard to conquer it. The significance of this campaign transcends imperial expansion, however, for it was this event, and the suffering that his hard-won invasion caused, that set Ashoka on a new path, inspiring him to abandon his pitiless past, embrace Buddhism, and follow a life of *Dhamma*—Buddhist righteousness or piety.

This event is recorded in the Rock Edicts, in a remarkable text that provides a particularly revealing view of royal thinking. In what is known as the 13th Major Rock Edict, dated to 260 BC, Ashoka—referred to here by the religious name Piyadassi—explains his new concern for following the path of Buddha:

> When he had been consecrated eight years the Beloved of the Gods, the king Piyadassi, conquered Kalinga. A hundred and fifty thousand people were deported, a hundred thousand were killed and many times that number perished. Afterward, now that Kalinga was annexed, the Beloved of the Gods very earnestly practiced Dhamma, desired Dhamma, and taught Dhamma. On conquering Kalinga, the Beloved of the Gods felt remorse, for, when an independent country is conquered, the slaughter, death and deportation of the people is extremely grievous to the Beloved of the Gods, and weighs heavily on his mind.

The Buddha left no writings himself. Despite this, the Buddhist canon is enormous, over ten times the length of the Old and New Testaments combined. His teachings were transmitted orally and were developed and elaborated over hundreds of years by followers in divergent schools of Buddhism until gradually set down on paper; the world's oldest surviving printed book is a Buddhist work, the *Diamond Sutra*, printed in a Chinese translation in AD 868. One of the central texts of the religion, compiled in the third century BC and thus roughly contemporaneous with Ashoka, is the *Dhammapada*, the "Path of Dhamma," a collection of aphorisms that encapsulate the struggle toward nirvana, the final release from the ego. In over 400 pearls of wisdom, the *Dhammapada* explains the way of righteousness; we can speculate that such a sentiment as this affected Ashoka as he considered his actions in Kalinga:

> If a man should conquer in battle a thousand and a thousand more, and another man should conquer himself, his would be the greater victory, because the greatest of victories is the victory over oneself; and neither the gods in heaven nor the demons down below can turn into defeat the victory of such a man.

Dhamma became the policy of Ashoka, and he used his Rock Edicts to exhort his population to follow the Buddhist path. Conversion was not required, the goal apparently being to persuade the people to live a life in accordance with the ideas of Dhamma, rather than actual recruitment into the ranks of the faithful. However, it seems that this involved some considerable and direct intrusion into daily life: a new class of official, the Dhamma-Mahamattas, toured the empire to ensure that Dhamma was being followed. Further, the Third Buddhist Council—a gathering of the senior men of the religion—was held during the reign of Ashoka in about 250 BC: with enormous significance for India and for the future of the outside world—especially China, Japan, Burma and other areas that came to adopt Buddhism—this assembly decided that theirs would become a proselytizing faith, and resolved to dispatch missionaries abroad. Mahinda, the son of Ashoka himself, is said to have introduced Buddhism to Sri Lanka. In the reign of Ashoka, therefore, Buddhism adopted a fresh activism, an energy to impress itself upon people, whether they wanted it or not.

One should not assume that his wholesale, even aggressive, adoption of Buddhism had cured Ashoka of his violent temperament. While he preached peace and tenderness, he may still have descended into savagery, for there are stories of the king exercising great brutality in the Buddhist cause during religious upheavals occasioned by the Dhamma policy. Stories they may be, since they cannot be verified, but they are too much reminiscent of the old Ashoka to be dismissed altogether. One such account tells of a man upsetting a statue of the Buddha in a city called Pundravardhana; it fell at the feet of a Hindu holy man, who took the opportunity to break the statue into pieces. When he heard of this, Ashoka ordered that every inhabitant of the city be killed, 18,000 people in total. The sources also relate a similar event happening in Pataliputra itself: Ashoka decreed that the *sadhu* responsible, along with the man who assisted him, their parents, friends and all of their properties, should be burnt. Every Hindu holy man that could be found was to be killed. Such tales, even after making allowances for their exaggeration, suggest that the population did not take kindly to an imposed righteousness. Indeed, the Hindu counterattack began within the royal household: Ashoka's queen, Tissarakha, cut down the sacred bodhi tree under which the Buddha was said to have received enlightenment.

This resistance to the policy of Dhamma came at a time when the means of enforcing the will of the government were declining through neglect, despite the appointment of the new agents of virtue. The emperor had too great a focus on his position on the Wheel of Becoming and not enough on the business of rule. The Buddhist sources themselves tell us that Ashoka donated the entire contents of his treasury to a Buddhist monastery and that at the end of his reign the only possession that he could give to a wandering holy man was a piece of mango. Delusion also affected the king: he apparently believed that he had secured the submission of the Hellenistic kingdoms to the west merely through sending missionaries there to preach Dhamma. In light of his waning government, the resistance to his holy authoritarianism, and his continued predilection for violence, we are faced inescapably with a picture of Ashoka at the end of his reign as a failed hypocrite who had reduced himself from imperial might to ownership of half a mango.

The decline of the Mauryan dynasty after Ashoka was dramatic. He died in 232 BC and the family remained in power for less than half a century, the empire breaking up during the reigns of a series of weak kings. The final end came when Pushyamitra, the Hindu army commander, murdered the last of the Mauryans, Brihadratha, during a parade in about 180 BC. Hindu resistance to Dhamma was one cause of the deterioration of Mauryan rule; another was the enervating effect of Buddhism itself. Princes schooled in otherworldliness—in a concern for Dhamma and the freeing of oneself from the ego—make bad rulers. The business of government is practical, deeply worldly, and often violent: inimical to the Buddhist withdrawal from the harsh realities of life. The neglect of things military that followed from Buddhist pacifism, and an inattention to daily governance, provided only for a royal line that ended in failure.

Ashoka gave advice to his successors. In the 13th Major Rock Edict, in which he had declared his shame over the carnage he had caused in Kalinga, he admonished his sons and their sons to abandon war:

This inscription has been engraved so that any sons or grandsons that I may have should not think of gaining new conquests, and in whatever victories they may gain should be satisfied with patience and light punishment. They should only consider conquest by Dhamma to be a true conquest, and delight in Dhamma should be their whole delight, for this is of value in both this world and the next.

Chandragupta and Chanakya had created the empire by following realist principles of practical government that bear comparison with Machiavelli; in his advice to princes, the Italian is forthright about the necessity of martial readiness:

> A prince, therefore, must have no other object or thought, nor acquire skill in anything, except war, its organization and its discipline. The art of war is all that is expected of a ruler; and it is so useful that besides enabling hereditary princes to maintain their rule it frequently enables ordinary citizens to become rulers. On the other hand, we find that princes who have thought more of their pleasures than of arms have lost their states. The first way to lose your state is to neglect the art of war; the first way to win a state is to be skilled in the art of war.

This passage has particular power as a critique of Ashoka and the impact of his insistence that his successors neglect war. When Machiavelli speaks of rulers "who have thought more of their pleasures than of arms," we can equate this "pleasure" with Ashoka's indulgent remorse—a luxury for a ruler in such an age—and with his pious self-satisfaction in turning his attention to his own ideas of salvation. Through being skilled in the art of war, Chandragupta had turned himself from an ordinary citizen—though one possessed of unusual talent—into a king; Ashoka had thought more of his own deliverance, and, neglecting the art of war, had caused his family to lose the kingdom he had inherited. Pacifism secures few thrones.

The northwest of the empire had already been lost even before the last Mauryan was murdered by his Hindu general, for events beyond the mountains had stirred a fresh force of invaders. A generation after Ashoka, Greeks would again march through the Khyber Pass, heralding a new era of invasions that would also see the first forays of the nomads from the north.

CHAPTER FOUR

Greeks and Nomads

A Bactrian Greek silver plate

Who fears the Parthian or the Scythian horde
. . . while Caesar lives?

HORACE, Odes, 4.5

As the Mauryan Empire and its Seleucid neighbor went into decline from around 250 BC, the Khyber Pass entered a long era of volatility in which kingdoms rapidly rose and fell around it. For 300 years, competing peoples arrived to contest control of the region and fought to establish new empires. The Greek settlers of Bactria made themselves independent of the Seleucid heirs of Alexander, and wrought a powerful kingdom out of their productive lands. Meanwhile, Scythian and Parthian nomads began to venture south off the steppes of Central Asia and a third great Iranian tribe—the Kushans—would appear on the horizon. These were the first of a series of nomad advances—a sequence of invasions of peoples from Central Asia—that would be the shaping force of Indian history for two thousand years.

The mechanism that propelled these tribes from their homeland was the erratic mobility inherent to nomad populations: as one tribe moved in search of grazing, it would collide with another and provoke a fight for possession of territory. Such a clash between two nomad groups would cause the expulsion of the weaker to find fresh lands in which to roam and graze their herds. Another contest would then be forced in neighboring territory and the process would continue, forming a violent chain of reactive migrations in which entire peoples streamed into fresh lands—families with horses, herds and all their goods and chattels, their big felt tents carried on carts. The essential mobility of the nomad thus amplified the impact of tribal conflicts in a manner impossible in sedentary societies, where defeated peoples could not uproot all and move en masse to find a new home with ease. In the nomadic world, a faraway battle could echo across continents, events in China or eastern Siberia reverberating in India or the Middle East, transmitted by the consecutive impacts of militarized migrations.

A hint that these Greeks and nomads had an impact in India can be seen in the *Mahabharata* itself, the famous epic poem that forms the founding myth of Indian civilization. In the *Mahabharata* we are told that at the battle of Kurukshetra, the climactic struggle to decide the fate of the Kaurava and Pandava dynasties, the army of King Sudakshina of Kamboja numbered among it Yavanas and Shakas—Greeks and Scythians. Despite such tantalizing glimpses, however, there are almost no documentary sources for the history of the Khyber region in this period: the principal evidence comes from numismatics—the study of coins. Examination of the legends, symbolism and metallic composition of coins from the different states of the time reveals a great deal about the era. Many conclusions remain hypothetical since numismatic data can be open to a variety of interpretations, but the distribution of coin finds is especially valuable in piecing together the rise and fall of kingdoms of the era.

Decline had set in on the east of the Seleucid realm by this time. Its size, as for all great empires of the age, created difficulties for government, stretching as it did from Asia Minor to Afghanistan, and the frontier provinces often hovered on insurrection in a bid for independence. Recognizing this difficulty, Seleucus had made his son Antiochus joint king—following Scythian incursions into Margiana and Aria in the 290s BC—and placed the young ruler in charge of the eastern parts of the empire. Antiochus took a special interest in Bactria and the surrounding region, no doubt in part because of the Iranian blood he inherited from his mother, Apama. On the death of Seleucus in 281 BC, however, much of the new emperor's attention was diverted to the west. This tendency continued under his son and successor, Antiochus II, setting the eastern fringes of the empire on a path toward independence.

The break came around 240 BC under Antiochus II or his son, Seleucus II. The powerful men of the eastern provinces had become much less fearful of the emperor's capacity to control the furthest reaches of the empire, and the satraps of Bactria and of Parthia—Diodotus and Andragoras—made themselves kings, throwing off an allegiance to the Seleucids that had in any case become tenuous. The territories north of the Hindu Kush would become the powerful kingdom of the Bactrian Greeks. The secession of Parthia, however, rapidly took a different form: no sooner had Andragoras proclaimed his independence than a major Scythian thrust into his lands displaced him from power. Arsaces and his tribe, who would come to be known by the name of their conquered land of Parthia—the Parthians—had arrived. The Seleucid hold on their eastern lands had been severed by a double blow: Bactria was in the hands of a breakaway kingdom of Greeks; Parthia was seized and settled by a Scythian people who would continue their gains westward, whittling relentlessly at Seleucid lands until they had made themselves masters of an empire.

The Bactria that Diodotus claimed as his own was very different from the barren north of Afghanistan that we recognize today. Fields and pastures were numerous and well watered by extensive irrigation networks (constructed by the Persians as well as the Greeks themselves). This productive agriculture brought wealth to the Bactrian rulers and provided for a sophisticated administration and army, as well as a developed culture. Startling evidence of a flourishing Hellenistic kingdom in Bactria was provided by the relatively recent discovery of the Greek remains of the city of Ai Khanum (meaning "Lady of the Moon") on the Oxus river. Excavations in the 1960s and 1970s revealed a highly developed town with many Greek features—an impressive administrative center, gymnasium, theater and much Greek statuary. From inscriptions discovered among the ruins, it seems clear that Greek literature—including Homer, Sophocles and Euripides—was read here.

In 208 BC Antiochus III, the martial and successful Seleucid emperor, arrived in the region to reclaim the lost provinces of the empire and found the house of Diodotus no longer on the throne. The Bactrian king was now Euthydemus of Magnesia, probably one of the many Greek adventurers who migrated to the rich lands of the east during these years. He ruled over a significant kingdom comprising Bactria, Sogdiana, Margiana and Aria and had fortified his capital city of Bactra well, for Antiochus besieged it for two years without success. Eventually, the king and the emperor came to an agreement in 206 BC in which Antiochus was forced to recognize Euthydemus as king in Bactria in return for an alliance. Euthydemus could not have resisted the emperor without considerable military resources and political strength, and his status would have been vastly bolstered by being party to negotiations with the emperor.

Following the agreement with Euthydemus, Antiochus turned south across the Hindu Kush and then entered India. Here he found a king by the name of Sophagasenus, either a Mauryan vassal king or—more likely given the rapid decline in Mauryan rule following the death of Ashoka— the ruler of a successor kingdom. Antiochus is believed to have renewed the treaty with the Indians made by his ancestor Seleucus—which is to say that he acquired some elephants to replenish those of the Seleucid army— and returned home. The real significance of this brief visit is that it demonstrated the vulnerability of India and prompted the rulers of Bactria to extend their dominions to the south of the mountain passes.

When Euthydemus died some time in the 190s BC, he was succeeded by his son Demetrius, an impressive figure who had represented his father in the negotiations with Antiochus and who would come to be known by the epithet Aniketos, meaning "the Invincible." It was Demetrius who led the Bactrian Greeks through the Khyber Pass in 190 BC to expand his kingdom into India. In the intricately rendered coins of his reign, Demetrius stares with a wide-eyed mania, as if he is constantly wary of threats to his indomitable reputation (see color plate 5). His mouth is shut fast under a nose that extends to a fine point; well-fleshed cheeks grow fuller in later coins. The invader is always shown in the elephant headdress that proclaims him to be the conqueror of Indian lands. Miniature tusks and a trunk stand forth around his brows.

Bactrian Greek soldiers continued to be armed and equipped in the traditional Greek or Macedonian style. They wore the muscled breastplate, or cuirass, of metal scales and skirts of leather strips to protect their thighs. The fertile pastures of Bactria certainly provided good mounts for the important cavalry arm, and evidence suggests that fighting horses were armored with iron in the Central Asian fashion. It is not known how far into India Demetrius led these soldiers; it may be that he conquered Gandhara, or the lands up to the Beas river that Alexander briefly seized over a century before. However far he got, Demetrius was forced to turn back.

While Demetrius was making his Indian conquests (around 170 BC), Eucratides usurped the Bactrian throne and split the kingdom of the

Bactrian Greeks into two. For a time, the Greeks of the region were divided into rival camps, supporters of Eucratides and the Euthydemids fighting a civil war. With Eucratides securely ensconced in the fortress of Bactra, a number of claimants followed his example and made their own bids for rule. The kingdom fragmented amid chaos. Once his hold over Bactria itself was firm, Eucratides set out to reduce these rebels; his success seems to have persuaded him to begin using the epithet "the Great."

Eucratides was an enigmatic king with a reputation as a warrior. Coins show him as a military figure, befitting a ruler who owes everything to his success in arms, and a pendulous nose and chin hang from a long face with a protruding brow. His numismatic signature is the Boeotian helmet, the flat, wide-brimmed headgear of the cavalrymen of Alexander the Great, suggesting that Eucratides was a cavalry commander before launching his coup. Plates of armor are visible under the folds of his tunic, and the fleshy curves of his face lend a comic pomposity to his stern gaze, at odds with his great reputation.

Now only in command of his most recent Indian conquests, Demetrius set out to recover his original lands, initially with some success. Eventually, however, he died in battle against Eucratides sometime in the 160s BC and his Indian conquests were captured by the victor. We can infer that Eucratides traveled through the Khyber Pass and occupied Gandhara, for we know that he held Taxila. At the height of his powers, therefore, Eucratides was master of a realm that straddled the Hindu Kush and the North West Frontier, and a Greek king was the ruler of the Khyber Pass.

Eucratides was himself killed in about 160 BC during an incursion by the Parthians, who had grown powerful to the west. The Bactrian Greek kingdom then fell into some disarray, with lands lost to the Parthians eventually being recovered by another Demetrius, perhaps the son of Demetrius Aniketos, before he too lost his throne and disappeared from view. A son of Eucratides named Heliocles seems to have restored Bactria to the Greeks, but by this time the Indian lands under Greek rule had followed a different path.

For almost two centuries after the invasion by Demetrius Aniketos in 190 BC, an Indo-Greek realm flourished in northwest India. The numismatic record shows over two dozen Hellenic kings of the region during this period, some utterly unknown except through one or two coins. One king who has achieved lasting renown, however, is Menander, famed in the Buddhist texts as Milinda, the Savior King.

Menander ruled for a sustained period (around 160 to 135 BC) and brought stability to the Indo-Greek kingdom, expanding its frontiers to include the Punjab, the Swat valley and lands in the Ganges region. For all the quality of his rule, though, Menander is best remembered for his adoption of Buddhism. In the *Milindapanha* (The Questions of Menander), an important Buddhist text, the Greek king converses with a Buddhist thinker, Nagasena. The work is a catechism, recording a discourse between king and holy man that is said to have resulted in the conversion of Menander to Buddhism. The *Milindapanha* gives us a rapturous account of the king, who ruled from his capital of Sagala (Sialkot in modern Pakistan):

> King of the city of Sagala in India, Milinda by name, learned, eloquent, wise, and able; and a faithful observer, and that at the right time, of all the various acts of devotion and ceremony enjoined by his own sacred hymns concerning things past, present, and to come. Many were the arts and sciences he knew—holy tradition and secular law . . . systems of philosophy; arithmetic; music; medicine; the four Vedas, the Puranas, . . . astronomy, magic, causation, and spells; the art of war; poetry; conveyancing in a word, the whole nineteen arts. As a disputant he was hard to equal, harder still to overcome; the acknowledged superior of all the founders of the various schools of thought. And as in wisdom so in strength of body, swiftness, and valor there was found none equal to Milinda in all India. He was rich too, mighty in wealth and prosperity, and the number of his armed hosts knew no end.

The recruitment of a ruler to the Buddhist faith was indeed something to celebrate: the religion of the king often becomes the religion of his kingdom through fashion or force, and such a text as the *Milindapanha* would have been very useful in proselytizing Buddhism among the new ruling class of Greeks. In the particular cultural circumstances of India, Buddhism had an advantage in attracting incomers: it did not recognize caste, whereas Vedic Brahminism, and, later, Hinduism could not readily absorb outsiders because of their lack of caste status. Invading kings and aristocracies might be granted caste, but it would be of a low order—hardly an attractive prospect for a successful king and his vigorous nobility. Buddhism had no such restrictions, and the welcome that the religion offered the Greek invaders explains the growing popularity of Buddhism among the Greeks in India, of which Menander is the paradigm.

Besides the Greeks, the inclusive attitude of Buddhism appealed to a rising section of Indian society: the merchant class. As international trade developed in these centuries, merchant wealth grew and dissatisfaction with the lowly place accorded merchants in traditional Vedic society grew accordingly. The disdain of the Brahmin caste encouraged merchants to favor the social flexibility of Buddhism, and their patronage—the endowment of great monasteries and monuments—caused the religion to gain in status, furthering its attraction to the rising mercantile elite.

Social inclusiveness explains the appeal of Buddhism to kings and merchants alike, but cultural inclusiveness was a feature too. Menander's coins were significantly syncretic, with Buddhist, Vedic, Jain and even Zoroastrian symbolism often employed along with Greek deities. Rulers of the time had to be patrons of numerous faiths, balancing the needs of their souls with pragmatic politics: the Greeks were a powerful but tiny minority and needed to attach the people to them. As with the Bactrian kingdom of the Greeks, the Hellenic component of these kingdoms in India largely comprised the ruling class and the army, governing an unchanged local population. A small Greek elite (to some extent Greco-Iranian through intermarriage) made up the state, while the population of Indians or Bactrians simply found one regime replaced by another. The desire to legitimate their rule, and to maintain quiescent subjects, led incoming kings to recognize or even adopt local religions: as with all states in all ages, religion became a tool of governance.

While the Bactrian Greeks were entrenching their independence and fighting their way into India, the Parthians were conquering westward and making themselves masters of the Seleucid realm province by province. After Arsaces brought his nomads off the steppes in 239 BC and defeated Andragoras with apparent ease, his brother Tiridates united the province of Hyrcania to newly seized Parthia, and Parthian Iran was born. Over the coming decades the new rulers would gain supremacy over much of the old Achaemenian Empire, once again giving Iran a ruling class of Iranian extraction. For five centuries, the

Parthians—horsemen not long off the plains of Central Asia—would govern the land of Cyrus and Darius.

The Seleucid response to the early Parthian advances was muted. Besides the Parthians to their east, they were beset by troubles to the west also, as the new Roman power arose in the Mediterranean to chip away at their other flank. The eastern advance of Antiochus III in about 208 BC, in which he besieged Bactra and entered India, did allow him to bring the nascent kingdom of Parthia under his suzerainty, but it was not long before the Parthians threw off his nominal rule and continued their expansion. Greatest among the Parthian kings was Mithridates I; during his reign between 171 and 138 BC, he conquered Aria, Drangiana, Gedrosia and Media. In 142 BC he captured Babylonia, the center of the Seleucid Empire, and the old Achaemenian title of *Shahanshah* (King of Kings) was revived for him. In the coin portraits Mithridates is bareheaded and his appearance is somewhat Hellenic, with trimmed hair and a crown around his head, reminders of the lasting impact of Seleucus and his successors in Iranian lands. This influence continued for many years under the Parthians: Greek remained the language of government and of coinage inscriptions, and Parthian kings posed as protectors of Hellenic traditions. In the course of time, however, this gradually gave way to an Iranian revival in language, religion and material culture.

In conquering an empire, the important advantage possessed by Mithridates—and by Parthian kings before and afterward—lay in the powerful cavalry that defined all nomad armies. Mounted archers—lightly armored, highly maneuverable and capable of delivering vicious blows from a distance—were a troublesome foe for many kingdoms forced over the centuries to fight nomad enemies. The horse archer of the Parthian Empire achieved particular renown. His signature tactic was to ride toward the enemy at speed before turning and firing an arrow behind him, across the rump of his horse, while galloping out of reach; from this action, the phrase "parting shot"—the *"Parthian* shot"—is in use over two thousand years later (see color plate 6).

The principal weapon of these cavalrymen—and later the scourge of Roman legionaries—was the Parthian bow, a recurved composite construction of wood, horn and sinew, assembled in layers to maximize the resistance of the materials. On a wooden core, strips of horn were laid on the inner curve to resist compression; dried sinew, teased into fibers, was soaked in glue and layered on the outer side to resist tension. These bows were made in such a way that when unstrung they would bend forward until the ends almost touched, reversing its shape. Strung, the bow was already full of latent energy, and enormous force was gathered in the drawing. This was unleashed to shoot arrows with such velocity that they had little difficulty in piercing the armor of the Roman legionary.

Despite the fame of the light cavalry, however, the fighting horseman of these ages reached its epitome in the Parthian *cataphract*, a name derived from the Greek word *kataphractoi*, meaning "covered over." These were battle-tank cavalry, mailed and armored all over, precursors of the knights of medieval Europe. A horse would be coated in a jacket of scales made of lacquered rawhide, iron or bronze, covering it completely, from flanks to face. A hemispherical lattice protected the horse's eyes while the ears poked unguarded through the armor. The rider—a nobleman of Parthia— wears a sleek round helmet in bronze, molded smooth over the skull, dropping low across the brow and sweeping down under the ears. A mail aventail armors his neck and throat, tied close under the chin. Scales of bronze are fastened to his leather tunic, overlapping upon each other and rippling with his movements. His arms from wrist to shoulder are wrapped around in curved plates, which flex as he stretches to deliver a blow below him with his long lance. A sword and battle-axe hang from his belt, ready to hand.

With such soldiers, armed and armored with advanced technology, the Parthian kings made themselves emperors as they fought their way across the Iranian lands of the declining heirs of Seleucus. It was the misfortune of the Seleucid Empire that it found itself caught between two expanding enemies: beset by the restless nomads to their east, the emergence of Rome to the west led to the end of the Seleucid dominion. It was the extinction of the Seleucid Empire between the onrushing Romans and Parthians that brought the Latin and Iranian worlds into a proximity by turns dismissive, uneasy and violent.

For as long as these nomad kings ruled Iran, the two powers coexisted in a state of unease. Rivalry was intermittent in Asia Minor and over Armenia, a kingdom of occasional power in the south of the Caucasus mountains, too important to both Rome and Parthia for either to leave it

The Parthian victory over the Romans at the battle of Carrhae

alone. In the early days of this antagonism, the Romans treated the Parthians as barbarians who deserved little respect. This view was shattered at the battle of Carrhae in 53 BC when the Parthian cavalry methodically destroyed a Roman army that had ventured into Parthian lands in what is now the southeast of Turkey. Wave after wave of arrows punched through Roman armor and decimated the ranks of the legions led by Marcus Crassus in search of glory to match his fellow triumvir, Julius Caesar. A Parthian force of about 1,000 heavily armored cavalrymen and 10,000 horse archers demolished a Roman army of 28,000 legionaries and 4,000 cavalry: perhaps 20,000 Romans were killed. The captured survivors were sent to Margiana to be forcibly settled. Carrhae was a terrible shock to Roman pride and it prompted drastic reform in military strategy, principally a greater attention to the use of cavalry. The disgrace was lasting, especially because of the captured standards—the eagles of the legions—that were taken and displayed in triumph in a Parthian temple. In a similar blow, more standards were lost when Mark Antony made another disastrous invasion attempt in 36 BC. These sensitive losses rankled with the Romans for years until the return of the standards was negotiated as part of a general improvement of relations in 19 BC.

Roman literature is an excellent source for this Persian period. Carthage, the contender across the Mediterranean, had been the enemy of Rome for decades until it was brutally destroyed; the now vacant role of principal foe was ably filled by the Parthians to the east. They became the shadow encroaching upon Roman paranoia and were mentioned often in Roman literature. The celebrated *Odes* of Horace make frequent reference to this enemy, in both respectful and resentful terms: the Parthians are variously labeled insolent, redoubtable, treacherous or perilous.

Despite the great power that they brought to bear against the Romans in the west, however, it was not the Parthians that would sweep away the Greeks from the Khyber Pass, but a kindred people from Central Asia. Tribal upheavals far away in Mongolia in the early second century BC led to a series of migratory impacts that eventually pushed two of the manifold Iranian tribes of Central Asia into India: the Scythian Shakas and the Kushans.

The Shakas—cousins of those against whom Cyrus the Great had died fighting—crossed the Oxus river into Bactria in the 130s BC. The Greek hold over Bactria itself was extinguished but Indo-Greek kings continued to rule fragmentary kingdoms in southern Afghanistan and India. The Shakas were, in turn, evicted from Bactria by the arrival of the Kushans in 127 BC and slowly migrated through the west of what is now Afghanistan until they established a kingdom in Drangiana. It is from this colonization—Shakastan—that the province derives its modern name of Seistan. From here, the Shakas developed their power into neighboring regions and fought the remaining Greek kingdoms for territory in India. By 65 BC, they had advanced northward along the Indus river, captured Gandhara and seized the Khyber Pass.

Shaka rule of Indian lands did not last long, but they left their mark nonetheless. It is likely—from linguistic evidence—that the Pathan tribesmen that occupy the Khyber region in the present day descend directly from these Shaka settlers of two thousand years ago. More immediately, it seems that a Central Asian deity named Surya, dressed in the Iranian style, was absorbed into the pantheon of Indian gods. The current of civilization flowed largely toward the Shakas, however, for they enthusiastically adopted the Indo-Greek culture that they found in their conquered lands. Shaka coins are models of numismatic syncretism, some showing the Greek god Zeus enthroned—copied from Eucratides—and the elephant helmet so beloved by Demetrius. Others bear images of Greek deities such as Poseidon, with inscriptions in both Greek and Kharoshthi.

The Greeks retaliated in the 30s BC. Under a king named Amyntas and his son Hermaeus, they took back provinces on the west bank of the Indus: once again the Khyber Pass was in the hands of the Greeks. This late blossoming of the Indo-Greek world was a transitory one, however, for just a few decades later, in the 10s and 20s AD, the Kushans descended the Hindu Kush, captured the Khyber Pass and finally extinguished the remnants of Greek rule in India. This incursion of the Kushans was the preliminary to a much greater empire, which will be explored in the following chapter.

The early Kushan advance through the Khyber Pass was countered by the eastward expansion of the Parthian realm. By AD 20 the Shaka province of Drangiana had been absorbed into the Parthian empire under a vassal king, Gondophares. He continued striking east, and by the mid forties AD had advanced into the Khyber area, expelling the Kushans from their lands in Pakistan and the Kabul valley. With these gains, the Parthian conquerors of the empire of Cyrus and Darius had restored its furthest boundaries and once more controlled the road to India: at the time that the Emperor Claudius was invading Britain to add it to the Roman Empire, his Parthian rivals were conquering the Khyber Pass.

By the time the Parthians expanded their power into India, a revival of Iranian culture in the rest of the empire had been firmly under way for a century. Through their strong adherence to Zoroastrianism, the Parthian kings oversaw a revitalization of the faith, and other Iranian traditions were strengthened alongside it. This is not to suggest that outside influences were thrown off, for the culture of the Iranian world was deeply syncretic and could not be separated easily by a political act or temporary popular preference. For example, Pahlavi—a cursive script modeled on Aramaic— replaced Greek on coins, but the Zoroastrian iconography on the same coins reflected a continuing and deep Greek influence: the Egyptian and Babylonian symbolism used by the Achaemenians had given way to anthropomorphic forms of the Hellenic style. The weightiest significance of the Parthian period to the Zoroastrian faith is that it probably saw the beginning of the attempt to record on paper the ancient sayings of Zarathustra and his followers that form the Avesta, the holy book of the religion. Having been transmitted orally for many generations by dedicated priests, it was written down some time in the early centuries after the birth of Christ, and was probably not completed until Sasanian times.

In parallel with the Zoroastrian reawakening in this era, Iranian beliefs impacted strongly on neighboring faiths. In Buddhism, the fresh promise of the *Maitreya*—the Buddha who would come to redeem the world— seems to owe inspiration to the Zoroastrian tradition of the *Saoshyant*, the World Savior who will lead humanity in the last battle against evil. Good relations between the Parthians and the Jews—following the Achaemenian custom—encouraged some Jewish works of the time to bear a Zoroastrian imprint, and it could be said that it was from a mingling of Judaism and Zoroastrianism over several centuries that Christianity was born during the Parthian era. The extent of the Parthian realm may have assisted the early Christians in their efforts to spread their new religion around the world by uniting much of the Middle East and northwest India and bringing it to border Palestine. It is said that St. Thomas, one of the apostles of Jesus Christ, met Gondophares while traveling to India, and this tradition variously has St. Thomas preaching Christianity in the realm of Gondophares, or proselytizing in the south of the Subcontinent, dying the death of a martyr in Malabar in AD 72.

Ancient Iranian ideas—stemming back to the Aryans on the steppe— came to animate the legions of Rome through a vigorous cult that developed in Asia Minor in the Parthian age, based on the worship of Mithra (called Mithras by the Romans, also Mitra in earlier times). Before the advent of Zarathustra—at least 1200 BC—Mithra was the god of fire for the Aryan tribesmen and was associated with the sun, the greatest of all fires. Evolving over time into the god of war, riding in a chariot drawn across the sky by white horses, Mithra migrated from Central Asia along with the Aryan peoples: in India, he became the Vedic sun god Mitra, keeper of the cosmic order; in Iran, he maintained his association with light and fire, and was the god of fair dealing and order. Although the divine status of Mithra was reduced when Zoroastrianism took hold in Iranian lands, the god remained in the pantheon, and returned to popularity in later years. In a manner still little understood, in the Roman period the worship of Mithras (in Latin *sol invictus* or "the unconquered sun") grew into an ascetic cult that was carried through the Empire by the Roman army. For a time in the first centuries of the Christian era, Mithraism—from which women were excluded—competed strenuously with Christianity in the Roman lands and the highest levels of Roman society, such as the Emperor Commodus, were initiated. It is intriguing to think that this mystery cult, dedicated to an ancient Aryan god found in India and Iran, might have triumphed over Christianity and become the religion of Europe.

This advanced degree of religious intermingling and cross-fertilization highlights the growing links between different parts of the world in this period. When both were at their height, the Parthians and the Romans divided between them Europe, western Asia and part of India. This unification of much of the world into just two political organizations assisted the trend toward connection: the hindrances and frictions caused by multiple borders and conflicting kingdoms were substantially reduced, easing travel across long distances. Trade was one of the great motive forces in linking together these distant parts of the world; it was also a motive for war, for the rivalry between Rome and Parthia was inspired in part by the desire to control the important trade routes to the east that passed through the north of Parthian territory. This was the age of the Silk Road, the network of caravan routes that covered thousands of miles between China and western Asia, carrying commodities and luxuries of all kinds through the deserts and steppe of Central Asia. Silk was not the only cargo, for amber, jade, diamonds, rhubarb, spinach, horses and exotic animals all traveled along these roads; in China, the ostrich was known as the "Parthian bird." The Khyber Pass provided for a branch line of the Silk Road system, Gandhara becoming a regional center of trade based on the route from Taxila through the Khyber Pass to Bagram, and thence north into Bactria where it joined the principal routes east and west. This was the means by which Indian precious goods were added to the flourishing international commerce, especially ivory, pepper and textiles.

During the tumult of these centuries—with Greeks, Shakas and Parthians all fighting for control of northwest India and the Khyber Pass— much was created amid the destruction and confusion that swept away one dynasty after another. Profound and lasting cultural compounds resulted as invaders brought ideas with their armies and took back influences with their booty, exchanges that leave their mark on the world today. After these years of changing fortunes and fleeting political organizations came a powerful empire that would for a time bring stability to the region: under the Kushans, this fertile entanglement of cultures would continue, and the Khyber Pass would see India export something altogether more important than ivory or peppercorns.

CHAPTER FIVE

The Kushans

A coin portrait of Kujula Kadphises, founding king of the Kushan Empire

. . . the great salvation, Kanishka the Kushan,
the righteous, the just, the autocrat worthy of
divine worship . . .

RABATAK INSCRIPTION

I stood by the roadside in the Khyber Pass, looking up at the grand brick mound, now crumbling, that houses the remains of an unknown Buddhist saint or holy man. This tomb, a *stupa*, dates from around AD 100 and marks the importance of the Khyber Pass as the route through which Buddhism was carried from its Indian homeland to Central Asia and thence China and the Far East. It sits above the road, near the scattered village of Zarai, deep inside the mountain pass.

For me, being inside the Khyber Pass was the realization of a goal of many years, and now I was in Pakistan at last, exploring the North West Frontier Province. With my growing beard, Chitrali hat and shalwar kameez (the loose trousers and long shirt traditionally worn in Pakistan), I was sometimes—to my great pride—mistaken for a Pathan, but most of the time it was clear that I was an outsider. Occasionally I was taken for a spy or a mercenary, and when I protested that I was researching a book, my claim seemed to carry little conviction. The U.S. military action against the Afghan Taliban regime in 2001 increased anti-Western sentiment in the region, especially because the fighting has developed into a long guerrilla campaign involving soldiers from the U.K. and other NATO countries. I received a number of lectures about American policy from angry Afghans and Pakistanis alike. The most common reaction to me was a profound and touching hospitality, but in places the hostility was palpable.

I felt that this reflected a larger and more ancient truth about the Khyber region: life is hard and people must treat others with some suspicion in order to survive. It is, and surely always has been, an unstable and dangerous place. The few Westerners who make it into the Khyber today are required to hire protection against kidnap or murder, and my armed guard from the Khyber Khasadar Force—the local militia—in Peshawar sat in the jeep with his AK 47 at the ready. A short but rugged soldier, he wore a shalwar kameez in the deep blue of the khasadars, and a black beret with the silver badge of his unit. On this first day in the Khyber I was also accompanied by Mumtaz, my guide and driver, blessed with a full moustache, perfect English and gracious charm. He kept the engine running, while I stepped out to admire the ancient Buddhist monument.

Built of bricks of a muddy brown, the domed mound is set on a platform of three tiers resting upon rock, and when excavated early in the twentieth century, it surrendered some beautiful statuary, now held in Peshawar Museum. Inside the solid dome, a small chamber once contained the body of a Buddhist holy man or teacher, along with decorative objects and statues. In some cases, a stupa can be built into a powerful edifice, as much as 30 meters across at the base; the Khyber stupa is smaller, but a solid testament to the faith nonetheless, despite the crumbling brickwork. We do not know for whom the Khyber stupa was built, but from its location and dating we can speculate that it contains the bones of a missionary or holy man who had been setting out to proselytize salvation to the fresh lands beyond the Khyber before meeting his end on the journey. As I stood looking upon this monument, occasional trucks whimpered past toward Afghanistan, following in the footsteps of the men who took Buddhism beyond its native soil.

The stupa was built during the era of the Kushan Empire, a strong realm that was itself an oblique result of political changes in China hundreds of years before. It was the success of Qin Shi Huang Di in making himself Emperor of China in 221 BC—through unifying several warring states that had been fighting for centuries—that began a chain of events that brought the Kushans to power in northern India and provided for the eventual arrival of Buddhism in the East.

Qin Shi Huang Di decided to improve his defenses against the nomadic tribes that harassed his northern frontier by mobilizing the resources of his newly powerful empire to build the Great Wall. By joining together and enhancing several existing fortifications dating from as early as the eighth century BC, he produced a single barrier to divide Chinese lands from those of the barbarians (the region broadly known to the modern world as Mongolia and Manchuria). Over the centuries, the Great Wall was extended and rebuilt (what we see today is largely the work of the Ming dynasty, 1368–1644) until it stretched across mountains and desert for over four thousand miles, studded with watchtowers and patrolled by soldiers standing ready to light the beacon fires that warned of attack. Tamped-earth construction was replaced first by brick and then by stone as each dynasty sought to develop its protection against the nomads, building higher and thicker walls at huge cost to the conscripted workers taken north for the construction. Many thousands died, their bodies simply being cast into the wall foundations; old Chinese tales are crowded with lovers or families cruelly separated by the imperial demand for labor.

The Great Wall evolved over time, but it had an immediate impact. In the early years, the wall was built to prevent the nomadic Xiongnu—a powerful tribe of Huns—from raiding the sedentary and wealthy Chinese lands with their swift horse-borne attacks, against which the slow-moving ripostes of a more pedestrian military were ineffective. Neighboring the Xiongnu, and similarly troubling the Chinese borderlands, were the Wusun and Yuezhi. All three suffered as the Great Wall grew to prevent the nomads from taking easy advantage of the settled Chinese. With China effectively closed to them by the early second century BC, the tribes were forced to look to the west, and the 170s BC saw the beginning of major migratory ructions in Mongolia, setting off a chain of tribal impacts that eventually careered into India. One tribe was displaced by another as they fought for possession of pasture lands in which to roam their herds and from which to launch raids on their neighbors.

In the course of these upheavals, the Yuezhi were forced westward, and in two generations had migrated hundreds of miles to Sogdiana. Here they came up against the Scythian Shakas in the 130s BC and pushed them across the Oxus river into the Greek kingdom of Bactria. The Yuezhi themselves crossed into Bactria in 127 BC—expelling the Shakas once again—where they paused for over a century and established a significant kingdom. It was in this period that the Yuezhi became the Kushans, the name under which they would go on to build an empire that would rank alongside the Romans, Chinese and Parthians as one of the great powers of the world.

Although known to us by a Chinese name, the Yuezhi was one of the numerous Iranian or Aryan nomadic tribes that roamed and dominated a broad swathe of Central Asia for many centuries. Having strayed further east than most, they came into the Chinese orbit and entered history with a Chinese title. During the century in which they developed their power in Sogdiana and Bactria, the Yuezhi—originally a confederation of clans in a loose tribal structure—were united into a more centralized kingdom under the leadership of a family known in the Chinese sources as Kui-Shan, from which we have the name *Kushan*. This Westernization of a Chinese term may have had lasting purchase in the minds of people of the time, as well as later scholars, because of its similarity to the Persian word *kushandeh*, killer.

The Yuezhi of the Central Asian plains resembled their Scythian kin: horseback warriors, marked and scarred by constant fighting, dressed and organized for continual warfare and for a life in flux. In their migratory lives they absorbed influences of decorative art and practical design from the cultures into which they collided, through the ransacking of Chinese villas or through picking up debris from the battlefield after defeating neighboring Scythians. By the time that the Yuezhi were being welded into the Kushans in Bactria and Sogdiana, they had a vibrant and astonishingly syncretic material culture. The excavations of Tillya Tepe have given us a remarkable insight into the art, craft and civilization of the Yuezhi of the first century BC, just before the rise of the Kushan Empire.

Tillya Tepe—or the Golden Hill—is the site of a royal cemetery in Bactria that contains the bodies of several princesses and warriors, all adorned with gold jewelry and ornate trappings. Given that the period during which the Yuezhi settled in Bactria is little known, lacking in both written and archaeological sources, the excavation of the Tillya Tepe site in late 1978 by a joint team of archaeologists from Afghanistan and the Soviet Union promised to transform our understanding of the time. Over 20,000 items were uncovered during several months of work. However, the exploration of the site was cut short by political troubles in Afghanistan in 1979 and the invasion by the Soviet Union later in the same year. The priceless artifacts were taken to Kabul where they disappeared. For years—through the war with the Russians, the Mujahideen civil wars, and the Taliban regime—there was no certainty about the whereabouts or the safety of the golden treasure. Rumors circulated that it had been melted down or was sitting on a warlord's shelf, that it had been taken to Moscow or sold on the black market. For twenty-five years, scholars lamented the loss.

It was thus with great excitement that, in 2003, the cache was rediscovered in a vault in the Central Bank in Kabul. It was intact, having been hidden and protected by a number of brave individuals, some of whom had been beaten by Taliban officials while refusing to reveal the secret whereabouts of the precious hoard; many of the fanciful rumors about the fate of the artifacts had been spread deliberately to put treasure hunters off the trail. The remarkable collection is now back under study, and has much still to reveal.

The treasures, combined with the archaeological exploration of 1978 and the painstaking artistic reconstruction of clothing from six of the discovered graves, give us an exceptional picture of the late Yuezhi and early Kushan nobility.

In Grave Six lay a woman in a long dress of dark red with the forearms, chest and shoulders heavily adorned with gold spangles; thick gold bracelets weighted her wrists and ankles and she wore highly fashioned earrings and elaborate necklaces, in gold set with delicate blue lapis lazuli. The splendor of her jewels alone marks her as an important individual, and her crown seems to confirm her royal status. Perfectly designed for nomadic life, it can be taken apart and stored flat, in pieces, to allow a princess to carry her mobile wealth in her saddlebags. Made of sheet gold, the crown has five filigree arches that slot into a headband, the whole being decorated by golden flowers with petals that rise glitteringly from amber or lapis lazuli centers. From each petal, and from many filigree points, a simply twisted strand of gold wire hangs a disc of gold, so that the whole construction becomes a shimmering array of light. One can imagine the princess turning her head, the Central Asian sun reflecting in cascades from her golden crown, drawing every glance to her.

In the six excavated graves, there was one warrior, a tall figure buried with his weapons. Every edge of his blue tunic was spangled with heavy borders of gold pieces, and he was waisted by a splendent belt of gold, metal wire woven into a band joining nine circular golden bosses, each one a high relief of a goddess jauntily mounted on a lion. Two Chinese buckles fasten his boots, thick hoops of gold studded inside and out with vivid teardrops of lapis lazuli. Each one frames a chariot, canopied in the Chinese fashion and bearing a Chinese driver, but drawn by Bactrian griffins. These pieces show the melding of borrowed influences into an eclectic local style.

To arm him against trouble in paradise, the warrior has a dagger that details scenes wrought with a dry humor. The blade is now rusted beyond use, but two millennia underground have not diminished the brilliance of the gold hilt and sheath. Adorned with lapis lazuli, dragons and chimeras form a line along both, each creature open-mouthed to maul or devor the one ahead. The knob of the dagger depicts a bear chewing upon a vine laden with grapes—a motif of Siberia.

A young woman, perhaps a teenager, was found in Grave Three wearing a tunic dress and loose trousers. The clasp at her throat to fix her dress is formed of two gold dolphins inlaid with lapis and with eyes of pearls. Each is ridden by a curly haired cupid of Greco-Roman appearance. That the dolphins have been given scales seems to confirm that the piece was made by a craftsman native to a land far from the sea.

Another clasp may portray Ares, the Greek god of war, or his Persian counterpart, Verethragna. Clutching shield and staff and dressed as a Greek soldier, he is surrounded by trees full of snarling animals. The gnashing lions, chimeras and coiling snakes show the Scythian influence that fertilized this Greek scene. That such a martial piece should decorate a young princess suggests the militarized nature of nomad life, and the importance attached to strength in arms.

Cosmetics and grooming items were also found with these princesses. An ivory comb, probably from India, is carved to show a bare-chested man with shaven head, perhaps a holy man or wandering ascetic, sitting under the branches of a tree. In another piece, cultures meld in a pot: a tiny golden jar shows Greco-Roman and Iranian inspiration. Laurel leaves make a single stripe around the vessel and decorate its lid, which is pommelled with a pomegranate handle—the Persian fruit that to the Greeks symbolized fertility, death and eternity.

Perhaps the most outstanding example of all the cultural amalgams in these graves is a tiny Aphrodite figurine found on the chest of the princess in Grave Six (see color plate 7). This Greek goddess of love is naked beneath a toga that falls to her thighs while she poses in the Greek style with limbs draped artfully, one arm resting on a plinth. Angelic wings have been added to the Greek figure, a Bactrian feature not found on Aphrodite in the West. Around her head she wears a circlet of twisted cord in the Persian fashion, and her forehead is adorned with the *bindi* of India, the ritual dot usually worn by women as a mark of marriage. Her Oriental eyes suggest an influence from still further east, and altogether this diminutive gold pendant manifests the crucible of civilizations that was Bactria in this era.

The king who united the ruling clans of the late Yuezhi under his Kushan family banner was Kujula Kadphises. We know very little about him, but it seems likely that it was in the first years of the Christian era, perhaps the 10s and 20s AD, that Kujula brought the Yuezhi clans together, crossed the Hindu Kush, and entered India through the Khyber Pass.

Though it was Kujula who wrought the Yuezhi into the Kushans, the nomadic tribes of the steppes had already undergone changes to fit them for rule over the sedentary population that they found in Bactria and neighboring lands. Traditional raids for seizing livestock and valuable items from farmers and townspeople became transformed into administrative control over them. Tax and tribute took the place of violent confiscation as the means of extracting wealth. With increasing organisation behind them, the heads of the Yuezhi clans became an aristocracy, developing systems of rule to support them, and Kujula rose above the others to make himself their king. By the time that they passed south through the Hindu Kush, the tribes were Yuezhi no longer, but Kushans.

Under Kujula they had early successes, ending Indo-Greek rule in Afghanistan and northwest India; it is likely that lands up to the Indus river became part of his new empire. At the same time, the rising Parthian vassal king Gondophares was conquering to the south, and both continued their advances until they shared a frontier. In Afghanistan, Gondophares held Arachosia and Kujula ruled the Kabul valley. Gandhara was split between them: Taxila was in Parthian hands, while the country west of the Indus was Kushan. It was not long before these encroaching empires fought each other, and Gondophares succeeded in expelling the Kushans from most of their recent gains by the mid forties AD: the Khyber Pass and the Kabul valley were in Parthian hands by this time. By the mid sixties AD, however, the Kushans had returned in force to reconquer southeast Afghanistan and northern Pakistan, razing Taxila to the ground in AD 75.

Kanishka, the greatest of the Kushan kings, began his reign sometime in the period AD 78 to 144. It may be that he assumed the crown of the expanding empire a few short years after Taxila was set aflame; other experts put him on the throne well into the second century AD. Under Kanishka, the Kushans pushed deeper into India from their conquests in Gandhara, attaching the Punjab and parts of the Ganges valley to the empire; it seems that Kanishka conquered as far as Pataliputra, the ancient capital of the Mauryans. The Indus river, all the way to its mouth at the Arabian Sea, became Kushan territory, along with Gedrosia to the west and an arc of lands through Drangiana and Aria to Khwarizm. The Kushan realm had expanded to cover all of modern Afghanistan and Pakistan, and significant swathes of India and Central Asia. The great cities of this empire included Mathura, on the Jumna near the later city of Delhi, and Bagram, close to modern Kabul in Afghanistan. The capital of Kanishka, however, was Purushapura, modern Peshawar, a telling demonstration that the Khyber Pass was at the center of this imperial project.

An inscription discovered in 1993 at Rabatak in Afghanistan, in ancient Bactria, celebrates this expansionary success and describes events in the early years of Kanishka's reign. It is carved in the Bactrian language, an Indo-Aryan tongue closely related to Persian and to Sanskrit. That it is written in the Greek script demonstrates the lasting influence of the Greek cultural imprint on Bactria. Indeed, legends on Kushan coins were written in Greek until Kanishka decreed that this language be replaced by their own Bactrian; it was natural for the Kushan to adopt the Greek alphabet to render their spoken language into written words. It is not well known today, but as the language of the Kushan rulers it would once have ranked as one of the most important in the world and its life continued long after the empire of the Kushans was a distant memory. Documents written in Bactrian and dating to the late eighth century AD show that the language was in active use for almost a thousand years.

The Rabatak inscription bears significant similarities to the Bisitun inscription of Darius the Great in the boldness of its diction. The emperor is hailed as the scion of the race of the gods and congratulated for having subdued all India to his will:

As for these gods who are written here—may they keep the king of

86

kings, Kanishka the Kushan, forever healthy, fortunate and victorious, and may the son of the gods rule all India from the year one to the year one thousand.

Kings who extend their domains are remembered as great rulers. Kanishka also showed greatness in his tolerance of the growing variety of religions and cultures that he found in his empire as it expanded. Coins from his reign display a striking willingness to embrace the deities and icons of his growing population: images from the Iranian, Indian and Greek pantheons are used regularly, including Mithra and Verethragna, Shiva and Buddha, Helios and Selena. Even Serapis, whose cult was popular in Hellenistic Egypt, can be found. It is not, however, for his tolerance that the Rabatak inscription declares him to be "the great salvation . . . the righteous." It is for his conversion to Buddhism.

Buddhism had been practiced for around 600 years by the time of Kanishka, but it was in the Kushan era that it underwent profound changes and became a truly global religion. The benefits of powerful royal patronage were no doubt significant, but the transforming change at this time was the development of the Mahayana (Great Vehicle) school. So named because it was held to be of a size great enough to carry all people to nirvana, this variant of Buddhist teaching is wholly different from the Hinayana (Lesser Vehicle) school, a more restrictive brand, which came to dominate in South India, Sri Lanka and Burma. Mahayana took root in northern India—it is associated especially with Gandhara—and truly laid the foundations for Buddhism to spread beyond India and become a world faith.

The fundamental change lay in the attitude to the laity, those who had not committed themselves to a monastic life in pursuit of nirvana. Although Buddhists had previously sought to make some compromises in order to encompass those who stood outside religious orders, it remained very much a monastic calling. Under Mahayana, this changed completely—lay people were drawn in and offered salvation readily, revolutionizing a monastic order into a broad church that had a role in daily life. No longer was it necessary to live the life of a monk to acquire nirvana.

Just as Ashoka was associated with the Third Buddhist Council of about 250 BC, Buddhists claim that Kanishka convened the Fourth Buddhist Council around AD 100, at which the developments were formalized. An outcome of the Council was recognition of, and support for, the missionary activities of some Buddhist sects, a decision that no doubt aided the transmission of Buddhism to new audiences.

It is said that the Fourth Buddhist Council was held at Peshawar, Kanishka's capital, and Gandhara was undoubtedly the center of an active and fertile Buddhist community that contributed significantly to these developments. Indeed, such was the extent of doctrinal innovation in the region that it amounts to a distinct school of Gandharan Buddhism. For many years there was some uncertainty about the character, or even the existence, of this trend of thought because the rich variety of archaeological remains in the area were not matched by texts. Without texts as evidence, doctrine and dogma remain hidden: they cannot firmly be divined from a statue or the ruins of a monastery.

This situation was suddenly transformed in 1994 when a set of Buddhist writings were discovered (probably in eastern Afghanistan) and passed through several hands until they came to reside in the British Library. The precise story of how the manuscripts came to light remains something of a mystery, but scholars have begun the long process of deciphering and analyzing the contents of what have become known as the British Library Scrolls.

The manuscripts comprise thirteen birch bark scrolls, tightly rolled and placed in three clay pots. It is possible that they had been discarded at the end of their useful lives: too sacred to be destroyed, they were perhaps buried ceremonially, having been copied on to fresh scrolls. The texts are written in the Gandhari language, one of the vernacular tongues (Prakrits) of the Indo-Aryan group; the significant difference is that it was written in the Kharoshthi script, an adaptation of the Aramaic of Achaemenian use, rather than the Brahmi used for other Prakrit texts. Together, the Gandhari language and the Kharoshthi script spread far beyond Gandhara in this period. Inscriptions have, for example, been found in China.

It will still be many years before the full significance of the British Library Scrolls is understood. Their very existence, however, confirms the reality and distinctiveness of the school of Gandharan Buddhism. The fact that the texts do not display characteristics of Mahayana Buddhism tends to argue against an early origin for the development of this form of the religion. Although the dating of the manuscripts themselves cannot be definite—the range is broadly between the first century BC and the second century AD—suggestions of references to historical figures, not least Kujula Kadphises, makes a dating of AD 10 to 30 possible. This, and an evident influence from the years of Scythian dominance in Gandhara, makes it necessary to revise our view of the development of the religion in this region: the flowering of Gandharan Buddhism was not restricted to the Kushan era, but had begun under the Scythian and Parthian dynasties well before the rise of Kanishka, even before Kujula Kadphises first conquered through the Khyber Pass.

The unification of many lands under Kushan rule, however, eased the passage of ideas and was crucial to the spread of Buddhism. That a monk or missionary could travel all the way from Pataliputra, through Gandhara, and as far as Kashgar under the protection of a single government was a major benefit to a religion that was setting out to proselytize. The Khyber Pass was essential to these missionaries and became the main means by which the Buddhist faith was exported from India.

The growth of international trade assisted its spread. Kushan coins have turned up as far away as Ethiopia and Scandinavia, and contacts with Rome were considerable: Kushan ambassadors attended the celebrations in the city after Emperor Trajan was victorious against the Dacians, and Roman coins have been found deep inside India. At Pompeii, an Indian ivory statuette of the Kushan period was excavated from beneath the lava, and Roman glassware has been discovered in the Kushan palace at Bagram. Of all the many trade routes and contacts that were being developed by the Kushans, however, one above all was of crucial importance in the story of Buddhism: it was along the Silk Road that the teachings of the Buddha were introduced to China.

According to Chinese legend, the Emperor Mingdi was led by a dream in AD 65 to send to India for Buddhist teachers, books and statues; this story may indeed be based on the dim memories of the earliest encounters with Buddhist wanderers, for it was at this time that contacts began to develop. Progress in attracting adherents was not, however, considerable until the Han dynasty collapsed in the early third century AD—no doubt a novel and pacifist religion was attractive to some amid a disintegrating feudal society with its consequent turmoil and disorder. Another possible reason for the receptivity of the Chinese to Buddhism is that is has much in common with Taoism. Indeed, the two systems of thought merged to become virtually a new type of Buddhism, the Amida or "Pure Land" school, by the sixth century AD.

Chinese writings give the names of several Buddhist monks from Kushan lands who translated religious texts into Chinese, and from linguistic analysis it seems likely that some of these translations were done from originals in Gandhari. Buddhist inscriptions in the Gandhari language and the Kharoshthi script have been found near Loyang and Xian, great cities of the Silk Road. Such inscriptions could only have been written by monks from Gandhara.

Buddhism benefited from the support—both active and tacit—of the Kushan kings, with Kanishka paramount among them. This raises the question of the motives behind this assistance: royal political ambition may have shadowed the proselytizing monks on their journeys into the east. With Kashgar already in the Kushan realm, Kanishka and his successors may perhaps have cast their eyes along the Silk Road, keen to extend their influence over more of the wealthy trading cities that it connected. This cannot be known for certain, but it is an intriguing possibility to set alongside the devoted efforts of missionaries.

Buddhism had itself achieved some considerable political power under the Kushans, as seen in the dominance it had acquired in Gandhara. Several hundred monasteries were established in the region during this period, some imposing themselves on the landscape like feudal castles. On the approach to the Swat valley, one of the most scenic parts of northern Pakistan, the crumbled ruins of Takht-i-Bhai speak of the developed wealth that Buddhist monks were living in by the early years of the Christian age. A once-grand monastery resting defiantly on knife-edge ridges, Takht-i-Bhai sits in the mountains that overlook the Malakand Pass and the lower Swat valley. An inscription of Gondophares tells us that this monastery dates from before the Kushan adoption of Buddhism under Kanishka, but we can suppose that this Buddhist site benefited also from royal patronage, for in its ruined form it has yielded wonderful examples of the Gandharan school of art that dates from these years (see color plate 8).

A particular doctrinal feature of the northern school of Buddhism contributed to the distinctive characteristics of Gandharan art, and its longevity. Whereas Hinayana Buddhists continued to consider the

Buddha a teacher only, under Mahayana he became a god. In early Buddhist art the Buddha is not represented in person but is symbolized by the Buddhist wheel or by a tree, representing his enlightenment. In the developing northern school, however, he is personified everywhere. His statue became ubiquitous, an idol adorning every holy place. The influence of Greek sculptural forms—and indeed, by these years, the associated aesthetics of Rome—were transmitted through Bactria to give a particular character to such carving. Thus the Buddha himself is the icon of the Gandharan school of art, swathed in draping folds of fabric as in a statue of a Greek god or Roman emperor. Without Greek influence, the Gandharan school of art could not have existed, and by extension Greco-Roman art was introduced to China and the Far East through the vector of Buddhism. It is curious that the legacy of the Kushans—ruthless nomadic invaders—should be the spread of the religion of peace and the flourishing of graceful sculptural forms.

Comparison is sometimes drawn between Kanishka and Ashoka, both being influential warrior kings who adopted Buddhism. Another comparison, though, is less flattering: neither provided for a lasting dynasty. After Kanishka, there came a much less successful line of Kushan rulers, dwindling into defeat in the early third century AD. Perhaps the enervating effect of Buddhist pacifism was again at work, reducing the capacity of rulers to rule, diminishing the necessary ruthlessness that must on occasion characterize successful kings. Certainly, the Kushans had no answer for the energy of a new competitor arisen to the west: when the Sasanian Persians came to power in Iran and set out to recover the eastern territories of the old empire, the Kushans did not long resist.

CHAPTER SIX

Sasanian Persians and White Huns

A Sasanian king, hunting

Shapur, king of kings, partner of the stars, brother
of the sun and moon

AMMIANUS MARCELLINUS, *Res Gestae*

They are the only ones among the Huns who have
white bodies and countenances which are not ugly.

PROCOPIUS, *Book of Wars*

The Parthians—the swiftly turning horsemen from the steppe—continued
to rule over Iran for another two centuries after the Kushans conquered
their eastern provinces and deprived them of their Indian lands. During
this time, the wars with Rome continued—stimulated especially by Roman
jealousy of the flourishing trade along the Silk Road—and nomads harassed the northern frontiers as they had done for generations. It was not,
however, invasion from without that ended the 500-year empire of the
Parthians but the rise of a dynasty from the ancient Achaemenian heartland of Persia itself.

Before their rapid ascent to power in the early third century AD, the
Sasanians held office as hereditary high priests in the temple at Istakhr,
near the old royal center of Persepolis. There is uncertainty about the
family relationships, but the eponymous Sasan was probably a senior
temple dignitary whose son Papak married the daughter of a local prince,
ruler of the province of Persia as a vassal king under the Parthians. It is
likely that Papak seized power from his father-in-law only to find that the
Parthian king of kings would not recognize his status, nor agree to the
accession of his son, placing the debutant dynasty in a state of revolt
against the overlords. Ardeshir, son of Papak, succeeded his father and
proclaimed himself king not just of Persia but of all Iran, and met the
imperial army in a battle in AD 224 in which the Parthian king, Artabanus
V, was killed. With startling rapidity, Ardeshir went on to smash a coalition
that had formed against him, composed of Romans, Armenians, Kushans
and Scythians. Just two years after Artabanus was killed, Ardeshir was

crowned as ruler of an empire that stretched from the Euphrates to Seistan.

Amid the uncertainty accompanying the origins of the dynasty, a number of myths developed. In one, Sasan—secretly a descendant of the Achaemenians—was said to be the shepherd of Papak, the king in Persia. Papak had a dream that the son of Sasan would one day rule the world, so he gave his daughter to Sasan and Ardeshir was born. This resemblance to the tale of the birth and rise of Cyrus the Great—the future greatness of an unborn son being foretold in a dream—illustrates a characteristic often attached to the Sasanian dynasty by later ages: that they were the real successors of the Achaemenians, a truly Persian family of kings arisen in a nationalist reaction against the centuries of rule by Seleucid and Parthian outsiders. Since detailed knowledge of the Achaemenian era has only been reconstructed through the archaeological and linguistic work of scholars of the modern age, the Sasanians can have known little about it, perhaps viewing the time of Cyrus and Darius as something of a mythical golden age. It may be, therefore, that royal propagandists in the employ of Ardeshir would have welcomed fables that highlighted parallels between the new dynasty and old.

Certainly, propaganda was a lively concern of the early Sasanians, and they carved rock reliefs to imprint their status on to the landscape. This was a deliberate effort to ape the Achaemenians: the earliest Sasanian relief is found at Naqsh-i-Rustam, where Darius the Great and other Achaemenian kings lie entombed three miles from Persepolis. Two horsemen have been cut into the rock cliffs, standing face to face, their mounts almost clashing heads, a body lying fallen under the hooves of each horse. In the sandy brown stone aging to grey, the relief is carved so deep into the cliff that the figures, and especially their horses, stand out almost as full sculpture. This bold scene shows the investiture of the Sasanian usurper by Ahura Mazda—God—himself.

The horseman on the left is Ardeshir, clad in a long gown that reaches below his feet, and wearing his distinctive crown, the *korymbos*—a skullcap surmounted by a large globe containing his hair. Ahura Mazda is mounted on the right, bearing a bundle of sacred twigs and offering the crown of royal authority to the new king. With right hand outstretched, Ardeshir takes the crown from the divine hand, his left arm raised with fisted hand, forefinger extended in a respectful greeting of the time. Beneath his horse, Ardeshir tramples Artabanus V, the defeated Parthian king, a lifeless body prostrated on the ground; under the horse of Ahura Mazda lies Ahriman, the devil, similarly inert and overcome. No grander comparison could be made: the monarch and god act together in crushing their enemies, of equal stature and on the same level, brother kings of different realms. The arrogance of this claim carries more than a touch of blasphemy.

Such familiarity was effectively repaid, however, for Ardeshir was a loyal ally to Ahura Mazda throughout his reign and began a royal patronage that saw the Zoroastrian church reach its zenith in the Sasanian era. Despite his rapid conquest of the Parthian realm, Ardeshir recognized the limitations of violence and the value of religion in legitimizing a crown seized by force: the Zoroastrian priesthood became his advocates, and were rewarded with greater power. Ardeshir forged a single, unified Zoroastrian church out of the existing fraternity of independent communities, and it became more amenable to king and priesthood alike. Firmly under priestly control but dedicated to royal service, Zoroastrianism was welded into a state religion.

The worship of cult images was banned: statues of numerous deities and idols—widely used throughout Iran in popular religious practices— were forcibly removed from temples and replaced with sacred fires of the Zoroastrian style. The Sasanians became enthusiastic iconoclasts, allowing the loyal priests to expand their own empire over souls. The sacred fires had other uses in propaganda: to proclaim his devout character to every one of his subjects who turned a penny in their hand, Ardeshir placed a fire altar on the reverse of his coins. This practice was followed by all his successors and was just one of the characteristics that gave later ages a sense of the Sasanians as especial protectors of the Zoroastrian faith. In making this claim, they also denigrated the righteousness of the Parthians in order to justify their seizure of power, describing their predecessors as little more than pagans: so successful were the Sasanians in spreading this prejudice that it has forever colored views of the Parthians.

Besides looking to the church to tighten his grip on power at home, Ardeshir made an early effort to shore up his borders; as the heir to the Parthians and their squabbles with neighboring kings, this meant war with Rome. After initial reverses, the new Persian empire made some territorial gains in several years of fighting, and Ardeshir maintained a vigorous focus on his western frontier throughout his reign. The eastern border was left to his successor.

With the major part of the old Achaemenian lands absorbed into his empire, a strong army built and tested, and the Romans to the west temporarily bested, Ardeshir is said to have retired from rule several years before his death, passing the throne to his son Shapur in AD 241. Having been associated in his father's rule for some time before becoming emperor, Shapur succeeded untroubled and inherited a centralized and organized state in the ascendant, shaped to do the royal bidding.

The western frontiers having been bolstered by his father, Shapur was free to look to the east from the start of his reign. The Kushan dynasty continued to rule in the former eastern territories of the Iranian realm, and Shapur had strong motives to seek to win them back: no empire sits comfortably with powerful rivals on two flanks, and with the Romans to the west and the Kushans to the east, the Sasanian lands were under the constant threat of assault. Moreover, the Kushan lands had become rich, benefiting from the flow of trade along the great routes that they controlled, including the road into India through the Khyber Pass. Success and riches can bring softness, and Buddhist pacifism may also have played its part in weakening Kushan armies. An attack on the Kushan Empire was an attractive proposition for Shapur, and it was his first undertaking.

His victory was rapid: Shapur seized Peshawar, the capital of the Kushan Empire, and the road to India was his; he marched into the Subcontinent and occupied the Indus valley. In the north, Bactria was conquered and Shapur led his troops across the Oxus river into Samarkand and Tashkent. The professionalism of Sasanian arms overcame a Kushan soldiery once triumphant but now weakened beyond a riposte, and much of their empire was absorbed into the Sasanian kingdom under vassal rulers. By the early 240s AD, the Sasanian Persians had restored to their empire the furthest eastern frontiers of the Achaemenians, and the Khyber Pass was Persian once again.

Success in the east seems to have persuaded Shapur to reopen war with the Romans, for it was very shortly after his triumph over the Kushans that he entered the Roman province of Syria and fought his way to Antioch.

After the murder of Emperor Gordian in AD 244, his successor Philip the Arab sued for peace with the Persians, ceding Armenia and Mesopotamia and paying a large tribute to achieve a settlement. This peace held for fifteen years, until war began again with renewed Persian success—Shapur seized several cities in Syria, including Antioch once again. It was, however, a victory near Edessa in AD 260 that proved unprecedented: Emperor Valerian himself was captured, along with 70,000 Roman soldiers. Never before had the person of the emperor been taken by an enemy, and the shock with which Rome heard the news must surely have equaled the pride taken by the Sasanian king in his unmatched triumph.

This victory, the capture of Valerian, takes us back to the rock reliefs at Naqsh-i-Rustam, for Shapur commemorated in stone all of his achievements. In a celebratory carving placed near the tomb of Darius the Great, Shapur is shown on horseback, a broad-shouldered and commanding figure. On the left of the relief are two Romans: one is on bended knee before Shapur, his arms stretched forward in supplication. He wears a short tunic of the Roman style and a cloak clasped by a brooch at the throat. This is Philip the Arab, shown beseeching the Sasanian for peace as he had done in AD 244. The other figure, clad similarly, stands before the royal mount, raising an arm that is clutched tightly by Shapur: this Roman is Valerian. With his left hand, Shapur grasps the hilt of his sheathed sword to remind us of his prowess in arms and the means of his success. Behind the king, and shown half obscured as if a shadowy onlooker at this scene of victory, is the Zoroastrian high priest, his fist raised in the finger greeting. ?

Shapur lost no time in exploiting the advantage that Roman disarray offered. After the capture of the opposing emperor, he marched deep into Cappadocia and scorched its earth. The Romans fought back and Valerian soon died in captivity, but by his efforts at publicizing his deeds in stone, Shapur ensured that the memory of his success was enduring.

After the death of Shapur I, the Sasanians faced a rebellion in their Kushan and Indian lands in support of a pretender to the throne. This trouble proved sufficient to warrant the making of a disadvantageous peace with Rome, who forced the Persians to cede Armenia and Mesopotamia, and later some lands to the east of the Tigris, an inroad that Rome had never made before. At the beginning of the fourth century, therefore, the

Sasanian Empire was not at its strongest, and it seems that the Kushan vassal rulers sought to take advantage of the succession in AD 309 of a minor, Shapur II. While internal weakness and disorders beset Iran, the rebellious Kushans briefly recaptured their former glories, making some territorial intrusions into Sasanian lands and freeing themselves for a time from their western masters. This independence was short-lived, however, for when Shapur achieved his majority he lost no time in returning to the east to impose himself as king. The Kushans were comprehensively destroyed, and were this time not trusted as vassal rulers; they were replaced with a line of Sasanian princes known as the Kushanshahs (Kings of the Kushans) who would henceforth govern the former Kushan lands as a province of the Sasanian Empire from their capital at Bactra.

The long reign of Shapur II was one of the most celebrated and eventful of the Sasanian period. His seventy years on the throne saw some of the most significant developments to affect the world outside Iran—the adoption of Christianity by the Romans, the rise of the Gupta Empire in India, the appearance of new nomad groups to threaten his northeast frontier—and events within his empire were determined especially by Shapur's reactions to these stimuli.

There are some excellent literary sources for this active reign, chief among them the writing of Ammianus Marcellinus. A Roman officer of Greek parentage from Antioch in Syria, Ammianus served in the continuing wars against the Sasanians in the middle years of the fourth century. He set out to chart the history of Rome from where Tacitus leaves off in AD 96; unfortunately, almost half of his work called the *Res Gestae*, or Histories, has been lost, but the surviving parts cover a twenty-five year period from the 350s AD and provide an excellent window on the Persian wars. Ammianus himself took part in the events he describes, giving a compelling immediacy to his account of Persian arms:

> The Persians opposed us with squadrons of cuirassiers drawn up in such serried ranks that their movements in their close-fitting coats of flexible mail dazzled our eyes, while all their horses were protected by housings of leather. They were supported by detachments of infantry who moved in compact formation carrying long, curved shields of wicker covered with raw hide. Behind them came elephants looking like

moving hills. Their huge bodies threatened destruction to all who approached, and past experience had taught us to dread them.

One of the most significant events during the reign of Shapur was the conversion to Christianity of the Roman emperor Constantine in AD 312. The consequent adoption of the religion across his empire altered the relationship with the Persians: previously, when Christians were a persecuted minority in Roman lands, they had been potentially useful to the Sasanians as spies, collaborators and secret supporters inside the borders of their regular enemy. With the changes wrought by Constantine's conversion, the position was reversed: Christians within the Persian Empire were suddenly looked upon as a potential fifth column, a dangerous sect of dubious loyalty, and they began to suffer intermittent harassment from the Sasanians. Although it seems that Shapur had no particular personal animosity for Christianity, he became troubled especially by Christian intrigues on behalf of Rome, and in AD 339 was forced to launch the first organized campaign of persecution against them in Iranian lands, a campaign that continued for the rest of his long reign.

Thus, a new epoch began on his western border early in the reign of Shapur. On his east, similarly, a new era commenced with the rise of the Gupta dynasty of India. The origins of the family are unclear, but they were possibly the rulers of a Kushan successor state in the western Ganges region, a small principality that they built into a great empire that achieved a cultural distinction to match its political success. The first Gupta ruler of note was Chandra Gupta I, who came to power in around AD 319 and ruled for twenty-five years, forging his small inherited principality into a kingdom. His son Samudra Gupta continued in the expansionary path and conquered his kingdom into an empire, acquiring mastery of the Ganges valley and subjugating rival kings to the north and south, receiving tribute from as far afield as Sri Lanka and Nepal. Under Chandra Gupta II, the territory of the empire was extended still further, into the western Deccan.

Despite sharing a border with the Sasanians, there does not seem to have been significant tension between the two powers. Indeed, the two can seem natural associates rather than rivals: just as the Sasanians are often seen as the instigators of an Iranian national renaissance, the Gupta period saw a truly Indian dynasty recover some of the glory of the Mauryan era after centuries of rule in northern India by Greek, Scythian and Kushan outsiders. Both are seen as the zeniths of their respective civilizations.

Under the Guptas, classical Sanskrit became dominant as the language of the literate elite, a position that it maintained for several centuries until Persian intruded into the central lands of India after AD 1000. A vibrant Sanskrit literature arose, centered on the court, aristocracy and urban rich, who consumed poetry, prose and plays. The political assistance enjoyed by the Sanskrit language parallels the privileged position that the Sasanians gave to Persian, and their efforts to impose it upon their subjects as the sole tongue of the official sphere. Developments in the Indian religious realm also parallel the Sasanian support for Zoroastrianism; Hinduism was developing under royal patronage, and some sacred texts were written at this time, in Sanskrit. Just as the Sasanians used a national religion to legitimize their rule, so too did the Guptas seek to acquire divine support, and the cults of Hinduism were a valuable and varied source of gods.

The Gupta years thus provided an age to rival the Sasanians for distinction even if they did not rival each other in arms. Freedom from wars with India was a blessing to Shapur II, for his energies were absorbed by fighting Rome and another people who troubled his northeast frontier. Having firmly defeated the Kushan revival early in his reign, forcefully taking their territories into a closer subjection to his empire, Shapur found a new band of nomads infiltrating Bactria later in his reign: the Chionites. The threat they posed was enough to bring Shapur to the east to campaign in person against them in about AD 356. The Sasanian emperor could not destroy them, and after two seasons of fighting, he was forced to cede Bactria in a treaty in which the nomads agreed in return to fight for Shapur against the Romans.

It seems that a flourishing Buddhist community at Bamiyan played a crucial role in making this peace. Bamiyan is a secluded valley in the mountains eighty miles from Kabul in Afghanistan; its enviable proximity to the tributary routes of the great Silk Road combined with the natural protection of its cliffs and peaks make it an ideal site for a religious retreat. It is not known when the valley began to fill with Buddhist monks, but during the Kushan years Bamiyan became an important community, benefiting from the nearby flow of peoples and goods. A remarkable

The Bamiyan Buddhas in a nineteenth-century engraving

feature of the Buddhist colonization of the valley was the use made of caves carved into the massive cliff, monks' cells cut directly into the rock and dotted about the side of the valley, sometimes hundreds of feet above ground. As the community grew, so more caves were cut in the rocky honeycomb, until hundreds of irregular rectangles and squares covered the valley sides. Their remains can still be seen today.

The most remarkable feature of Bamiyan in the 350s AD, however, was a colossal statue of the Buddha carved into the same cliff face. A truly stupendous undertaking, it stood 125 feet high and was hewn deep into the sandy stone. This grand Buddha dominated all around it, a powerful testament to strength in faith, a sight to inspire awe in pilgrims and travelers walking the valley beneath; alongside it, the caves seem like the burrows of tiny animals. Despite the vast size in which they worked, the sculptors lent an aspect of delicacy to the statue, the folds of gown—owing its style to the art of Gandhara—falling lightly around the commanding body. In a method that must have multiplied the impact of the huge figure—raising even more powerfully the sensation of a divine presence—

it seems that the face was not carved into the rock, but was painted on to a banner fixed to the head.

We do not know when the great Buddha was carved—it could have been as early as the time of Kanishka—but certainly it was in place by the time that Shapur agreed his treaty with the Chionite nomads. A mural painted high up in the niche of the Buddha, by the head of the statue, is thought to show the very occasion on which the leaders of each side met to parley. Rendered on the stone in bright colors—the blues and reds remaining vivid even today—is a scene of seated figures, some bejeweled and crowned as kings or princes, some wearing monastic robes, princesses sitting among them. It is a great banquet, probably showing Shapur II himself, his vassal king Bahram II Kushanshah, and the Chionite king Grumbates, sitting together to agree the terms of their treaty. The restoration of peace—and the presence in Bamiyan of the King of Kings—would certainly warrant celebration through the commissioning of such a work of art. The location, and the monastic presence in the mural, suggest that the Buddhist community hosted the peace conference and mediated the negotiations.

Although it cost him Bactria, Shapur II successfully diverted the Chionites from making further inroads into his territories—and, incidentally, India—and attached them to him for an assault on Rome. Shapur thus marched into Roman lands with Grumbates by his side in AD 359, and advanced on the fortress town of Amida on the Tigris river—modern Diyarbakir in southeast Turkey—that he attacked and destroyed. Ammianus Marcellinus was himself present at the siege of this powerful town and gives us an exciting account of the fall of the city and his own dramatic escape across the desert; he tells us also that Shapur was "reinforced by the wild peoples on whom he had imposed peace." In this campaign, the provinces of Armenia and Mesopotamia were restored to the Sasanians and the Roman emperor Julian was killed in battle.

The lengthy and distinguished reign of Shapur II came to an end in AD 379 with no further inroads against his northeast frontier. His pact with the nomads, however, did not long protect the Sasanian realm. A few decades later, Bactria had again become a looming threat in the hands of a newly arisen tribe of conquering nomads: the White Huns.

The origins of the White Huns are somewhat mysterious, but it seems that they were another of the multitudinous Iranian tribes of nomads, following so many of their fellows off the steppe into the advanced civilizations of the south. In this they were noteworthy as being the last such group, for after them came Turkic nomads distinct in ethnicity and language, the peoples that would come to dominate so much of the Middle East and India in later centuries. For now, though, the Iranian tribes were still paramount in Sogdiana and Bactria, and used their hold on these territories to raid into Persian and Indian territory. Thus, the White Huns were not properly Huns (a Turkic people that harassed the Romans in the west with success) but formed the border tribe, the easternmost group of Iranian nomads, in closest contact with the Turkic populations who pushed them westward. We can suppose that the White Huns absorbed some considerable influence from these neighbors. Cultural borrowing, intermarriage and trade would have led to some similarities in dress, ornament and lifestyle that may have confused observers at the time; the very name "White Hun" seems to speak of some confusion and an admission of their Iranian origins but with some Turkic cultural adoptions: the Roman historian Procopius labels them White Huns on account of their "white bodies" while at the same time pointing out their differences from true Huns.

While there is some doubt about their origins, it is certain that the White Huns were a fearsome people, inured to war and the hard life of nomads from their very earliest days: young White Hun boys had deep gashes cut into their faces so that they would grow into scarred and frightening warriors. The most unsettling practice of the White Huns was the binding of heads: infant skulls were tightly wrapped around the sides to force growth in height, producing adults with slim, towering heads that presented a profoundly disturbing sight to their enemies. Curiously gashed and cone-headed, White Hun fighters must have seemed terrifyingly alien, and their coin portraits bear out this bizarre appearance. The White Huns appear to have been poorly endowed with the crafts of some of their Central Asian fellows, and they had a less developed metalwork culture. They seem to have relied on facial disfigurement for their impact of appearance rather than on wrought-metal decoration or sophisticated animal symbolism.

It seems that clashes with the White Huns began during the reign of the Sasanian king Yazdagird I (AD 399–420). By AD 425, the nomads had infiltrated Bactria, absorbing or displacing the Chionites. From Bactria, they continued to strike into Iranian territory, reaching deep into the empire. In AD 427, during the reign of the legendary Sasanian hunter-king Bahram V, the White Huns penetrated as far as the modern city of Tehran, before the Persians agreed to pay tribute; as the White Huns returned home, Bahram ambushed them and destroyed their army, the White Hun king being killed and his queen captured. A large column was erected on the border between the two realms, and it was said that no White Hun might pass beyond it, on pain of death. This underhand defeat kept the invaders out of Sasanian territory for the rest of the reign, and Bahram V died in AD 438 without having to look again to the northeast frontier.

Troubles with the White Huns recommenced under his successor Yazdagird II, but it was after he died that a new and disturbing era began, in which the White Huns came to have an increasing influence in the affairs of the Sasanian polity. A succession struggle arose between the sons of Yazdagird, and one, Piroz, fled into the White Hun domain. After two years in exile, he persuaded their king to assist him in his ambitions on the crown, and in AD 459 Piroz made himself emperor of Iran at the head of an army of White Huns. Piroz paid his new friends a generous tribute in return, and for some years there was peace, but war broke out again and recurred frequently.

In the 470s AD, the two sides came together to negotiate and a treaty was settled; the agreement required Piroz to give the White Hun king one of his daughters in marriage, confirming an alliance that was intended to keep the peace between them for many years. It seems, however, that the reality of this provision appalled Piroz, who came to feel revolted by the prospect of a Sasanian princess being married to a barbarian. He instead contrived to send a slave girl, dressed and ornamented as a princess, in place of his own child. With great ceremony, the marriage went ahead before the deception was revealed; the slave-girl queen remained in the harem, but war broke out once again, and the Sasanians fared badly: Piroz himself was even captured and ransomed, before making war again and dying in battle against the White Huns in AD 484.

By these years, the White Huns were able to exercise some considerable influence over the Sasanian kingdom—if war was not under way, there was always the threat of a fresh campaign, or the enforcement of tribute payments, to sustain pressure. The most dramatic success of the White Huns, however, was their conquest of the Sasanian province of Gandhara: by around AD 465, the tower-headed nomads had seized the Khyber Pass and marched into India. Through failing to keep the White Huns in Bactria, Piroz had lost his Indian lands, and his enemy was commensurately augmented in their power and resources. As so often in this murky area of history, there is no written account of this occasion, no witness who saw their advance into these new territories: imagination must suffice, and we can conjure a picture of these wild people as they rode through the Khyber, the scars on their cut faces perhaps reddened by the snowy cold of winter or sweating in the vigorous sun of a violent summer. Their strangely tall heads swing lightly as the horses under them pick their way over the uneven track, and their bows—the weapon of all steppe horsemen—knock against their thighs. Clad in furs and leathers, their weapons at the ready and free of extraneous ornament, these horsemen would have presented a fierce sight, a vision of self-inflicted violence that would leave an onlooker in no doubt about their willingness to harm others.

The White Huns did not stop at the conquest of Gandhara: the riches and cultural splendor of the Gupta Empire of India were an attraction not to be denied, and war broke out late in the 460s AD. The Gupta armies had initial success in holding back the onslaught under their king Skandagupta, but then began a long series of defeats that ended with the destruction of the empire. Although the Gupta dynasty survived into the sixth century, Skandagupta was their last important monarch. In its short life, the Gupta state reached a level of advancement in art and science that has placed it high in the memory of India ever since, but its achievements were no insurance against the committed warring of the White Huns.

When the White Huns were successful in their Indian invasion, they appointed a viceroy—or *Tegin*—to rule over Gandhara and their Indian conquests, under the suzerainty of the great king in Bactria. This official was Toromana, a vassal ruler who would come to outshine his nominal superior and make himself the greatest king in northern India through prowess in war. It was he who smashed the Gupta power, and after the death of Skandagupta, found himself opposed by a weak set of disunited successor principalities. These Toromana reduced one by one until he was paramount in north India, a process that was complete by around 500 AD.

The coins of Toromana show him with a severely elongated skull, tapering upward into his crown; he has heavily arched eyebrows and the flattened nose of a boxer above a pinched mouth with fleshy lips. Later coins of the White Huns show even more extreme representations of the tower head, resembling cartoons in their disturbing deformations.

Under the White Hun dominance of India and Afghanistan, Buddhism fared badly: the invading barbarians had little incentive to spare those who could not defend themselves, and many Buddhist communities were destroyed; unknown numbers of monks and lay followers perished. This was a very damaging blow for the religion at a time when it had already been under pressure from the support given by the Gupta dynasty to the developing faith of Hinduism; the decline of Buddhism in its homeland of northern India dates from this period. With royal patronage extended to a rival, and the lasting impact of the vicious depredations of the White Huns, Buddhism rapidly lost out to Hinduism and survived into later ages only in other regions of the world. It was not extinguished completely, however: some communities survived, among them that of Bamiyan, benefiting perhaps from its relative isolation from the Indian lands that most attracted the White Huns. It may even be this period that saw the carving of a second great Buddha into the cliff face of the valley, a monument of yet larger size, a splendid defiance by the Buddhists of Bamiyan of the attacks on their fellows. Over 170 feet in height and set deep into the cliff, this second figure commanded even more attention than the first.

Toromana died shortly after he had achieved his martial dominance, in AD 502, and was succeeded by his son Mihirakula, a paradigm of tyrannical excess who sought to consolidate the conquests of his father. His oppressive exactions and his enthusiasm for bloodshed eventually provoked a rebellion: after Mihirakula had ruled for three decades, his suffering subjects rose under an obscure leader named Yasodharman and overthrew him as their king; he escaped to Kashmir with his armies and displaced the local prince, ruling there until his death ten years later. Mihirakula is said to have pitched elephants over cliffs so that he could watch their death agonies, a form of entertainment in keeping with his

A coin portrait of Toromana, showing typical White Hun skull deformation

bloodthirsty ways. The White Huns were thus forced out of India in AD 532, but they maintained their hold on Gandhara and Bactria for some years: it was during the reign of one of the most celebrated Sasanian sovereigns, Khusrau I, that they were finally defeated.

After their success in Gandhara, the White Huns had been enticed from their armed antagonism with the Sasanians by the rich prospects of India, sparing the Persians from the full brunt of their rising power. Their rivalry did not end, however, and White Hun interference in Sasanian affairs continued. In the 490s, the Sasanian king Kavadh was deposed by his nobles and fled to the White Huns; as a prince, Kavadh had spent two years living among them as a hostage left as a guarantee of Persian tribute payments, and knew them well. The White Huns provided him with an army to recover the throne, and thereby acquired a say in Sasanian affairs for the rest of the reign. It was after Kavadh died in AD 531 that the relationship began to change, for he was succeeded by his son Khusrau I, a great king who would come to be known as Khusrau the Just.

Khusrau I did much to restore the status of the Sasanian crown after decades of debilitating warfare with the White Huns and rivalry with the potent nobility. In this, he was aided by the experiment of his father with

109

Mazdakism—a strange brand of religiously inspired communism—which served to reduce the power of the nobility and clergy alike. Although the internal disorders caused by this movement had disrupted the state finances and created significant upheaval, Khusrau gained from a quiescent aristocracy and more cooperative priesthood. He returned much of the property that had been seized during the times of Mazdakite excess, accruing to himself a store of credit as the just restorer of equity and stability: he was able to rule with absolute authority and became known even outside the Sasanian Empire as a king of justice.

By AD 540, Khusrau was sufficiently confident to end the regular payments of tribute to the White Huns, made by the Sasanians for many years in order to keep the nomads from Iranian lands. Perhaps the loss of their Indian provinces had evidently diminished their powers, and Khusrau felt he could take advantage. It was to be a further two decades, however, until Khusrau was able to seek a conclusive end to the constant White Hun threat, and he did this with the help of the Turks, a rising new force from the steppes who would conquer widely in later centuries. Following behind them on their migration westward, in the continual flux of nomadic life in Central Asia, the Turks had run up against the northern frontiers of the empire of the White Huns, and made war against them. Seeking the assistance of the Persians against their common enemy, the Turks sent ambassadors to Khusrau to ask for an alliance; accordingly, in around AD 558, the Turks and the Sasanian armies made a joint attack on separate fronts, and the White Huns were crushed between the two. The Turks acquired Sogdiana, and Khusrau recovered Bactria and Gandhara for the Sasanians. The borders of the Iranian empire once more rested on the Oxus river, and the Persian power was restored in the east. After almost a century in the domain of the White Huns, the Khyber Pass was again in Persian hands.

Besides his victory against the White Huns, Khusrau was successful in extending his empire to the south, pushing his rule along the coast of the Arabian peninsula as far as the Yemen. The seemingly inevitable wars with Rome—now in its later eastern form, the Byzantine Empire—continued also. The achievements of the years of Khusrau were not only in matters of state, however, for it became an era known for art and culture, flourishing vigorously in a time of internal peace and order in the empire. Many books were brought from outside to be translated into Persian, including works from India and the Psalms from the Christian West. Khusrau was a great builder, and architecture benefited from his interest. Commerce developed amid the stability he introduced, improving the systems of banking: the bill of exchange became a more sophisticated financial instrument, and the check was invented—indeed the very word we use today is from the Persian. It is possible that the game of backgammon dates from this period of innovation and cultural developments great and small. At a time when the Christian church of Rome was persecuting the philosophers of Greece, they found a welcome in the empire of Khusrau and added their contribution to the cultural mix; after aggressive early backing for Zoroastrianism, Khusrau appears to have adopted a tolerant attitude toward religions, and in this time of openness the intellectual gains were many.

Thus under Khusrau I, the Persians had recovered their standing, and he died in AD 579 with the Sasanians in the ascendant once more, having survived the White Hun threat and won out in the internal struggles against the aristocracy and overmighty priests. The regeneration continued, the dynasty following the rising trajectory set by Khusrau. By the turn of the seventh century, Persian power was seemingly unassailable: in wars with the Romans, the Sasanian armies invaded the Holy Land and seized Jerusalem, massacring 50,000 Christians and carrying off a piece of the True Cross. Egypt was conquered and Persian territory was extended deep into Africa, to the borders of Ethiopia. Much of Asia Minor was captured and Constantinople itself was besieged. With vaulting successes in the military realm being matched by advances and innovations in arts and science, the Sasanian dynasty had again made Iran an expansionary civilization, its cultural energy and military ambitions bursting its borders east and west. Then in AD 632 the Prophet Muhammad died in Medina, and the world changed.

CHAPTER SEVEN

The First Muslims

Caliph Harun al-Rashid in a nineteenth-century edition of
A Thousand and One Nights

Slay them wherever you find them. Drive them out of the places from which they drove you. Idolatry is more grievous than bloodshed . . . Thus shall the unbelievers be rewarded: but if they desist, God is forgiving and merciful. Fight against them until idolatry is no more and God's religion reigns supreme.

THE KORAN, 2:191

Ali Masjid, the narrowest part of the Khyber Pass, where the cliffs close up tightly around the roadway and the white fort sits high above, is named for a tiny place of Muslim worship—the name means "Mosque of Ali"—that stands nearby (see color plate 9). Driving along the Khyber, I saw this scruffy green and white building below us; Mumtaz pulled up by the side of the road, engine running, so that I could look down upon it. Surrounded by such natural grandeur, it was a humble human presence. A curving roof, painted bright green, stood duty for a dome above cracked walls peeling their white paint, scuffed and in need of restoration; this was not a towering edifice of the faith but was almost lost among the trees nearby. The walls were cornered with miniature towers, and a tiny minaret—just a few feet high—formed a statue atop a wall like a toy version of the grand minarets found on mosques elsewhere. I could see only one or two tribesmen padding about.

This lackluster mosque is associated in legend with Ali, the cousin and son-in-law of the Prophet Muhammad, who is said to have traveled through the Khyber Pass and paused to build it with his own hands. History contradicts this story as Ali cannot have ventured here, but the fable nonetheless carries its power to believers. I had no doubt of this influence: the religious significance of the place combined with the prevalent tension of the Khyber to make Mumtaz anxious to hurry on, keen to avoid attracting attention for his inquisitive feringhee at such a holy place. We drove on, his unease making me reflect on the meaning of this modest mosque.

Ali Masjid is symbolic of one of the most significant of all the many passages through the Khyber Pass: the introduction of Islam to South Asia. It was an event that would enrich the South Asian interior world and which would go on to define the politics of the region to the present day. To understand how Islam came to the Khyber Pass, it is necessary to go back a few hundred years even before the Muslims began their forays into India, all the way back to the earliest days of the faith and its prophet.

Muhammad was born in about AD 570 in Mecca, a town in western Arabia. A member of the powerful Quraysh tribe, known especially as merchants, he was orphaned as a boy and raised by his grandfather and then by his uncle, Abu Talib. As a youth, he traveled with the trading caravans from the sparse desert lands of Arabia into the fertile and wealthy countries to the north—the Holy Land and Syria—and gained success in business. At the age of twenty-five, he married Khadijah, a rich widow fifteen years his senior, having impressed her through his management of her commercial affairs.

Despite his worldly achievements, Muhammad evidently perceived something lacking in his life, for he made a practice of withdrawing to a cave in the mountains for periods of solitary meditation and prayer, a man searching for meaning and vocation. In this era, the Arab tribes of Mecca maintained a compound of religious beliefs derived from their position on the frontier of the Holy Land: a fusion of Judeo-Christian influence with ancient pagan customs. They worshipped the supreme God of the Semitic tradition alongside a number of female deities, enshrined as idols in the sanctuary in Mecca. It was into this confused spiritual milieu that Muhammad delivered his transforming revelation: there is no god but God. In AD 609, while alone on his wanderings in the hills, Muhammad is said to have been visited by the Angel Gabriel, who gave to him the word of God, recited in beautiful Arabic that became inscribed upon his heart. It is this message from God—along with many more received by Muhammad in numerous visitations—that comprise the Koran, the sacred text of Islam; as the chosen vessel of holy communication, Muhammad became the Prophet of God. This status of Muhammad, and the uncompromising monotheism at the center of the creed, is daily affirmed in the Muslim declaration of faith: *there is no god but God, and Muhammad is his messenger*.

Following the first of his revelations—on the occasion known later as the Night of Destiny—Muhammad confided in some close companions, including his wife Khadijah and Abu Talib. Though it was only a small number who initially accepted his mission and became his adherents, Muhammad delivered to them a growing body of divine revelation, and gradually a group of committed believers came to surround the Prophet. The message of Muhammad was that God the omnipotent had created all humanity and would judge everyone when the world ended: those who had submitted to the will of God could expect his mercy, and a place in Heaven; those who had refused to accept the authority of God would go to Hell. The centrality of this requirement to yield to God is expressed in the very name of the faith—*Islam* and *Muslim* are derived from the Arabic for "submission" or "surrender."

Support for Muhammad grew, and his modest coterie of devotees expanded, drawing in some members of the Quraysh and related tribes, and others such as craftsmen and slaves. As the following and power of Muhammad grew, the leaders of the Quraysh became antagonistic, increasingly troubled by the threat that the new religion posed to their accepted beliefs as the differences became plain; Muhammad attacked their idols and the ceremonies devoted to them, and new forms of worship were enjoined. When both Khadijah and Abu Talib—who had become the protector of Muhammad among the Quraysh—died in AD 619, his position became difficult. Finally, in AD 622, Muhammad and his followers were forced to flee Mecca and journey 200 miles north to an oasis settlement that came to be called Medina, the City of the Prophet: this was the *hijra*, the flight from the unbelievers of Mecca from which the beginning of the Muslim era is dated.

In Medina, Muhammad found a more welcoming reception, and it became the center for his growing power. As the Muslims increased in capacity and reach, violent conflict began with the Quraysh and continued for some years, no doubt exacerbated by a struggle for control of the lucrative trade routes of the region. Such vicissitudes—the escape from Mecca and the necessity of war—influenced the development of the teaching of Muhammad, and it acquired a hardened characteristic: it was evidently necessary to fight for one's beliefs, and Muhammad declared that God would come to the aid of those who fought in his name. Idolaters—

those men of Mecca who refused to submit to God—should be slain, and driven from the places from which they had driven the Muslims. The Koran (9:14) requires the faithful to fight against unbelievers without mercy, but decrees that God is compassionate and may extend forgiveness:

> Make war on them: God will chastise them at your hands and humble them. He will grant you victory over them and heal the spirit of the faithful. He will take away all rancor from their hearts: God shows mercy to whom He pleases. God is all-knowing and wise.

This time of struggle was thus crucial to the final form taken by Muhammad's teaching, and in the parts of the Koran thought to have been revealed in these years there is a particular concern with rules of behavior, and with morality and ritual observance: the means of defining and controlling his increasing body of devotees. The basic religious duties that are laid down for Muslims are known as the five pillars: the declaration of faith; prayer, five times daily while facing toward Mecca; the giving of alms; fasting during the daylight hours of the month of Ramadan; and the *hajj*, the pilgrimage to Mecca, required by all able Muslims at least once in their lives. These duties, as much as anything, are what identify and define a Muslim to the outside world, in the modern day as in the old.

After several years of conflict and discord between Mecca and Medina, a reconciliation took place as the number of Muslims in Mecca grew, and as the Quraysh seemed in danger of losing their control of trade due to the growing Muslim reach over important routes. In AD 629, relations had improved sufficient to allow the Muslims to enter Mecca on pilgrimage; in the following year, the city was surrendered to Muhammad without resistance. Medina remained Muhammad's capital, but the submission of Mecca to Islam was a powerful landmark in the rise of the faith.

At this time, there was no organized Muslim polity—government was centered on the person of Muhammad himself, exercising authority through his unique status and without the aid of a developed administration or structured organisation. Indeed, of the several marriages that Muhammad made after the death of Khadijah, some at least were political, designed to strengthen his support among the tribes. The Muslim military force was gaining considerable strength but remained a private army, a band of volunteers under the direct command of Muhammad and his close advisors.

1 *The rugged Khyber landscape is scattered with the forts that have provided a clear shot on to the roadway for generations of tribesmen.*

2 *Inside the Khyber Pass: the author at Michni, with the border town of Torkham and Afghanistan in the distance.*

3 *A stone relief from the Apadana at Persepolis, the great Achaemenian palace in southwest Iran.*

4 *The Alexander Mosaic from Pompeii, showing Alexander the Great in battle, dressed as a member of the companion cavalry.*

5 *A Bactrian silver tetradrachm from around 190–180 BC, showing Demetrius Aniketos in his customary elephant-scalp headdress.*

6 *The Parthians in the popular imagination: a 1939 collectable card from the Liebig meat extract company, showing the Parthian shot.*

7 *The tiny Aphrodite figurine from the Tillya Tepe excavations in Afghanistan: a perfect illustration for Bactria as a cultural crucible in the first century BC.*

8 *A statue of Buddha at the ruined monastery of Takht-i-Bhai in northern Pakistan, showing the graceful styling of the Gandharan school of art.*

9 *Ali Masjid—the Mosque of Ali—inside the Khyber Pass: not a grand monument, but symbolic of the crucial role played by the Pass in spreading Islam into India.*

10 *A fourteenth-century Persian manuscript showing Genghis Khan in battle.*

11 *The battle of Panipat of 1526, from a late sixteenth century edition of the* Baburnama, *the memoirs of the founding emperor, Babur.*

12 *Some of the memorial stones inside the Khyber Pass, commemorating the British and Pakistani regiments that have served there.*

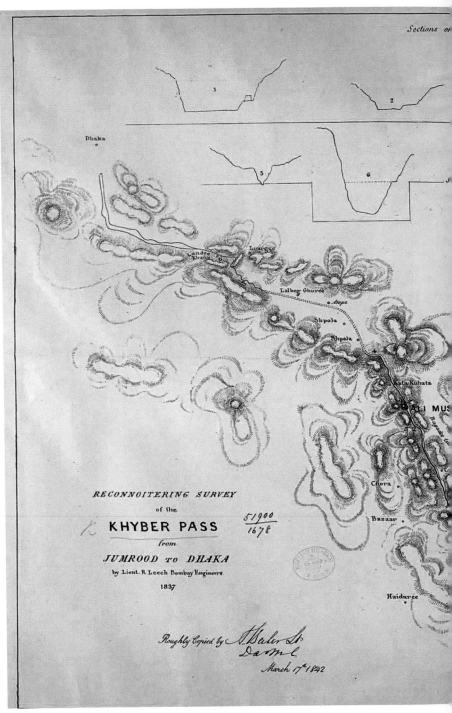

13 *The map of the Khyber Pass drawn by Lieutenant Leech in 1837. Part of the British preparations for an aggressive policy toward Afghanistan, it was of great value in the war that broke out just two years later.*

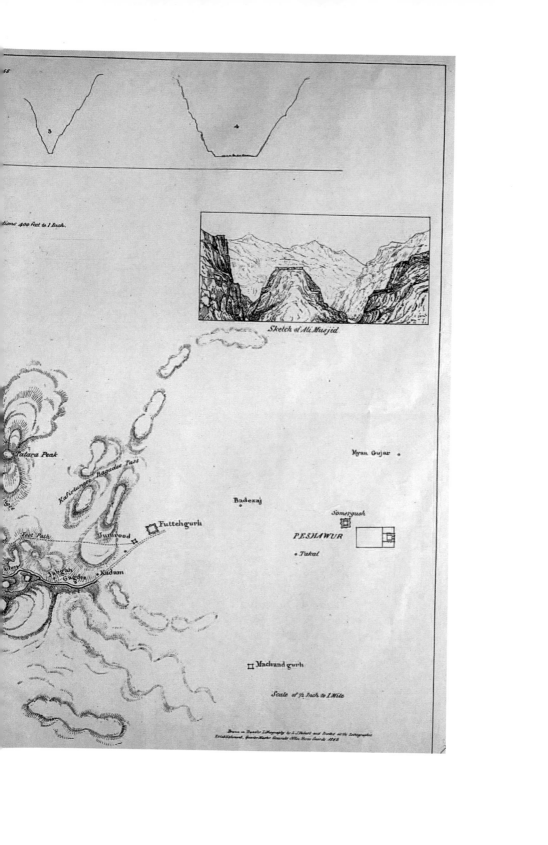

14 *Major Louis Cavagnari (second from left) with the Afghan king Yakub Khan (center) during negotiations at Gandamak in 1879.*

15 *Craftsmen in a typical workshop in Darra, the gun town in the Tribal Areas of Pakistan.*

16 *In Kabul: a game of* buzkashi, *the wild and violent Central Asian version of polo.*

It was through these means—the personal appeal of the Prophet and the mounting power of his army—that Muslim rule was stretched over a wide area of western Arabia, the tribes submitting to Muslim arms as much as to God. Muslim control over the important oases, market towns and trade routes forced numerous local chiefs to make terms with them, under varying conditions and different degrees of submission to Muhammad and his faith.

Muhammad made his last pilgrimage to Mecca in AD 632; he is said to have enjoined unity upon the Muslim brethren and to have declared that he would fight until all men confessed that there is no god but God. He returned to Medina and died later that year. The death of the Prophet came at a time when Muslim power dominated in Arabia but had not yet truly extended its reach beyond the peninsula into the advanced and settled societies and empires to the north. In a sense, the explosion of the Muslims out of Arabia and into much of the rest of the world happened because of the death of Muhammad, for it was in the fighting that followed it that the Muslim army and nascent state was forged into a power that would sweep away kings and emperors. Muhammad had established no succession, and had no sons to assume leadership; in a meeting of his close associates, Abu Bakr—an early adherent of Muhammad, and father of his wife Ayesha—was chosen as the first caliph, the successor to the Prophet. This consensus ensured his authority over the community of Muslims, but the death of Muhammad threatened to destroy the delicate network of tribal submissions and treaties that had been the basis of a very personal power; many tribes rejected political control by Medina when shorn of the figure of Muhammad, and not a few alliances were dissolved. Thus Abu Bakr had to fight to ensure that Muslim rule was continued: in rising to the challenge of apostasy, a collection of tribal volunteers was transformed into a professional army that gained a momentum of conquest that carried the Arab empire of Islam as far as Spain in the west and India in the east.

The empires to the north were those of the Byzantines and the Sasanians, two forbidding powers, each one centuries in the making and established in its territories. As the impetus of the Arab wars of reconsolidation carried the Muslim armies into the frontier regions of these grand empires, they found resistance to be slight, a surprise that inspired bolder penetration. Very soon, the Muslims were making deep thrusts into the center of these puissant neighbors, increasing their muscle as they went.

There can be little doubt that the outstanding success of the early years of the Muslim effervescence was their destruction of the Sasanian Empire. In AD 636, perhaps as few as seven or eight thousand Arabs met 40,000 Persians in battle at Qadisiyya, south of the Euphrates in what is now Iraq. Three days of fighting followed, during which the Sasanian general was killed and his army routed; this Persian defeat was just the first in a series of startling Arab victories that saw Muslim forces sweep across Iran in a brief span of years. Fierce resistance was offered in places, but the Persian king Yazdagird III had little riposte, and was reduced to a refugee in his own land, fleeing repeatedly before the onrushing Arab forces. For several years he remained at large, king only of a diminishing domain and dwindling band of loyalists, until eventually he fled to Margiana, the furthest reach of his former empire. Here, Yazdagird is said to have taken refuge with a miller; unaware of the identity of his guest, but noticing his rich possessions, the miller murdered the king while he was asleep to rob him of his last belongings. This was in AD 651, and marked the final end to the dynasty. The Muslim conquest of Iran was total: no rump of the Sasanian state remained, and Islam was carried to the traditional Persian frontier with Central Asia: the Oxus river. Zoroastrianism was all but extinguished, surviving to be practiced only by a tiny minority.

The speed and comprehensiveness of the Sasanian collapse was astonishing: it is difficult to find explanations for how an army of inferior size and weaponry could conquer one of the most powerful empires of the era. This, moreover, when the Arabs were also engaged elsewhere, pushing Islam into Byzantine lands and along the coast of North Africa. Certainly, the Sasanians had been beset by a crisis of succession in the years before the death of Muhammad: between AD 628 and 632, the crown passed violently between perhaps ten kings before Yazdagird settled on the throne to become the last Sasanian emperor; this period was dominated by fractious nobles who exacerbated such conflicts in their pursuit of their own rivalries and influence. External problems had added to these internal troubles: the Byzantines made some bold military gains in the 620s, thrusting deep along the Euphrates and besieging the Sasanian capital. However, these ills in the Persian state in the years before Islam burst its Arabian bounds do not explain the swiftness of its disintegration. It is perhaps something that will never be fully understood, but the uncompromising certainty that God was on their side no doubt gave Muslim fighters a special strength and vigor.

By the death in AD 644 of the second caliph, Umar ibn al-Khattab, the Arab conquests had been carried across all Arabia, the Byzantine provinces of Syria and Egypt, and much of the Sasanian Empire. The rest of Iran fell to them in the following years, and they also pushed north into Armenia and Azerbaijan. Not content with these sweeping gains, the Muslims continued to test the frontiers of the Byzantines and struck west from Egypt, advancing through the Maghrib: over several decades they reached the Atlantic coast of Morocco. In AD 711, they crossed into Spain and brought most of the Iberian peninsula under Islam; in the same year, far to the east, Arab armies crossed the deserts of Gedrosia, entered Sind and established Muslim rule in this corner of India. The expansion of Muslim arms at the furthest extent of the new empire came to an end only when they crossed the Pyrenees into France and were defeated by the Frankish ruler Charles Martel at the battle of Poitiers in AD 732. Thus, a century after the death of Muhammad, the Arab armies of Islam had spread his message across a grand swathe of the world, from Iberia to the Indus, besting the strongest kingdoms of the age until the Caliphate of Islam became the greatest power in the world.

Meanwhile, with the Sasanian empire crushed by the Arab assault from the west, the eastern lands of the Iranian realm were set adrift from the former center of rule. The Persian king could exercise no control over the extremities of his collapsing polity, and Gandhara and the Indian holdings of the Sasanians experienced a vacuum of authority, the focus of affairs being elsewhere. Having been a strategic imperative and essential possession for many centuries, the Khyber Pass was for a time on the margin: though they seized Bactria, the Arabs did not march through the Khyber into the heart of Gandhara and India beyond it; their modest bridgehead in Sind was the extent of their advance into the Subcontinent. This void in government at Gandhara was filled by a dynasty descended from the White Huns, remnants of the former rulers who had remained when their empire was smashed by the Sasanians and Turks. Taking their opportunity to recover power after their Persian masters were destroyed, a line of kings emerged from among the White Huns who had settled in the region after losing power. This Shahi dynasty ruled Gandhara by the middle of the eighth century, extending their influence to Kabul.

For three centuries after the collapse of the Sasanians, northwest India was relatively untroubled: the Khyber Pass saw no invasions. With the world to the west occupied by the rise of Islam, Gandhara gained an unparalleled respite from outside aggression through its mountain pass; Indian and Islamic politics and polities developed for a time in separate spheres. Toward the end of the ninth century, the Shahi line was displaced not by invaders from without but by a local Hindu family of Brahmins, known with simple logic as the Hindushahi dynasty. This family would go on to consolidate their rule over Gandhara and extend it into the Punjab, and still controlled the North West Frontier when the assaults from the west began again late in the tenth century.

The extraordinary successes of the Muslim armies were achieved despite disunity in the higher reaches of the Islamic empire. As they burst out of Arabia, the leaders of Islam were transformed from a small band of Muhammad's followers into the rulers of a vast and complex empire: shifts in the locale of power became likely as they conquered regions vastly more fertile and populous than the original Muslim heartland of western Arabia. Rivalries emerged while the conquests were still being undertaken: in AD 656 the third caliph was murdered, and the first period of civil war among the Muslim community began. Ali—the cousin of the Prophet, married to his daughter Fatima and celebrated by the mosque inside the Khyber—was the claimant to succeed as caliph, but was challenged. Despite the disputed succession, Ali established himself as caliph in Kufa, in what is now the south of Iraq, and fighting broke out with the forces of Muawiya ibn Abi Sufyan, the governor of Syria. Since the conflict proved inconclusive, the two sides agreed to meet to negotiate a settlement, but months of discussion culminated only in the murder of Ali in AD 661, whereupon Muawiya proclaimed himself caliph and established a new capital in Damascus. From this time, the office of caliph became in essence hereditary, and passed through the family of Muawiya. Under the dynastic name of Umayyad, this line of caliphs ruled from Damascus for almost a century.

The murder of Ali is the origin of the division in the Muslim world between the Shia and Sunni. The Shia—or *Shi'at Ali*, the followers of Ali—believe that authority over Islam rightly descends through the line of Ali, being of the family of the Prophet; the rift persists today. The early Shia differed in their degree of opposition to the Umayyad caliphs: some opted for peaceful acceptance, while others took up arms against them. Husein, the second son of Ali, launched a rebellion against the rule of Damascus in AD 680, but he was killed with his followers in Karbala in the same year. The tomb of Ali in Najaf and that of Husein in Karbala—both in the south of modern Iraq—are of especial importance to the Shia, second only to Mecca as places of pilgrimage.

The establishment of Syria as the center of Islamic rule was, in one sense, a natural shift of power from the arid deserts of Arabia to the wealthier and more productive regions to the north: as government and administration grew in scope, the court and bureaucracy required the resources of a wealthy country to support it. Moreover, Damascus was better located in the expanding empire, enjoying a central position and lying on the trade routes to the Mediterranean; by comparison, Medina was isolated. Syria had the advantage of fertility and population, and—in the Muslim world—was rivaled in this respect only by Iraq: when the Umayyad caliphate was brought down by civil war and revolt, it was thus Iraq that became the center of power, a second gravitation toward wealth and population. In AD 750, the Abbasid dynasty of caliphs—descending from Abbas, an uncle of the Prophet—established itself in Iraq, and built a new capital, the city of Baghdad. This eastward transfer of the locus of power marked not just the obvious advantages of Iraq in population and commerce, but also a recognition of the growing strength of the eastern lands of Islam. As the conquered Iranian population began to reassert itself in its new Islamic identity, the cultural influence of Iran could not be ignored, and the east of the empire grew in importance: it was an eastern army that put the Abbasids into power.

The capital of Baghdad was built to display the splendor of an empire at its height, sited where the two great rivers of the Euphrates and the Tigris ran close together, a rich countryside of canals and agriculture. In a city within the city, designed to separate the ruler from the mass of his subjects, the caliph was surrounded by gardens, halls and courtyards. In a palace staffed by eunuchs and surrounded by his soldiers, chamberlains, slaves and elephants, the caliph lived a luxurious life of absolute power and intricate ceremony, his executioner always close by. The most famous of these caliphs was Harun al-Rashid, the celebrated ruler of *A Thousand and One Nights,* at the turn of the ninth century. In his reign, material

A nineteenth-century engraving of a story from A Thousand and One Nights

splendor was accompanied by intellectual brilliance, and Baghdad became renowned for its Arabic literature and its learning in science.

Under the Abbasid caliphs, the Arab empire reached its zenith. By the early ninth century, the territorial unity of the early Muslim world was in decline, as independent dynasties emerged at its furthest fringes to challenge the supreme authority of the caliphs. The last surviving members of the Umayyad family had fled to Spain and established rule over Iberia; they would later claim once again the status of caliphs, issuing a direct challenge to Baghdad over the rightful succession to Muhammad. In the east, in the developed Iranian regions, several minor principalities arose and achieved a measure of independence, such as the Tahirids and Saffarids of Khorasan. The relationship between such nascent states and the rulers of Baghdad was not characterized by simple antagonism:

political sovereignty waxed and waned with circumstances, and often events brought autonomy to a temporary end. A pattern developed in which ambitious families arose and established independent rule, but then sought the blessing of the caliph for their actions and for their continued possession of their thrones, seeking to attach the spiritual authority of Baghdad to powers won in a very worldly way. That the caliphs often granted this recognition demonstrates their growing inability to maintain a real grip on regions of the empire that sought to rule themselves. Although it shows the weakness into which the caliphate descended, this pattern also explains its longevity: while the caliphs were prepared to accept a purely nominal status, and to legitimize the rule of rising states, they need not be removed. Thus, the caliphate survived to supply a figurehead of Islam while its lands, and Baghdad itself, were absorbed into new empires; it was not until 1258 and the arrival of the Mongols that the Caliphate of Baghdad came to a violent end.

One such family of independents that arose in the ninth century was the Samanid dynasty. Iranian chiefs from Bactria who began to expand their power by cooperation with the Arab rulers, they were initially encouraged in their ambitions by the caliph of Baghdad, who was seeking a counter to more threatening seceders in his eastern territories. Through honors and office granted by Baghdad, and through conquest, the Samanids built an empire that encompassed modern Afghanistan, Khorasan and neighboring territories. The lands north of the Oxus river became the heart of the rising dynasty, and as they grew in authority and stature, their chief cities of Samarkand and Bokhara became cultural centers to rival even Baghdad. As the leading nuclei of a resurgent Iranian civilization, now fused and fertilized with Islam, these cities became the focus for a new Persian literature, written in the Arabic script, that would achieve a lasting power and is still celebrated daily in the modern world. Moreover, it was from the Samanid court of the late tenth century that perhaps the greatest mind of the Islamic world emerged: Avicenna, the Persian philosopher, scientist and physician who became known as the "Supreme Master" for his influential studies in medicine, logic, mathematics, psychology, botany, astronomy and other fields. His principal work, the *Canon of Medicine*, was widely read in medieval Europe, and was frequently cited in Latin texts of the time. Indeed, the name Avicenna is a Latin rendering of Ibn Sina, by which he should more properly be known.

With the decline of the Samanid dynasty, toward the end of the tenth century, a new people came to prominence, a people who would go on to change fundamentally the history and ethnic character of the Middle East and India, and conquer much of Europe: the Turks. As with many nomadic peoples of the steppes of Eurasia, the precise origin of the Turks is uncertain: long centuries of migration in a preliterate age makes reconstruction of the details very difficult. It seems clear, however, that a region of Inner Asia comprising the Altai Mountains and parts of modern Mongolia saw the emergence of groups speaking Turkic languages during the early centuries BC. Tongues such as Turkish, as members of the Altaic language family, are related to Mongolian, suggesting a degree of common descent between Mongols and Turks or at least a considerable level of cultural borrowing between two neighboring populations. Since this region forms a frontier between China, Mongolia and lands to the west ranged by Iranian nomads, a population of inextricable ethnicity undoubtedly developed.

The Huns who ventured west and harassed the Roman Empire in the early centuries AD were a Turkic people, but not yet known under that name: the first known use of the term "Turk" dates from the mid sixth century, when the Turk khanate was established on the Orkhon river in Mongolia. In the fifth century, the people of this principality had lived in the Altai Mountains and western Mongolia and were subject to the Avars, a powerful Mongol kingdom. The Turks served as the blacksmith slaves of their overlords, and the few historical sources that mention them emphasize the importance of their ironworking industry. By the 540s AD, the Turks had become sufficiently strong to throw off Avar mastery, beating them in battle and expelling them westward in a forced migration that would later impact brutally on Europe. The Turks rose rapidly after this success, under their first emperor, Bumin, and quickly gained the recognition of the Wei dynasty of China. Their lands expanded apace, and soon they ruled over a vast stretch of Central Asia from the Great Wall of China to the borders of Iran.

Thus it was these rapidly ascending Turks who allied with the Sasanian emperor Khusrau against the White Huns. Together they destroyed them in AD 558, and after the Turks gained the former White Hun territory north of the Oxus river, they ruled all Central Asia. This was a landmark in the story of the steppe: the domination of the Iranian nomads had been ended. After more than a thousand years of supremacy over the wide grasslands of Central Asia, the multitudinous Scythian tribes of the steppe were masters no more. This region—once known broadly as Scythia—had become the realm of the Turk, and would in later years acquire the name Turkestan, the Land of the Turks, a term still used to describe the region today.

The original Turk khanate quickly divided into western and eastern halves. That these separate regimes each became sustainable states by the 580s AD suggests that even the early Turk polity possessed a structured and flexible political system that could be adapted to evolving circumstances and emerging centers of power. The western Turks had formed into the Khazar khanate by the early eighth century, and it was this kingdom that halted the advance of the Arabs as they swept north through the lands of the defeated Sasanian empire. The frontier between Islam and infidel mirrored the traditional boundary between the settled Iranian world and the realm of the nomad: the Arabs pushed across the Oxus river but not much beyond the Jaxartes. For a time, this border between Muslim and Turk was relatively stable, but was crossed by regular raids and counterraids. It was not a tale of relentless war, however: Turks allied with the Arabs in AD 751 to fight the Tang Chinese at the battle of the Talas river, an event that marked the beginning of a growing assimilation of Turks into the sedentary Muslim domain. The Muslim religion was also assimilated into Turkish lands; already exposed to Zoroastrianism, Christianity, Buddhism and Manichaeism, most Turks became Muslim over the course of two centuries of conversions.

For over 200 years after their respective spheres gained a common border, the principal means by which Turks entered the Muslim world was through the institution of the *ghulam*: the Turkish slave soldier. The use of ghulams began under the Abbasid caliphs, from which time they were purchased in slave markets or seized in war. In the Muslim writings of the time, there is considerable unity on the subject of Turkish characteristics: all agreed that the Turk was militarily superior and skilled both with horse and bow. They were said to be hardy, brave and proud, and to possess an inordinate love of violence; for a time, the term "Turk" became synonymous with "soldier." The value placed upon the Turkish slave soldier was so great that they often served at the highest levels, as palace guards to the caliph or in the courts of the local rulers that sprang up across the Muslim empire.

From the visual evidence of such service, we can picture the palace ghulam at work in the ninth century, perhaps standing broad-shouldered across a doorway, denying entry with a superior air. He wears a round iron helmet that rises to a point, with a long guard descending in front of his nose; the entire helm is covered in scarlet silk that falls in a sweeping aventail about his neck, transforming metal protection into a display of status. A mail shirt covers his shoulders and upper arms, and a lamellar cuirass protects his chest: tiny rectangles of bronze and iron tightly lashed together make a flexible defense. Skirts of the same lamellar construction drop over his thighs. Underneath his armor, the ghulam wears a tunic of red silk patterned in gold, flowers and suns intricately picked out in expensive metal thread, speaking of the prestige of his corps. Below his fine tunic he wears wide breeches and leather boots laced to the knees. Belted to his waist, he bears a sword and dagger, and in his right hand—the butt planted forbiddingly on the ground before him—a long spear, wooden shaft gripped firmly, the polished spearhead decorated with black ostrich feathers.

The military success of these ghulams spilled over into politics, and in the ninth century they came to dominate the Caliphate, capitalizing on their military value to exercise influence in other spheres. This ambition of their slave soldiers was troublesome to the caliphs, but to the Samanids it was fatal: it was through their overmighty ghulams that the dynasty came to an end. The Samanid rulers or *amirs* of Bokhara had sought to use slave soldiers as a counterweight to the powerful landed class of their realm, upon whom they were becoming reliant for military strength and the taxes that could buy it. Having no local interests or personal loyalties beyond his owner, the ghulam was widely supposed throughout the Muslim world to be of exemplary reliability, ruthlessly devoted to his master; often he was, and the necessity for rulers to keep a palace guard of slaves was never questioned. The ghulams of the Samanid *amirs*, however, became too substantial in their powers to balance the political scales, and they gradually sought to be kingmakers in succession disputes, developing into a force for instability, sometimes even with schismatic tendencies. The ability of senior ghulams to acquire their own retinues of slave soldiers—while still slaves themselves—made them dangerous, providing the means for ambitious commanders to make an attempt on power. Alptigin, a senior ghulam of the Samanid army who was appointed governor of Khorasan in the mid-tenth century, had a personal following of 2,700 slave soldiers, loyal not to the *amir* in Bokhara, but to Alptigin himself.

It was Alptigin who set the separatist trajectory that would lead to the rise of a new empire: the realm of the aggressive Ghaznavid sultans, the Turkish conquerors who would be the first to carry Islam deep into India. In AD 961, the Samanid amir Abd al-Malik died in Bokhara; Alptigin sought to exercise his armed influence to place his own candidate on the throne through a violent putsch. The plot failed, and Alptigin was forced to quit his headquarters in Khorasan and march east into the mountains of what is now Afghanistan, withdrawing to safety in the fringes of the Samanid lands with his following of loyal ghulams. Here he seized the town of Ghazni—in the southeast of modern Afghanistan, on the road from Kandahar to Kabul—and rapidly established himself as a sovereign ruler. The Samanids dispatched an army to bring the renegade commander to heel, but Alptigin and his slaves beat this force in battle in front of the gates of Ghazni. The *amir* subsequently legitimized Alptigin in his status by issuing him a patent of authority. The willingness of the Samanid state to accept the separatist ambitions of its officers demonstrates its deteriorating power, and paralleled that of the Caliphate itself: the last of the Samanid rulers or *amirs* were used to legitimize the rising Ghaznavid sultans.

The Islamic proscription against representative art has meant that many hundreds of the leading figures of the Muslim world were not celebrated in portraiture. In contrast to even some of the most ancient kings and emperors—even back to the Achaemenians—we cannot gain a clear picture of the likeness of the great men of the Islamic empires. Characterized by his actions, though, Alptigin was a thrusting leader, ruthless and pragmatic in his use of power. Certainly he was ambitious, and skilled in warfare and politics; from being a lowly slave he had risen to acquire important office and the means to make himself an independent sovereign. His dynastic intentions were suggested when his son Ishaq succeeded him as ruler of Ghazni.

Alptigin was not the first Turkish ghulam to achieve a measure of independence from the Samanid empire, but his establishment of Ghazni as the center of a fresh line of rulers was highly significant. Since the new capital lay on the mountainous frontier with the Subcontinent, India was a natural direction of expansion, and the long peace that had reigned over the Khyber Pass was soon to come to an end. It was not long after Alptigin died in AD 963 that conflict began with the Hindushahi rulers of Kabul and Gandhara, presaging an extrusion of Islam into India that would develop into a violent rhythm of regular assaults that carried the Muslims across the mountains.

In the decade after the death of Ishaq in AD 966, several ghulam commanders ruled Ghazni: the regime had not yet properly acquired a hereditary character, but was passed between Alptigin's leading slaves. In AD 977, Sebuktigin—both slave and son-in-law of Alptigin—became king and set about placing the nascent sultanate on a solid foundation of lands and revenues. While Alptigin was the progenitor of the Ghaznavid state, Sebuktigin could be said to be its true founder in that he forged a powerful domain and was succeeded by his son: the throne of Ghazni was hereditary thereafter. Sebuktigin extended his borders north to the Oxus river—taking Kabul from the Hindushahis—and west to the borders of modern Iran and Afghanistan. In AD 986, Sebuktigin again raided Hindu territory—perhaps through the Khyber Pass, it is not known—and carried away much plunder and many slaves. Toward the end of his life, he also acquired supremacy over the Samanid province of Khorasan, appointing his eldest son Mahmud as commander of the army in this rich and fertile region.

Sebuktigin died in AD 997, having provided his heirs with a strong kingdom and a sovereign throne (despite the occasional Ghaznavid request for the blessing of the *amir* of the decaying Samanid empire). Sebuktigin may not, in fact, have intended his family to become an independent dynasty, for he divided his lands between three sons and a brother, treating each more as provincial governors than as imperial rulers. Were it not for the ambition and skill of his son Mahmud, the empire of the Ghaznavids may not truly have taken shape: unsatisfied with his inheritance of the province of Khorasan, he set out to reunite all the territory of his father and to weld it firmly into his realm as sultan. It was this aggression and confidence that would make Mahmud the greatest of the Ghaznavids, and his enthusiasm for raiding India would see him enter history as the man who carried Islam deep into the Subcontinent.

Sebuktigin had appointed his son Ismail to rule in Ghazni. While this was accepted by many of the senior ghulams and nobles of the court, some favored the more skilled and energetic Mahmud; the superior resources of his wealthy province of Khorasan were also to count in Mahmud's favor. With noble support, Mahmud demanded that his brother surrender Ghazni to him, and, when Ismail refused, marched on the city. The armies of the two brothers fought a battle outside Ghazni in AD 998 and Ismail was defeated, Mahmud having him locked away for the rest of his life. At the age of twenty-seven, Mahmud of Ghazni had made himself sultan.

Mahmud spent the first three years of his reign consolidating his powers and adding to his territory. It was necessary for him to regain Khorasan from the Samanids, who had sought to take advantage of the disputed Ghaznavid succession to recover the province, and in AD 999 he marched south and took possession of Seistan. Although in his early years Mahmud seems to have felt it politic to offer homage to the Samanids, he also sought confirmation in his status as sultan from the caliph of Baghdad, attempting to gain the backing of the most august spiritual authority of all. This bid was successful and Mahmud was granted a patent of title and a robe of investment, the symbols of divine sanction of his rule. When this caliphal favor was received in AD 999, Mahmud is said to have made a vow that he would undertake yearly an expedition into India to make war on the idolatrous Hindus. Mahmud did not launch his aggressive incursions into India *every* year, but his reign saw perhaps as many as seventeen violent assaults on Hindu territory, attacks of such force that—even though they seem to have been conceived largely as raids for iconoclasm and plunder— Muslim rule was eventually established over much of northwest India. Despite the Arab foothold in Sind, it was to be the Turks who would properly introduce Islam to India.

The first of these invasions was in the autumn of 1001: Mahmud assembled his army of 15,000 horsemen and marched through the Khyber Pass to Peshawar, where the Hindushahi army was waiting, headed by their king, Jayapala. As the first crossing by Sultan Mahmud of the mountainous border between his lands and India, this event was one of the most consequential in history: it was the beginning of the percussion of assaults over many years that would make much of northern India Muslim, changing forever the character of the Subcontinent and determining the political divisions of South Asia in the modern day. We can conjure an image of the sultan's hardened gaze as he entered the Pass and slowly climbed the hillside above the Torkham gap, and imagine his face when he caught his first sight of the plains of India as the mountains of the eastern entrance parted before him. Picture him dressed with splendor, luxuriously armored for battle, silk and iron wrapping Mahmud and his mount in a sleek, unyielding cover. Perhaps he wears the black cloak that declares his allegiance to the caliph of Baghdad, over a silken coat of canary yellow worked and embroidered in gold thread, a shining demand for attention and respect. The soft sheen of this tunic belies the hard iron mail underneath, for even in his finery, the sultan is dressed for war: a king born of a ghulam. On his head, he wears a rounded iron helmet edged in gold studded with tiny jewels, a piece of practical protection that nonetheless displays his wealth. Mahmud is trousered in silk and booted in kid leather, and as a fighting sultan, is armed with sword and dagger close to hand at his belt, a long mace dropping weightily from a strap around his wrist. His horse is caparisoned in a soft armor of quilted silk, yellow to match its master, covering its entire body and rising up its neck to a leather face-guard chased in gold.

Although they did not make up the bulk of the Ghaznavid army, the ghulams were a potent and formidable nucleus and generally took the center in battle, remaining close to their king. On the autumnal campaign of 1001, we can imagine the palace guard marching through the Khyber Pass on the heels of the sultan, watchful for any threats to his person. We know that the Ghaznavid bodyguards wore headdresses of peacock feathers, rising above a close-fitting cap of black silk embroidered with gold thread. Long gowns of dark silk fall below the knees, decorated with ornate designs picked out in light blue thread, and broad collars of white open across the chest. As they trot their mounts behind the sultan, their long swords knock against their thighs, suspended from leather belts hung with golden ornaments. Maces were carried by the palace ghulams as a symbol of their status, silvered or gilded depending on their rank or the fame of their regiment. Borne on their other arms, or perhaps slung across their shoulders for this journey through the mountain pass, are small round shields plated in gold, with a vicious spike rising from the center and black fur trimming the edge. The outfits of these palace ghulams combined a display of their position in the Ghaznavid court with the practical needs of professional soldiers.

As the sultan and his army debouched from the eastern end of the Khyber Pass on to the plains of Peshawar, Jayapala was awaiting reinforcements and sought to delay the imminent battle, even though his forces already outnumbered the Ghaznavids: perhaps the fierce reputation of the Turkish ghulams was enough to panic the Indian king. Jayapala had an assembled force of 12,000 horsemen, 30,000 foot soldiers and 300 elephants, but still he avoided an engagement in the expectation of allied support. Maneuver and countermaneuver continued for some weeks, until Mahmud forced the Indian army into battle at the end of November: the Hindus were soundly defeated and Jayapala was captured along with a dozen relatives. 15,000 Indians were left dead on the battlefield.

After this victory, Mahmud struck east to plunder in the region of Attock, the Hindushahi capital, but soon went home to Ghazni with his treasure; Jayapala gained his freedom for a large ransom of gold and 150 elephants. For the Hindu king, however, there was little to celebrate in his release. Defeat and—even worse—capture by a Muslim was considered so shameful that he put himself to death on a funeral pyre, having appointed his son Anandpal as his successor.

This was the first of the grand raids that Mahmud launched into India, and raids they were, not conquests: the Turks began to settle garrisons on captured Hindu territories only from about 1013 onward. There is much uncertainty about the dates of campaigns and the boundaries of rule that they shifted, but with Mahmud's firm authority extending early into the border lands, we can say with confidence that the Khyber Pass was in Muslim hands by the early 1000s. Mahmud, the Turkish sultan of Ghazni, had seized the road into India. For years, he was content only to launch swift assaults and return to his capital with little thought of staying in India to rule, but, with the Hindu rulers worn down by the Muslim attacks, the Turks gradually began to fill the governmental vacuum. In 1021, Mahmud formally annexed the Punjab after putting the Indian king Bhimpal the Fearless to flight: from this time on, he can be considered fully an Indian ruler. The city of Lahore was to become an important Ghaznavid center and later, indeed, the Ghaznavid capital when they were reduced to their Indian lands in the twelfth century.

Mahmud showed a creative commitment to his war-making that made him something of a master tactician, often finding unusual means of effecting victories. In a siege in Seistan, he ordered that his catapults hurl sacks full of snakes into the enemy city to frighten and demoralize the opposing population. During his last expedition into India, in 1026, he caused a grand fleet of river boats to be built on the Indus for an expedition against the Jats of the Multan region; the sultan ordered his boats to be prickled with large iron spikes, protruding all round from the prow and gunwales, and armed his soldiers with hand grenades of naphtha—Greek fire. With these innovations, his fleet of 1,400 boats destroyed a Jat armada of over 4,000 vessels, annihilating them so completely that virtually none of the enemy army survived.

Besides his soldierly renown, Mahmud acquired a reputation for greed: the bountiful plunder that he seized on his Indian raids became the stuff of legend, and the sultan seemed never to be satisfied. Every assault into the Subcontinent gathered gold and jewels to add to Mahmud's treasury, but some were especially productive; the 1008 campaign against the fortress of Nagarkot in the upper Indus valley yielded 700,000 gold coins, large amounts of gold and silver ingots, an expensively decorated throne, much rich clothing and a folding house made of silver. On his return to Ghazni, Mahmud displayed this vast haul of treasure, piled upon carpets in the courtyard of his palace for all his subjects to see, an exhibition both of his great wealth and superior military skills. Slaves too were brought home to Ghazni: during the 1013 campaign, the Ghaznavid army carried home Hindu captives in such plentiful numbers that they became cheap enough to allow even a humble shopkeeper to buy some.

In other campaigns, the sultan took many millions of gold coins and an unknown value of jewels, such was the wealth of India. The Koran offered Mahmud an explicit justification for taking this treasure: in a chapter of the Koran (48:20) that was to be carved upon minarets in later years for display to the public, such plunder is said to be of divine origin:

God has promised you rich booty, and has given you this with all promptness. He has stayed your enemies' hands, so that He may make your victory a sign to true believers and guide you along a straight path . . . And God knows of other spoils which you have not yet taken. God has power over all things.

Mahmud was therefore doing the work of God by seizing the treasure of the Indians. Moreover, many of his campaigns combined plunder with iconoclasm, exploiting the happy coincidence that some of the wealthiest targets in India were the many temples richly endowed to service and celebrate a Hindu idol. There was therefore a strong element of convenience in Mahmud's claim to be a hammer of idolaters—he was willing to make war on Muslims too when they had bounty to be seized—but he was nonetheless awarded titles and honors by the caliph in gratitude for his violent furthering of the cause of Islam.

In the campaigning season of 1018, the sultan allied iconoclasm with profit when he struck deep into India to attack the city of Mathura, eighty miles south of Delhi on the Jumna river. As the reputed birthplace of Krishna, Mathura is one of the holiest shrines in India, but Mahmud found it barely defended and was able to plunder freely and destroy its temples without hindrance. There can be no doubt that the treasure taken was plentiful, but it is hard to believe the stories that tell of the seizure of five gold idols, each five yards in height, and of a sapphire weighing over 16 pounds. Nonetheless, the booty was great, and it may well be true that the gold seized weighed over 548 pounds, as is recorded. Plunder taken elsewhere on this campaign included over 380 elephants and an extraordinary 53,000 slaves.

The most famous iconoclastic effort of Sultan Mahmud was, however, not his attack on Mathura, but his 1024 campaign against Somnath. Sitting on the coast of the Indian Ocean in what is now Gujarat, the great temple of Somnath might have seemed safely removed from the arena of regular Muslim raids; hundreds of miles separated the city from the Punjab and the Ganges valley, the areas that bore the brunt of the Turkish incursions. The temple of Somnath was dedicated to Shiva, Lord of the Moon, and stood above all others in India for its rich endowments and the extravagance of its worship: 3,000 Brahmin priests prayed at the temple every day, and over 300 dancing girls and religious prostitutes were in constant attendance on the idol, working in relays to ensure that dances were performed without end. The endowments of the temple that provided for such dedicated worship were said to amount to the revenues of 10,000 villages. The idol that stood at the center of all this attention, the sacred object of the devotion of thousands, was a giant penis, carved in stone and standing three yards high.

The stories of the wealth of Somnath had reached the ear of the sultan, and he launched a bold thrust all the way to the sea to seize these legendary riches, an arduous undertaking that required a hazardous desert crossing. With his ruthless ability to find means of overcoming obstacles—in this case, 30,000 camels loaded with water—Mahmud's army reached the city walls of Somnath in around January 1025. They were met with jeers from the people of the city, who crowded on to the ramparts to heckle their attackers. This confidence was misplaced; although it took Mahmud's army two days of hard fighting, they breached the walls and entered the city with much slaughter, driving the Hindu army back toward the temple. Many of the defending soldiers would enter the temple to pray to the idol before charging forth to die under a Muslim blade or arrow. Very few were left alive.

When Mahmud entered the temple, he is said to have raised his mace and brought it down upon the idol with such force that the huge stone phallus was smashed into two. He ordered the idol destroyed, despite the desperate Brahmins offering him a huge ransom to spare it; an embellishment of the story—no doubt apocryphal—has the idol being broken open and revealing a stash of riches, gold and jewels worth a hundred times the proffered sum. Two of the fragments of the smashed penis were sent to Ghazni to be used as steps in the great mosque and the royal palace, righteous Muslims thus treading upon an idolatrous outrage. Two other fragments are said to have been sent to Mecca and Medina for a similar purpose, and the large gates of the temple were hauled back to Ghazni.

This grand attack on Somnath brought Mahmud further honors from the caliph, and served his dual purpose: iconoclasm for Islam, and material wealth for Mahmud. It was not, however, just gold and jewels that the sultan seized: he became known for filling his court with men of letters, sometimes by force. Poets and scholars were taken as living booty from beaten enemies or demanded as tribute from vassal rulers. Through such means, Mahmud's court came to be a glittering center of the rising Persian literature of the age; he is said to have had 400 poets in attendance at court. This number included perhaps the most famous Persian poet of all: Firdausi, the author of the Shahnameh, the *Book of Kings*, the Iranian national epic that is read and savored every day even now. Behind the writing of the Shahnameh lies a tale of the selfishness of the sultan: he is said to have promised Firdausi a gold coin for every couplet of the great work, but the completed poem ran to a lengthy 60,000 couplets. When he heard this, Mahmud is said to have offered Firdausi silver instead of gold, whereupon the famous poet fled the capital, wrote a sharp satire on the meanness of the sultan, and died in poverty.

Under Mahmud, Ghazni became a leading city and a cultural center of some brilliance. Besides its artists and poets, architecture too was a strength: as Mahmud and his senior soldiers enriched themselves with Indian booty, they built mosques and palaces, gardens and courtyards, until Ghazni was a lavish capital fit for the powerful rulers who had raised the city from its humble past. It was not just Indian treasure that contributed to this building, for a distinctive Ghaznavid architecture developed that combined brick building of the Iranian style with techniques of working marble that were learnt in India. Moreover, Indian statuary seized in raids seems to have been displayed in Ghaznavid palaces as trophies of war or incorporated into public buildings along with gold and other precious materials.

Some of this cultural standing would live on into the time of his successors, but the imperial power of the Ghaznavid state reached its apex under Mahmud: the lands under his rule comprised all Afghanistan, the Punjab, the east of modern Iran, Seistan and lands beyond the Oxus river as far as the Aral Sea and Samarkand. He died in 1030 and the decline of the dynasty began soon afterward. His son Masud ruled until 1040—after a disputed succession that resembled Mahmud's own—and his reign saw the rise of the Seljuq Turks, a new wave of invaders from beyond the Oxus, who would come to conquer much of the Muslim world, including all Iran and the caliphal heartland of Iraq. This broad movement of conquest tore the desirable province of Khorasan from the Ghaznavid domain in 1038, and the Seljuqs continued their advances until Masud was deposed by his ghulams in 1040 in the act of fleeing for Lahore, by then a disgraced monarch who had failed to live up to the reputation of his father.

Seljuq pressure continued on the declining kings ruling Ghazni thereafter, and as Ghaznavid lands to the west dwindled, their Indian territories acquired a corresponding importance. By 1118, Seljuq suzerainty was established over Ghazni, but the dynasty whimpered on.

It was not the Seljuqs that ended Ghaznavid power, however, but a rival family who had arisen in the mountains of Afghanistan: the Ghorid dynasty. An Iranian clan of mountain dwellers from the region of Ghor in what is now the west of Afghanistan, the Ghorids rose as local rulers and paid homage to both Ghaznavid and Seljuq rulers while they increased their powers. Eventually, in the middle years of the twelfth century, they felt able to throw off the bonds of vassalage and emerge as sovereign rulers. They made war on Ghazni in the 1140s, and in 1150 the Ghorid leader Ala ad-Din Husain burnt Ghazni to the ground, a deed of such ferocious comprehensiveness that it earned him the sobriquet *Jahan Suz*, the "World Burner." From around 1160, the Ghaznavids were reduced to their Indian lands alone, for the Ghorids ruled in Ghazni. Once overlords of a grand empire, these Turks from Afghanistan had been whittled down to the Indian province they had once treated as their annual battleground. Lahore became the Ghaznavid capital.

With Ghazni in their possession from the 1170s, the Ghorids followed the example of their Ghaznavid predecessors and used it as a convenient springboard from which to launch attacks into India under Muizz al-Din Muhammad, the ruler of the eastern territories of the expanding Ghorid empire. Their armies were also similar: the nucleus of the Ghorid force was formed of Turkish ghulams, and they would come to play a crucial role in the future of the Ghorid state. War between Ghaznavid and Ghorid continued, but with the rump Ghaznavids still in possession of Peshawar and the Khyber Pass, the Ghorids could make no headway in India: an invasion through the minor Gomal Pass ended in disaster. Only when Muizz al-Din succeeded in wresting control of the Khyber Pass in 1180 could the Ghorids advance with vigor into India; after almost two centuries in the realm of the Ghaznavids, the Khyber Pass had changed hands once again, and the final extinction of the house of Sebuktigin and Mahmud followed close upon the loss of the crucial border route. Muizz al-Din captured Lahore in 1186 and the rule of the Ghaznavids was over; the last king of the line was later murdered, probably in 1191.

Muizz al-Din had extinguished Ghaznavid rule and extended the Ghorid domain over the Punjab. It was, however, one of his senior Turkish ghulams who would go on to entrench Muslim rule over a wide swathe of northern India: Qutb al-Din Aybek. While Muizz al-Din was occupied elsewhere in the Ghorid realm, Aybek advanced into the heartland of India and seized Delhi in 1193. From this time, Aybek forged a virtually independent power and turned Delhi into a Muslim capital in all but name, a part of the Ghorid domain but troubled little by the decrees and depredations of rulers far away. When Muizz al-Din was murdered in 1206, leaving no heir and an undecided succession, Aybek assumed the authority of a sovereign ruler over the Ghorid lands in India. He founded the Slave Dynasty, which became the Sultanate of Delhi, a wholly Indian realm ruled by Turkish slave soldiers from Afghanistan. This was a landmark: the establishment of a Muslim state in the heart of India, separate in itself and independent of rulers of Islamic lands to the west. Thus through the violent introduction of Islam by the Ghaznavids and the entrenchment of Muslim rule by the slave soldiers of the Ghorids, the creation of a Muslim realm in India was the work of the Turkish ghulams. Although racked by internal dissension and war, and invaded by the great conquerors of legend, the Delhi Sultanate was to last as the ruling power in northern India for 300 years. The founding of an Islamic state in the Subcontinent had been a long time in the making—more than two centuries since Mahmud began his raids—but it had barely been founded when it was threatened by the expansionary empire of Khwarizm, a brief flowering from what is now Uzbekistan. It was not this polity that next struck into India, however, but a shocking new force arisen from the ancient homeland of the Turkish soldiers who fought to make India Muslim: the fearsome Mongols of Genghis Khan.

CHAPTER EIGHT

Genghis Khan and Timur

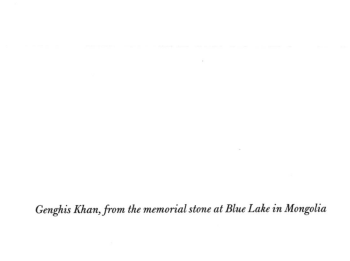

Genghis Khan, from the memorial stone at Blue Lake in Mongolia

In the Year of the Hare Genghis Khan went to war
with the Muslims
THE SECRET HISTORY OF THE MONGOLS

I that am termed the scourge and wrath of God,
The only fear and terror of the world
Tamburlaine the Great by CHRISTOPHER MARLOWE

I looked down on the final mile of the Khyber Pass, toward the eastern
entrance, as the sun behind me cast a weakening light upon the winding
road ahead. It was late afternoon and the bright winter sky was beginning to
deepen in color, presaging dusk. We had parked the Landcruiser and stood
by the roadside for a last view of the Pass before we returned to Peshawar.
The armed guard waited silently beside me, AK 47 over his shoulder, while
Mumtaz walked about restlessly, making a few comments in guidebook style.
I was, this time, paying no attention. Like a schoolboy trying to contain his
excitement, I was absorbing what I could of a sight that all of the many
Khyber conquerors had enjoyed across the centuries: the first glimpse of the
plains of South Asia through the narrow entrance of the great pass. Of all the
many armies that have marched through the Khyber, the one that sprang first
to my restive mind was that of Genghis Khan. Abandoning any pretence of
scholarly composure, I became a child again and pictured many thousands
of rugged and terrifying horsemen, dusty and weather-beaten, jostling along
the meandering road, impatient to reach their goal. Far from home and
blooded in many campaigns, these Mongols must have inspired a dreadful
terror in the Khyber tribes as they passed through with hurried determination.

How was it that these nomads from Inner Asia should be descending
upon India? What gave Genghis Khan such a powerful command over his
followers that he was able to bring them thousands of miles from their
homes and pastures? As we returned to the jeep and began the drive back
to Peshawar, I thought of the Mongols riding the same road 800 years
before, and of the steely character that drove them on.

The story of the Mongols as an overwhelming, conquering force begins with Genghis himself. Before he rose to rule over the nomads of Mongolia they were not a united people and had not troubled the outside world with the sweeping invasions that characterized them under Genghis and his successors. To an unusual degree, the creation of the Mongol nation was the work of one man and is a story of a remarkable triumph over adversity, a story that begins in the late twelfth century when the great warlord Genghis Khan was just a boy named Temujin.

A famous story from Temujin's childhood signals the ruthless nature to come. Picture him on a hillside in the grassy steppes of Mongolia, some time in the 1170s, creeping up behind his half-brother Begter, with bow and arrow in hand. Earlier that day, they had quarreled over a fish and a bird that Temujin had caught; as the elder, Begter had claimed them for himself, leaving Temujin to slink away and brood, taking his younger brother Kasar with him. Now they had returned to advance stealthily on their bullying sibling, who was sitting on a rise watching over some horses. Temujin and Kasar closed in on Begter, drew their bows and killed him where he sat. They returned home, leaving the body of their brother abandoned on the grass.

The murder of his half-brother was just one among many early signs of the merciless temperament that would see Temujin bend the Mongol people to his purposes in the coming years and set them on a path to savage and shattering victories against advanced civilizations everywhere. This inexorably flinty character—formed out of the harsh life on the inhospitable steppe of Inner Asia—was allied to an impressive political facility that allowed him to gain followers of great loyalty and lead them with skill. These qualities combined to enable Temujin to transform himself from an outcast living in poverty into the emperor of millions, the founder of a dynasty that would come to rule the ancient and powerful civilizations of China in the east and Iran to the west, strike deep into Europe, and raid India through the Khyber Pass.

In the late twelfth century, the Mongols lived a nomadic life divided into tribes and clans, ranging their herds across what is now northern Mongolia, especially between the Onon and Kherlen rivers. Mongolian and the Turkic tongues form two branches of the family of Altaic languages, denoting a close ethnic affinity between the respective groups; Turkish tribes to the west such as the Naiman and Kerait bordered on the Mongol pastures in this era. Related also were the Tatars and Manchus to the east: all these peoples shared a common linguistic and cultural heritage. They also shared a migratory life on horseback, shifting camp as the seasons changed in search of fresh grazing. Hunting and the tending of their livestock were the daily preoccupations, with this pastoral routine being interrupted by tribal wars or by raids on their neighbors to seize the mobile wealth manifested in horses and herds. Earlier in the century, the Mongol tribes had been united under a leader named Kabul—the great-grandfather of Temujin— who had plunged his people into war with the Jin dynasty in China and with the Tatars to the east. In this way, the Mongols were brought to the brink of power but were then comprehensively defeated by the Jin Chinese in around 1160: their unity was abolished and they fragmented into tiny family groups, returning to their herds and pastures with their ambitions for empire abandoned.

The countryside in which these nomads fed their herds and fought their wars—roughly modern Mongolia—was loosely bounded by the Altai Mountains and the Gobi Desert, characterized by extremes of height and aridity respectively. Much of it, however, comprised the great plateau of steppe grassland, undulating and treeless, stretching for hundreds of miles. This was the classic terrain of the Mongol nomad: wide swathes of swelling hills and open plains reaching far into the distance under the broad firmament for which Mongolians sometimes name their country the "Land of the Blue Sky." This steppe is grassy but not always verdant: only in the brief spring do the sweeping hills turn a vivid green, as new pasture leaps into life to provide the herds with a few weeks of plush feeding. When long, the grass gives a lively dance under the stiff steppe wind, the blades being swept together, one way and another in unison, as if a giant invisible hand were stroking an expanse of velvet back and forth. This time of luxuriance is brief, however, for the steppe passes through extremes of climate: scorching heat in summer and blankets of snow in the long winter. The sharp sun and uncertain rains in the summer threaten a desiccation that can ruin livestock; the harsh winters imperil the herds—and their herders—through their icy bite and the hungry isolation caused by snowdrifts and stiff Siberian winds.

It is from this landscape of frequent hardship that the Mongol tribes of the twelfth century sought to eke out a living. The principal source for this period of Mongolian history is *The Secret History of the Mongols*, and it tells of this time as one of especial strife and difficulty following the defeat by the Jin, the losses of war adding to the natural constraints upon life on the steppe. Probably written in 1228 by unknown bards or scribes, the *Secret History* gives a vivid account of the origins of the Mongols and the rise of Genghis Khan, their unifying leader who had died the year before. In this colorful text—one of very few pieces of written evidence for the history of Genghis and his people—the period after the defeat by the Jin is remembered as a time of discord, a leaderless age of disharmony and poverty. With no central authority or overarching ruler in these years, we can suppose that quarrels between tribes and families were fierce as they sought to survive on the inhospitable steppe, competing desperately for the scant resources it offered. It was during this turbulent time that Temujin entered the world; indeed, his very conception was brought about through an act of violence, his father kidnapping his mother and forcing her into marriage.

His father died when Temujin was just eight years old, and the young boy and his family were cast out by the tribe, set adrift on the cold ocean of grassland where they struggled to survive. The *Secret History* tells us much about their sufferings and leaves little doubt that the motive for the steely rise of Temujin lay in these years of privation; his willingness to murder even his own kin showed that Temujin was capable of acting with amazing ruthlessness to secure his interests. Allied to this, however, was his undoubted skill in politics and fabled charisma; as he grew into a man, Temujin exercised these talents to the full in gaining the adherence of a growing number of the Mongol tribes. Over the years, he fought battles and demanded acquiescence until he had achieved a dominance over the Mongols that was beyond dispute (see color plate 10).

The final act in this rise was the legitimization of his power. Temujin called a mass gathering of the clans in 1206, the culmination of the rise to power of the young steppe outcast: he was acclaimed by his swollen population as the great khan of all the Mongols, undisputed ruler of the realm of the people of the felt tents. His unparalleled power demanded a new classification, and Temujin was given the title of Genghis Khan—

more accurately Chingis Khan—a term invented afresh for the occasion and of disputed meaning today, but doubtless reflecting his untrammeled dominance. In this triumph, he had achieved his grand goal, the strident ambition burnished by his early years of hardship and poverty. He was supreme in his powers, at the mercy no more of the whims and fancies of others, but a ruler commanding terrified respect from a million subjects and the committed devotion of a mighty army.

The rise of Temujin to Genghis Khan—from fatherless outsider to ruler of all the Mongols and many other tribes besides—was all the more remarkable because it was necessary for him to fashion a state to grow alongside his influence. Most kings and emperors achieve power within an existing polity, either by inheritance or violence, and work within its institutions to secure their authority and achieve their aims. Even the greatest founders of empires tended to acquire power through the extant system—Cyrus the Great, Alexander the Great, Chandragupta Maurya all included. Temujin, however, found no such polity among the peoples of Mongolia and set about building a state for himself, organized to serve his ends. Tribal formations were refashioned and an army was created to promote the Great Mongol Nation and his own universalist worldview. The pastoral population of this nascent political system maintained their migratory life but were now mobilized behind the ambition of their new ruler.

Genghis adopted a strategy of detribalization to ensure the fidelity of his population. The focus of loyalty was no longer to be the tribe but the khan himself: Genghis promoted his most devoted adherents, regardless of their tribal origin. The organization of the army was an essential element of this program since every able-bodied tribesman was also a soldier during the fighting season, and the structure of the army determined that of society. Immediately upon his accession to supreme authority, Genghis established his Grand Army, based around a decimal structure of *tumans* of 10,000 men containing *mingans* of 1,000, composed of squadrons of 100 and sections of 10. Although in some cases the manpower of each unit came from the same tribe, often they would not, and every man was expected to abandon previous tribal rivalries and focus everything on serving Genghis Khan.

Given that Genghis would later become known as a paradigm of murderous ferocity, elements of his social policy were surprisingly enlightened. By 1206, his subjects were drawn from several ethnic groups, including Turks and Tatars along with the Mongol tribes. In the new structure, such differences were ignored as families of varied origins were expected to work together. Religion too was removed as a source of discord: since Buddhism, Islam, Christianity and Manichaeism had all found some converts on the steppe by this time, Genghis decreed complete freedom of worship. Potentially disruptive religious squabbles were forbidden and the energies of his population were focused on matters more profitably worldly.

Having secured his position in Mongolia, Genghis Khan began to look outside the traditional lands of his people: conquest abroad was a requirement of his claim to universal rule. Moreover, conquest was essential to reward the loyalty of his adherents and to pay his army: in a nomadic country that lacked developed agriculture and industry, wealth was limited largely to herds of horses and cattle. For luxuries and manufactured wares, the steppe nomads had to turn to the settled regions beyond their own grassy sphere. Raids on these areas of China had been launched for generations to seize just such material injections of craft and culture. Given the size of the polity that Genghis had assembled behind him, the next Mongol intrusion was to be of an unprecedented scale.

At the turn of the thirteenth century, China was divided into three states. The north was dominated by the Jin from their capital of Beijing, while the south was in the hands of the rival Song dynasty. To the west of the Jin lay the Tanguts, a people of mixed Tibetan, Turkish and Mongol stock who had developed a sophisticated urban culture based along the Yellow river, in what is now the province of Gansu. Advanced, wealthy, but vulnerable, this was the first target of Genghis Khan, and he marched his army across the Gobi Desert in 1209 to bring the Tanguts under subjection. Handicapped by their inexperience of cities and their ignorance of siege warfare, the Mongols were unable to capture the Tangut capital of Yinchuan, but succeeded in gaining tribute, including a daughter of the Tangut ruler as a new wife for Genghis. Next, the Mongols advanced on the Jin in 1211 and swarmed across northern China, driving the Jin back upon their capital and sending out columns to raid the countryside as far away as Manchuria. Beijing itself was besieged for a year and then captured in 1215, the Jin emperor having fled to found a new capital in the south of his domain. This war would continue past the death of Genghis, but by 1216 he had brought much of northern China, including Manchuria and the kingdom of Korea, under his sway as vassals.

The mechanism of conquest having been set in motion, the Mongols next turned to their west, where they were bordered by a Turkic state named Kara-Khitai, an extensive domain that comprises the modern country of Kyrgyzstan, overlapping into Kazakhstan, China and Tajikistan. The rule of Kara-Khitai had been seized by Kuchlug, a refugee from the ruling family of the Naiman tribe that had been destroyed by Genghis in 1204. Having escaped the Mongols at that time, Kuchlug fled with a small number of followers for several hundred miles across Central Asia and succeeded in establishing himself in Kara-Khitai, marrying the daughter of the ruler before mounting a coup to place himself on the throne. Kara-Khitai was thus a natural target for Genghis, to complete the reordering of the tribes of his realm and to punish recalcitrants. With the Mongol army augmented in numbers and experience after the campaigns in China, Kara-Khitai proved an easy conquest, and the invasion of 1218 brought to a close the rivalry between Genghis and the Naimans. It also demonstrated the length to which Genghis would go to effect his revenge.

The greatest significance of the addition of Kara-Khitai to the empire, however, was that it gave the Mongols a border upon Khwarizm and thus upon the Muslim world. The consequences of this development would be profound: in the decades after the death of Genghis Khan, the Mongols would strike deep into the lands of Islam, destroy the Caliphate of Baghdad and install a ruling dynasty over Iran. Furthermore, a veneer of Mongol rulers would be laid across Islamic Central Asia, from which, in the following centuries, emerged both the Timurid dynasty that came to rule much of the Muslim world, and the Mughal empire, the most powerful Islamic state ever seen in India. It is possible that all this would not have happened had the neighborly reaction of Muhammad the Khwarizmshah been guided by tact and judgment rather than by an intemperate and dismissive scorn.

It seems that—with China still only subdued in part, and the war there continuing—Genghis Khan sought a peaceful relationship with Khwarizm, made profitable by commerce: both sides could benefit from the trade routes into China opened by Mongol conquests. Accordingly, an embassy was dispatched to Khwarizm along with a large number of Muslim merchants keen to establish trade. With remarkable lack of foresight—for Khwarizmian ambassadors had visited the newly captured Mongol city of Beijing and knew their military capacity—Muhammad had the envoys and merchants killed, and their goods seized. Such an act was tantamount to a declaration of war, and news of the deed is said to have sent Genghis into a vengeful fury.

So it was in 1219—year of the hare in the Chinese calendar—that Genghis Khan went to war with the Muslims, marching west with a massive army of perhaps as many as 150,000 horsemen, bolstered by siege engines gained in the Chinese campaign. This formidable force made short work of a Khwarizm weakened by the unpopularity of its king: many of the greatest cities of the realm surrendered to the Mongols rather than risk death in the service of an unloved monarch. Nevertheless, the deaths that accompanied the Mongol advances were ghastly in their scale and comprehensiveness. Otrar, the city in which the envoys and tradesmen had been killed, was reduced to rubble and its life as a flourishing urban center came to an end forever. Bokhara and Samarkand, the two brightest cultural jewels of Central Asia, were captured in the spring of 1220, and Muhammad was sent into flight, reduced from the status of ruler to that of refugee. The cities of Ugrench and Merv both decided to resist the invaders, and thus provoked the worst catastrophes of the campaign. Ugrench fell after a siege that lasted around five months, and had its opposition repaid with Mongol savagery: the Muslim sources record that craftsmen and others were saved for their skills, but the rest of the population—perhaps over a million people—was slaughtered, the Mongol soldiers dispatching dozens of townspeople apiece in a grim bout of methodical murder. In a similar episode of destruction, Merv was razed after the population had been led outside the city walls to be killed systematically—again, perhaps over a million Muslims were slain.

Muhammad the Khwarizmshah was hounded across his declining domain, Mongol pursuers chasing him to the Caspian Sea, where he died on a small island with just a few followers around him. His son Jalal al-Din proved to be an inspiration greater than his father, and rallied a resistance to continue the fight against the Mongols, hopeless though it seemed. Having previously been governor of the lands that now comprise

Afghanistan, the prince set out for his old province and sought to win back the lost kingdom. At Ghazni he succeeded in assembling a force of perhaps 60,000 men, composed of local hill tribes and the legions of refugee soldiers from Khwarizm. At Parvan, fifty miles to the north of Kabul, Jalal al-Din defeated a Mongol army. It was the only defeat suffered by the Mongols during this extended campaign.

It was not Genghis who commanded this beaten army, and when the khan heard the news, his furious desire for revenge caused him to set out with his own force to end the impertinence of Jalal al-Din. He marched into Afghanistan, pausing in his pursuit to destroy the Buddhist community at Bamiyan when it failed to submit. The town was leveled and all the inhabitants down to the cats and dogs—were slain. Once a flourishing settlement dedicated to spiritual peacefulness, Bamiyan was now a town of silent dead and lifeless ruins. The great statues of Buddha, however, were too grand to submit even to the ferocious depredations of the Mongols and remained untouched, looking out upon the destruction as sturdily as ever.

Genghis next moved on to Parvan to review the battlefield, Mongol corpses still lying where they had fallen. In Ghazni he found that Jalal al-Din had escaped into India, having traveled through the Khyber Pass with his army. Genghis continued the chase, his need for vengeance triumphing over grand strategy. India had not featured in his ambitions, but now it was revenge that drew him into the Subcontinent.

Thus it was that Genghis Khan and his army of Mongols swiftly journeyed through the Khyber Pass in 1221. We can envisage the Mongol vanguard, alert and eager, entering the Khyber through the Torkham gap, riding keenly over the ground where now stands the little border town. Pressing forward, they glance about the mountains that rise grandly from the track, seeking for signs of resistance as they ride onward. A swarm of dust heralds to distant onlookers the approach of yet another army through the Pass. This was a forced march in which the mobile Mongols made best advantage of their speed of travel: relentless hours in the saddle gave them a chance of closing in upon Jalal al-Din before he found refuge deep inside India.

Successful campaigns in China and Khwarizm had added to the Mongol wardrobe. Fur, felt and leather were now enlivened with silk and cotton, dyed and decorated in the styles of the conquered cultures. We can picture a Mongol horseman in a tunic of blue silk tricked out with threads of gold in swirling patterns of arabesque, tiny starbursts covering him in rich splashes. Stained and dusted now by almost constant campaigning, this stolen garment is fastened by a belt of fine leather clustered with gold ornaments, taken perhaps from a prosperous Khwarizmian as he lay dying outside Merv. Underneath this magnificent garb, however, the horseman wears the traditional Mongol felt trousers tucked into his stout boots, having found no replacements in his looting during the long campaigns of the previous years. His weapon remains the trusted and deadly Mongol bow, and a quiver of arrows bounces against his thigh as his horse trots along the Khyber road.

As the great army of Genghis Khan funnels through the narrow strait of Ali Masjid, imagine a swarming press of horses, their jostling flanks filmed in sweat as they squeeze through the slim channel. Their riders—the tribesmen hardened in battles across half of Asia—urge their mounts into tiny gaps in the crowd of men and animals. Hooves flick impatiently at the stony trail, and clothes that already reek from uninterrupted and energetic war become only more pungent in the hot sun. Driving forward, these horsemen will pass through the Khyber as rapidly as its constrictions allow. Imagine an officer of the heavy cavalry attempting to regulate this crush while urging his men on. He wears a tabard of scarlet silk, adorned with looping swirls of metallic thread, splitting open along the vents to reveal glinting armor underneath. This officer is armored with sparkling sheets of lamellar construction, oblong fingers of iron fastened by leather bindings into taut protective plates that shine under the bright sun. He wears a helmet seized in the Khwarizm campaign, curved like the dome of a mosque, spiked with a feather and trimmed with fur. Hanging by his side, along with the ubiquitous bow and quiver, is a fine sword of Arabic crafting, the lustrous hilt damascened in silver and gold. Workmanship such as this is unobtainable on the steppes of the Mongol homeland. Mounted on a horse armored similarly, this officer is an advert for the spoils of conquest.

These soldiers of the Mongol khan poured from the eastern end of the Khyber Pass, thousands of horsemen debouching into India without pause. Their speed bore fruit, for they succeeded in overhauling Jalal al-

Din at the Indus river before he had time to make a crossing and escape. At the battle fought on the banks of the river, the Mongols were exhausted after their frantic ride and the Khwarizmians fought well. Jalal al-Din was among their finest, and rallied his men strenuously. With Genghis in command, however, the Mongols were stronger. When all was lost, Jalal al-Din made a desperate bid for escape, launching his horse into the river from a twenty-foot bank and setting out to swim the great Indus amid a hail of Mongol arrows. Genghis himself witnessed the act and was so impressed by this princely bravery that he ordered that Jalal al-Din should be allowed to go free, declaring that every man should have such a son. Although Genghis later sent a force to pursue him, the prince of Khwarizm would live on for another decade of adventures.

The escape of Jalal al-Din at the Indus river is the origin of a curious eventuality. After his flight, the prince reassembled the stragglers that had survived the battle, and they became a force of wandering mercenaries, following their fortunes through the Punjab and in Iranian lands over the next years. Eventually, in 1231, Jalal al-Din was murdered by a Kurd in what is now northern Iraq, but his small army continued in their escapades. One of their adventures is especially remembered, for they had a crucial role in the history of the Holy Land. In 1244, in the final days of the Christian Crusaders, the Hospitaller knights were defending Jerusalem from Muslim attacks when the old soldiers of Jalal al-Din were employed to attack the city. In the account of the Christian leader, the approach of the mercenaries—*Khwarizmian* here being rendered as *Choermian*—is recorded with lasting fear:

> After our vow of pilgrimage was fulfilled, we heard in the Holy City that a countless multitude of that barbarous and perverse race, called Choermians, had, at the summons and order of the sultan of Babylon, occupied the whole surface of the country in the furthest part of our territories adjoining Jerusalem, and had put every living soul to death by fire and sword.

Shortly afterward, the Khwarizmians assaulted the city, and Jerusalem fell to the forces of Islam. The holy city would remain in Muslim hands for almost 500 years until captured by the British in 1917 during World War I. It was the traveling army of Jalal al-Din, free as they were to wander in search of military opportunity, that ended the Crusader hold on Jerusalem. Had Genghis Khan not traveled through the Khyber Pass in search of vengeance, Jerusalem might have remained in Christian hands for a few years longer.

After his victory over Jalal al-Din, Genghis did not penetrate further into India, though columns were sent to sack Multan and to probe the countryside of the Punjab. It seems that the Mongols did not find India to their liking; perhaps it lacked sufficient grazing for their horses. Genghis also faced insurrections in Afghanistan, where the population had been provoked by Mongol savagery and inspired by the resistance of Jalal al-Din. He decided to return through the Khyber Pass, and India was spared a full Mongol invasion.

The winter of 1221 was spent in Afghanistan, suppressing uprisings with lasting brutality. It was in this period that the irrigation system that had made the country a land of flourishing agriculture was destroyed. The impact of this lives on into the present day. After a year of rest, Genghis then turned east once again, looking to punish the Tanguts for their refusal to send troops in tribute in 1219, and to continue the war against the Jin. In the next few years, the Tanguts were crushed—receiving no mercy, treacherous vassals that they were—and advances were made against the Jin. It was in the midst of this dual campaign, in 1227, that Genghis Khan fell ill and died after a few days of sickness, having divided his grand inheritance between his sons. The creator of the Mongol state, the man who had taken himself from poverty on the steppe to the rule of much of Asia, was dead.

When he died, his realm stretched across the continent from the Caspian Sea to the Pacific Ocean. It encompassed all Central and Inner Asia and much of the Far East; the great cultural centers of Bokhara, Samarkand and—thousands of miles distant—Beijing were joined in the same state. Bordering the Song dynasty in China, the empire of the Mongols was also within raiding range of the hearts of both Europe and India. The sons and grandsons of the founding khan continued to win bold victories that expanded Mongol rule in every direction. By the end of the thirteenth century, all China was conquered, along with Tibet, Iran, Iraq, the Ukraine and much of European Russia. The Seljuq Sultanate in Anatolia, the Russian principalities and parts of Indochina were made vassal states. Japan narrowly escaped invasion on two occasions, and a

Mongol expeditionary force even landed on Java. At the height of Mongol power, most of the known world was under their rule.

They were, however, no longer united. The divisions of the empire bequeathed to the heirs of Genghis grew apart into separate states as the paramount power of the Great Khan became increasingly nominal: the realm of the Great Khan in China and Mongolia, the Il Khanate in Iran, the Golden Horde in the West and the Chagatai Khanate in Central Asia. Assimilation, too, caused these imperial quarters to develop along divergent paths: the Il Khanate rulers adopted Islam, while the regime of the Great Khan was absorbed deeper into the traditions of culture and governance in China. Competition between the four fractions of the Mongol realm increased their differences and introduced decline. By the fourteenth century, the power of the Mongols was on the wane as their conquering energies came to an end and as their subject populations gained confidence in their own political ambitions.

The dilution and gradual disappearance of the Mongol polity did not, however, return their conquered lands to the status quo. The complexion of Asian politics had been changed forever. A powerful Turco-Mongol aristocracy had been spread across Central Asia, a cadre from which dynasties would spring for centuries, even reaching into India to establish a powerful empire three centuries after the death of Genghis Khan. Mongols and Turks were joined in this class through the wholesale adoption of Turkish tribes such as the Kerait and Naiman into the nascent state of Genghis. This process continued as the empire grew, bringing other Turkish peoples under Mongol domination, including the Kara-Khitan and the Seljuqs. The manner in which such peoples were accepted into the Mongol nation combined with the determination of Genghis Khan to reward loyalty above origins to produce a diverse elite, united in the early days by their adherence to the khan rather than ethnic or geographic origin, and growing apart into local dynasties as Mongol power declined.

It was out of this Turco-Mongol elite, stretched and assimilated across Central Asia, that another great conqueror arose: Timur, the ruler of legendary cruelty, comparable to Genghis Khan for his shattering successes in battle and for the rapidity with which he brought his world under his subjection. Timur—known often as Tamerlane from the Persian

Timur-i-Leng, meaning Timur the Lame—was born in 1336 near Kish in Transoxiana, to the south of Samarkand. Just as the young Genghis was of a family of chieftains that had fallen into straitened circumstances, Timur was born into the powerful Muslim Barlas clan but found himself in reduced circumstances early in his career. He was not himself a descendant of Genghis, but married into his line in order to associate himself with the glories of the golden family. Proving an able warrior and leader, Timur experienced various romantic adventures as a young man—including the acquisition of the arrow wounds that rendered him lame—hence his name—before becoming ruler of Transoxiana in 1370. The comparison with Genghis extends further, for just as it took Temujin several years to assemble his power in his homeland before bursting into the outside world as Genghis Khan, Timur spent the next decade strengthening his authority in Central Asia before setting out to invade Iran in 1380. This was the beginning of constant campaigning across Eurasia that saw Timur vanquish Iran, shatter the Golden Horde, subjugate the Ottoman Turks in Anatolia—even capturing Sultan Bayazid himself—and conquer Baghdad and Syria. When he died in 1405, he was setting out to invade China.

The two conquerors, though, differed in the depth of their ruthlessness. Both the Mongol hordes and the forces of Timur whipped a vicious storm across the lands they subdued, with devastating outrages abounding, but there is a difference in their attitude. Genghis Khan seems to have been motivated by a need for the security that power brings, Timur by anger. Whereas Genghis seems to have been simply indifferent to the suffering that he caused in his drive to success, Timur celebrated it, reveling in his cruelty. Thus when Isfahan in Iran revolted against his rule, Timur had the entire population of the city put to death and piled 70,000 severed human heads into 120 great towers outside the walls. When Baghdad was reconquered in 1401, pyramids were built from 90,000 heads.

His swift, violent conquests and his cruelty became legendary. Nearly two centuries after his death, the English playwright Christopher Marlowe painted a glitteringly fierce and imperial Timur, delighting in his role as heavenly avenger, in his play *Tamburlaine the Great*:

And till by vision or by speech I hear
Immortal Jove say "Cease, my Tamburlaine,"
I will persist a terror to the world,
Making the meteors that, like armed men,
Are seen to march upon the towers of heaven,
Run tilting round about the firmament
And break their burning lances in the air
For honor of my wondrous victories.

We can put a face to this terror: for while there are only generic portraits of
Genghis Khan, there is an intriguing source for the likeness of Timur—his
own skull. In 1941, Soviet scientists opened his magnificent tomb, the Gur-
i-Amir in Samarkand, and identified the skeletal remains of the long-dead
conqueror. Based on the skull, the anthropologist Gerasimov was able to
build a reconstruction of his face. Arched eyebrows sweep into a frowning
stare that asserts his dominance even through the medium of a clay model,
his eyes narrowing in Turkic fashion. He has high cheekbones of an
aristocratic cast and a full beard sharpened to a point. A stiff moustache
arches over full lips bearing the trace of a petulant pout. We can picture
this pitiless man at his ease in camp toward the end of his life, during the
incessant campaigns that were his norm, stretched out upon cushions to
rest his lame right leg. Wrapped in a loose silken gown of deep Islamic
green that is waisted with many slender belts in a fashion of the time,
Timur wears a tall, conical cap embroidered with metallic threads. Wide
white trousers are tucked into boots that rise about his calves, tan leather
etched in elaborate swirls. About him lie his sword and a symbolic mace,
weapons always close to the hand of this warring king. In attendance upon
his relaxation, Timur has just a few members of his guard, the most trusted
of his many soldiers. They are clothed and armored in a Central Asian
style that betrays a Chinese influence, speaking of the transcontinental
reach of the empires of this age. Each has a scaled cuirass worn over a
short mail hauberk, the whole surmounted by a tunic of blue silk, em-
bossed with a centerpiece of shining gold. Bowled helmets of Iranian
crafting are curtained with an aventail of rustling iron mail, and heads turn
continually in watch over their precious charge. Timur may perhaps have
been sitting thus in 1398 when he decided to invade India.

Timur, from the reconstructed head by Gerasimov

In India, the Sultanate of Delhi continued to dominate the north of the Subcontinent, relatively isolated from the ructions caused elsewhere in Asia by the Mongols and their successors throughout the thirteenth and fourteenth centuries. Although the raid through the Khyber by Genghis Khan had divested the Sultanate of important lands in the Punjab and given the empire of the Mongols a border in India, the rise of Genghis in fact assisted the Sultanate of Delhi in one crucial respect: the nascent Sultanate, established by the slave soldiers of the last Ghorid sultan at the turn of the thirteenth century, had been instantly in danger of absorption by the suddenly rising power of Khwarizm. Just as it had swept across the former Ghaznavid and Ghorid lands in Afghanistan and Khorasan, Khwarizm might well have reached into India and brought the new power of Delhi under its control, exploiting links of religion and Turkish ethnicity to force a claim over its sovereignty. Such a possibility was destroyed by Genghis Khan's Muslim war: instead of journeying through the Khyber Pass as an invader, the Khwarizmian prince came as a refugee. The Mongol explosion into Asia therefore allowed the Sultanate of Delhi to develop alone as a distinctive Muslim state in northern India, at a remove from the Islamic lands that came under the sway of Genghis and his heirs. Although sporadic Mongol raids troubled India for decades after the 1221 incursion, it was not until Timur turned his gaze toward India that the real cataclysm came.

Timur set out to invade the Sultanate in 1398, now an old man but still vigorous in his body and ambitions and still motivated by the riches of India; a veneer of piety was useful, the Central Asians claiming that Indian Islam was verging on apostasy. The year before, Timur had sent his grandson—Pir Muhammad, just fifteen years old—to prepare the way, and the young prince entered India with his army, placing Multan under siege. Stiff resistance at this city persuaded Timur to deal with India himself, and his grand army—perhaps 90,000 strong—entered the Khyber Pass, yet another invading army marching through its narrow confines. Heavy baggage trains and the royal ladies traveled in its wake, all the paraphernalia of an imperial court being dragged along the rocky trail. Timur reached the banks of the Indus in September 1398 and camped on the very spot where Jalal al-Din had leapt into the river to escape from Genghis Khan many years before.

At this time, numerous local rulers submitted to the invader as fear of his reputation easily overcame their loyalty to Delhi and Sultan Mahmud. Timur did not march directly on the capital, but went to the assistance of his grandson who was still besieging Multan, ransacking the cities of the Punjab as he went. The approach of the conqueror terrified Multan into submission and everywhere in the Punjab fell to the forces of Timur. His unjust treatment of those who submitted, however, provoked revolts that brought a cruel response, and many cities were devastated. The countryside was scoured and its towns and cities laid waste: the advance of Timur and his army was truly the visitation of a scourge. Many prisoners were killed where they were captured, and many thousands were gathered as slaves, accompanying the army in its progress toward Delhi.

Timur arrived in the Delhi region in December and spent some time preparing his dispositions and choosing his ground for the fighting ahead: wishing to avoid a lengthy siege of the city, he maneuvered for a battle in the open. After some days, Timur set out with an escort of several hundred horsemen to make a reconnaissance outside the city; noticing this party, and determining to seize the chance of a quick end to the encroaching danger, the commander of the Delhi army, Mallu Khan, made a sortie in force. Timur's party was beaten back to camp, but the Indians failed to make headway against reinforcements sent out to meet them. Such was the initial appearance of success, however, that the numerous prisoners held in the camp of the invaders thought they might be freed, and jubilation broke out among them; their joy was fatal, for it raised fears among their captors that they might prove a liability in the coming battle. Timur decided to slaughter all these prisoners in one terrible act—perhaps as many as 100,000 captives were slain: every soldier who had taken slaves during the campaign was required to kill them where they stood. The dreadful massacre lasted scarcely an hour: even those with scruples against such cruelty rapidly obeyed for fear of Timur, though most found little psychological obstacle to the butchery of despised slaves.

Several days later, the two armies advanced for battle outside Delhi. The forces of the sultan were entirely inadequate to meet the powerful and experienced army of Timur: Delhi fielded just 10,000 cavalry, 40,000 infantry and 125 elephants to meet 90,000 invaders. On December 16, the battle was joined; the Indians fought bravely, earning the praise of Timur, but were outnumbered and overwhelmed by their opposition. Sultan Mahmud and Mallu Khan fled to fight again in later days, and on December 17, Timur made a triumphal entry into the defeated capital. A great pavilion was erected at one of the gates of the city, and the conqueror received the submission of the important men of Delhi: noblemen, religious leaders, bankers and traders all came to offer their deference, throwing themselves at the feet of the invader to ask for quarter. Timur granted the city protection and freedom from ransack in return for a vast indemnity. Delhi was his.

However, the promises of protection were not to last. Most of the invading army was encamped outside Delhi, with just a few units of soldiers allowed to enter the city to assist the collection of the indemnity and to acquire provisions. Trouble started, apparently when some soldiers became rowdy while buying sweets, and looting began, which spread rapidly as the occupying army took the chance of exploiting a defenseless populace. For four days, Delhi was ransacked as the army of Timur swarmed in to pillage and burn. Ruthless looting brought immense profit in gold and silver coins and bullion, jewelry and fine fabrics, captive women and other slaves; many soldiers were so burdened by their precious haul that they could not carry all they had looted. The response of Timur was rage at the futile resistance that the population was able to offer: he ordered that those who had sought refuge in the Jama Masjid—the great Friday Mosque—be massacred. Their severed heads were piled into pyramids.

With little more profit to be had from a razed and ruined city, Timur marched his army away on the last day of 1398. Along with the material booty, craftsmen and artisans were marched off too, to beautify the cities of Samarkand and Bokhara. Ironically, Timur was much impressed with the splendor of the Jama Masjid, and wanted to replicate its beauty in his own cities. Accordingly, he took a model of the mosque back to Samarkand, and his captive craftsmen from India were put to work on building a grand mausoleum, the very Gur-i-Amir in which Timur was buried just a few years hence.

The violence continued as Timur headed back toward the Khyber Pass. Several other cities received a visitation no less destructive, and revolts were raised against the cruelty of the invaders in many towns in the region. Even during this return journey, the killing went on as before, and every opportunity was taken to seize yet more booty. However, news of revolts in other parts of the vast empire had been reaching the emperor, and his army was no doubt keen to return home to enjoy the spoils of war. Timur held his last court in India at Lahore in March 1399 and returned to Transoxiana, leaving northern India desolate and ruined.

While the rise of Genghis Khan had unintentionally ensured that the Sultanate of Delhi remained independent of Khwarizm, Timur's savage raid was a catastrophe from which it never fully recovered. The Sultanate stumbled on through the fifteenth century, shedding territories to revolt and to rising local dynasties, racked by internal dissension and rivalries. A Muslim ruler who made much of his religion, Timur in fact impeded the cause of Islam in India, for the decline of the Sultanate allowed a number of strong Hindu kingdoms to emerge. Despite this deterioration, the Sultanate of Delhi persisted into the sixteenth century, only to face another onslaught from Central Asia. Genghis Khan and Timur did not enter India to remain as rulers, but another Turco-Mongol—descended from them both—was to travel the Khyber Pass to found the greatest empire India had ever seen.

CHAPTER NINE

Mughals and Sikhs

The Badshahi Mosque, Lahore

In the year I first came to Kabul, I went through the Khyber to Peshawar intent upon entering Hindustan . . .

THE BABURNAMA

There is neither Hindu nor Muslim

B40 JANAM SAKHI

Lahore is a beautiful place. So renowned is it that in Pakistan it needs no explanation: as the saying goes, "*Lahore is Lahore.*" On my way to the North West Frontier, I traveled through the city, admiring its sights, and was astonished by the perfect beauty of the Badshahi Mosque: I knew nothing of it before I arrived, for it is much less famous than it deserves, but when I stepped into the impressive red sandstone courtyard, I was instantly captivated. I was also, however, immediately waylaid by a tiny, boisterous old man who scampered up to me, leapt to attention with a noisy stamping of his feet, and saluted with a flourish. His face was extremely comical, like a very amused child, and he had only a few teeth. I judged him to be an old soldier by his khaki shalwar kameez and tatty army jumper, and he had a blue rag arranged on his head in a form of turban.

I smiled at him, and he asked me my name in—for reasons known only to himself—French. I replied with one of only two Urdu phrases that I had available: *mera naam Paddy hai* (my name is Paddy). His laughing eyes and grinning mouth both opened wide in exaggerated awe, and so impressed was he with my basic Urdu that he declared me to be a *Haji*— literally, one who has completed the pilgrimage to Mecca; loosely, a man of distinction. He joked that while I was a Haji, he was a *baji*—a bad man, or as he said, a "crime man." Laughing away merrily, he then declaimed a couple of sentences about the mosque, florid phrases—I caught the words "sublime," "splendor" and "magnificence"—that had no doubt been used many times, then held out his palm for a tip. I gave him ten rupees; he looked at the note in his hand with crestfallen disgust and asked for 500, as a policeman arrived to shoo him away.

The Badshahi Mosque lived up to the old man's description. Breath-taking in its grand simplicity, the vast courtyard is said to hold up to 100,000 worshippers. The mosque itself stands at the far end, its red sandstone walls inlaid with intricate decorations, and an enormous squared arch surrounding the entrance. A huge dome of white marble rises in the center, flanked by another two almost as large. These full domes, nearly spherical, are drawn into tapering points topped with golden pinnacles. The mosque is guarded by four towers, each one capped with a roof of white marble, and the courtyard is cornered by immense octagonal minarets.

This beautiful scene could not have come into being without an invasion through the Khyber: the Badshahi Mosque is one of the architectural gems of the Mughal Empire, the great realm fashioned by Central Asian intruders who followed Genghis Khan and Timur through the Khyber Pass. The mosque was built in the late seventeenth century, but the origins of the Mughals go back to the end of the fifteenth century, when Umar Sheikh Mirza was the ruler of Ferghana, a fertile kingdom in what is now Uzbekistan. One day in the summer of 1494, Umar stepped into his dovecot, which was perched over a steep ravine. It collapsed under the weight of the stout king, and he fell to his death in a shower of feathery rubble. It was this almost comical demise that brought Zahiruddin Muhammad to the throne of Ferghana at just eleven years old. He would become famous under his sobriquet Babur, "Tiger."

By the end of the fifteenth century, Timur's empire had long since dis-integrated into fragments ruled separately by his many descendants. Ferghana was one such successor state, Umar being a great-great-grandson of Timur, and it was surrounded by cousin kingdoms competing for land and power. With no thought of dynastic loyalty, these petty kings and princes fought each other for the choice cuts of the corpse of empire; when Umar died, Ferghana was under attack by two of his brothers.

Outside Timur's Central Asian heartland, the unifying effect of his conquests had also waned. Iran had thrown off her Turco-Mongol rulers and saw the rise of the Safavid dynasty in the early years of the sixteenth century. In India, despite the ruthless wound inflicted by the invasion of

Timur a century before, the Sultanate of Delhi still persisted in its rule, by this time under the Lodi dynasty. After years of decline in which its territories were beset by rebellion and chaos in the wake of the great raid through the Khyber Pass, this royal house introduced some prospect of recovery for the Sultanate, but it was fleeting. It was Babur who would arrive to end this rising hope, and to establish the Mughal Empire, the greatest that India had ever seen. This dynasty—the name being the Persian for Mongol—provided India with a fresh set of powerful rulers from Central Asia who would go on to unite the Subcontinent under their command. The Mughal period saw India reach enviable heights in art, architecture and literature, and lasted for over three centuries—although in severely reduced and largely powerless form in the later years—until the British brought the dynasty to an end in the middle of the nineteenth century. This, however, was all some way off when the young Babur came to the throne of Ferghana in 1494.

Descended from both Timur and (through his mother) Genghis Khan, Babur had the perfect pedigree for conquest. Such an ancestry was a strong claim to rule, but was not enough by itself in the cauldron of kingdoms that was Central Asia in this era: a prince needed to prove himself in action. Thus the fearsome pedigree of Babur did not prevent his uncles continuing their attack on Ferghana after his father's death, but the youthful ruler succeeded in seeing them off.

Despite his ancestry—and his eventual subjugation of India—Babur was not a relentless pursuer of conquest. He was certainly ambitious, and soon recognized that the small kingdom of Ferghana could not contain him, but his career as a young king was characterized by adventurous forays and desperate reversals of fortune. A haphazard progression of losing one kingdom and gaining another lends his early life a quixotic quality, and he found happiness even when reduced to the status of a vagabond, wandering the mountains with a mere handful of loyal retainers. His memoirs, the rich and engaging *Baburnama*—the *Book of Babur*—are full of such tales. Babur was a highly literate prince, a poet of distinction, and the *Baburnama* is a beautifully written view into his life of royal adventures and misadventures, disarming in its frankness and charming in its style.

Babur's romanticism combined with his royal ambitions to make his eyes turn toward Samarkand—the great city of Timur and ancient center of arts and letters, then in a neighboring kingdom ruled by a cousin. In 1496, when just thirteen years old, the boy-king of Ferghana set out to attempt its conquest. It was a bold effort that ended in failure. Success came, however, in the following year and Babur captured Timur's capital. This triumph was only brief: he held the city for a hundred days until Ferghana went into rebellion in support of his brother Jahangir, and in setting out to put down the revolt, Babur lost Samarkand to his cousin Sultan Ali Mirza. Having reached a symbolic peak in the conquest of Samarkand, Babur had been reduced suddenly to nothing. This was the beginning of his years as a vagabond prince, searching the mountains and valleys of Central Asia for a kingdom, living sometimes as a destitute beggar and sometimes in the luxury of royalty. In these years, Babur recaptured both Ferghana and Samarkand only to lose them both once again, and his life as a royal desperado continued until he chanced upon the throne of Kabul in 1504. Ulugh Beg Mirza, King of Kabul and uncle of Babur, died in that year with only an infant son to succeed him: the kingdom fell into disorder and attracted adventurers and speculators from the surrounding regions who sought to gain from the confusion. Babur was among them, and he succeeded in claiming the kingdom. At the age of twenty-one, with several years of adventures behind him, Babur at last sat upon a secure throne as King of Kabul.

For the next twenty years, it seems that Kabul sated his ambitions. In this era, it was a beautiful city of gardens and palaces, surrounded by snow-capped mountains and with a temperate climate. Babur had clearly not surrendered to relaxation altogether—within a year of capturing Kabul, he led a raid on India through the Khyber Pass—but it was to be two decades before he mounted a full invasion. In part, these years were occupied with Central Asian affairs—the Uzbek ruler Shaibani Khan was marching through the region, displacing the descendants of Timur—and, in part, with pleasure. Although as a young man Babur had refused alcohol on religious grounds, later he ignored the Koranic proscription and enjoyed it with gusto; opium too became a favorite, and the *Baburnama* is replete with descriptions of courtly revelries and literary licentiousness. Mughal fondness for drinking parties became legendary, and it began with Babur and his carousing. One such night of mirth in the company of his princely friends—in 1519 during a raid into India—is described by Babur himself in the *Baburnama*:

At midday we rode off on an excursion, got on a boat, and drank spirits
. . . We drank on the boat until late that night, left the boat roaring
drunk, and got on our horses. I took a torch in my hand and, reeling to
one side and then the other, let the horse gallop free-reined along the
river bank all the way to camp. I must have been really drunk. The next
morning they told me that I had come galloping into camp holding a
torch. I didn't remember a thing, except that when I got to my tent I
vomited a lot.

Babur launched another raid through the Khyber Pass in 1507, but then
for a decade the King of Kabul turned his eyes from India, distracted by
Uzbek advances and his enthusiastic dissipation. From 1518 his eastern
ambitions recovered, however, and the pace and degree of his Indian
adventures quickened until, in November 1525, Babur set out on what
would become one of the most consequential of all Khyber crossings.
With a small army of just 12,000 men, he reached Peshawar in early
December, where he paused for a rhinoceros hunt. Finding little military
resistance in his way, Babur continued to the banks of the Indus river,
which he then crossed. In the first days of January 1526, he led his modest
army in a successful battle against the forces of the Lodi governor of the
Punjab and seized the chance to advance on Delhi. Having been blooded
in battle early in his life, Babur was more experienced in war than Sultan
Ibrahim of Delhi, but nonetheless showed great boldness in thrusting
deep into the capital territory of the Sultanate with such a limited force
behind him. The years in Kabul had evidently not diminished his daring,
and the march upon Delhi continued.

Several local nobles defected to Babur with their private armies in expectation of his continued success, but the invading army remained
meager at around 15,000 or 20,000 men. Since his force was too small to
fight in the open, Babur decided to choose a battleground that covered
both his flanks to allow him to fortify his front and await an attack from the
Lodi troops. A clash with the sultan himself was a necessary climax: only
when the two kings had met in battle would the future of India be decided.
By the time that Babur had to make his choice, it was April, and he elected
to fight at Panipat, fifty miles north of Delhi, close to the Jumna river.
Arraying his army so that the town covered his right flank, Babur had
ditches dug and palisades erected on his left, arranging his guns between

field defenses to his front. The sultan drew up his force opposite, and for a week the two sides simply remained in their positions, looking out across the empty field of battle, awaiting the start of the fighting. Needing his fortifications to compensate for his disadvantage in numbers, Babur could not take the battle to the sultan; perhaps lacking in audacity, the sultan would not seek to advance. Eventually, Babur tired of waiting for his patrols to provoke an attack and decided upon a night assault. A force of perhaps 5,000 men was sent in on the night of April 19 in an action that proved a miserable farce. The column lost its way in the dark, was unsuccessful in its bid to engage with the enemy, and had to be escorted back to camp when dawn broke.

This effort seems, however, to have coaxed the sultan into making an attack. On the morning of April 21, the army of the Sultanate advanced in full array. The battle of Panipat had begun (see color plate 11). The sultan started by directing his principal attack on the right flank of Babur, hoping to detach the invading army from the cover of the town. The Mughal right held its own, however, while the Sultanate advance in the center was contained by the fortified guns. The sultan's own superiority in numbers, meanwhile, began to tell against him, as his men could not withdraw in good order on the crowded battlefield. When Babur ordered a wheeling movement to take the enemy in the rear, the bulk of the Sultanate army became trapped between this attack and the guns to the front. At the same time, their own elephants proved a dangerous liability as they trampled indiscriminately in the crush. The battle became a rout, as the Mughal forces almost leisurely cut down an enemy with no means of escape nor chance of maneuver. By noon, the army of the Sultanate was broken and the sultan himself lay dead on the field. When Babur's soldiers found the body, they severed the head and carried it to their ruler as proof of his victory. Babur was no longer merely king of Kabul. He was now emperor of India, and the Mughal dynasty was born.

To a large extent, this new empire was accidental. It is likely that the limit of Babur's aims—even when he had set out in late 1525—had been to incorporate the Punjab into his kingdom and rule it from Kabul, rather than to penetrate deep into India: as opportunistic as ever, Babur took his chance to seize a greater prize. This development was not welcomed by all, however. India did not appeal to Babur's commanders except as a place to raid for its riches, and many of them were aghast when it emerged that he intended to remain in the new country to rule, rather than return home with their booty. Babur himself was unimpressed with his conquest, complaining in the *Baburnama* that it lacked good bread, melons, dogs, horses, grapes and candles. More seriously, he felt that India had little to offer in art and culture, and he was offended by the manners of the people. The hot climate also horrified the Mughals, used as they were to temperate Kabul. Nonetheless, Babur decided to stay in India as the founder of a dynasty. For him, the accidental conquest of India represented a chance of glory, an opportunity to exceed the modest boundaries of the kingdom of Kabul and to ensure lasting fame. Although he would have preferred an empire centered on Samarkand, India would suffice.

It was undoubtedly wealthy, and it was in the early days of the Mughal conquest that one of the legendary treasures of India first emerged into recorded history: the Koh-i-Noor, or "Mountain of Light," the most famous diamond in the world. After the battle of Panipat, Humayun, the son and heir of Babur, had been sent ahead of his father to secure the central lands of the Sultanate in preparation for the triumphal advance of the conqueror. In restoring order in these areas, he did a service to the royal house of Gwalior, vassal kings of the Sultan, and the family gave him the wondrous jewel in their gratitude. When Babur arrived in Agra, Humayun presented the Koh-i-Noor (although it was not yet known by that name) to the new emperor. Babur declared that such a magnificent diamond must have a value of the full expenses of the entire world for two and a half days, and—with his characteristic generosity—returned the gem to his son. Over the following centuries, the possession of the Koh-i-Noor marked the shifts of rule in northern India.

The victory at Panipat and the occupation of Delhi and Agra made Babur emperor but did not deliver him a quiet conquest. Lodi loyalists were marching against him from Bengal in the east, and the Hindu Rajputs to the south, themselves keen to make a kingdom out of the Lodi remains, were also in resistance. Numerous other princes lay outside Mughal rule, and the regime had to fight to absorb them. It took over a century for the Mughal dynasty to extend their rule over all of India, but by the spring of 1527, Babur had won enough victories to sit securely on his throne.

At the very time that Babur was entrenching his claim and founding a dynasty, the Punjab saw the gradual emergence of an unlikely threat that would later come to contest the Mughal hold on northwest India: the Sikh religion. While Babur fought battles along the banks of the Ganges and Jumna, the rivers of the Punjab were gently watering the seed of an emerging faith, which would grow to supremacy in the Punjab by the late eighteenth century. This seed was planted by Guru Nanak.

Nanak was born to a Hindu family in the Punjab in 1469 and grew up in the village of Talvandi near Lahore. When he came of age, Nanak initially entered the service of the Lodi governor of the province, before setting out to travel widely. On his return to the Punjab, he settled in the village of Kartarpur, on the Ravi river, where disciples and supporters—both Hindu and Muslim—began to gather around him as the fame of his religious insights and teaching spread; such was the power of his philosophy that he was soon acclaimed as a guru—a spiritual guide. The followers that coalesced about Nanak would become the Sikh community (*sikh* meaning disciple), and he became the first of a line of ten Sikh gurus. As an inward creed, it did not threaten the temporal powers in its early days, but over the course of two centuries or so, the faith assembled a community that grew into an alternative state, a martial and active establishment that became a potential replacement for Mughal rule in the Punjab. The competition between Sikh and Mughal was to become prolonged and bloody.

For Babur, of course, this was all impossibly far in the future. He had other very immediate threats to his rule, as well as great areas of India that he wanted to bring under his control, and his time was short. In December 1530, only five years after bringing his army across the Khyber Pass to found a Central Asian line of Indian emperors, Babur died after a period of illness. He was buried first at Agra, and a few years later the body of the accidental emperor was returned to his beloved Kabul and interred in a beautiful park—the Bagh-i-Babur, or Garden of Babur—on a hillside over-looking the city. The royal grave can still be seen there, though its setting has suffered from years of neglect.

Humayun succeeded his father—overcoming fraternal threats of disruption—and proved to be an affable but capricious king, talented but lacking direction. He could be brave—as when he led a daring night assault at the siege of Champanir during his pacification of Gujarat—but

An imagined scene of Guru Nanak (right) and Guru Gobind Singh

could fall into indolence caused by the opium to which he was addicted. Fond of revelry and ease, Humayun was committed neither to the exercise of government nor the protection of his state and status. He was a skilled mathematician and astronomer but did not produce any lasting contribution in these fields. He was inventive and sometimes designed a useful item such as a collapsible bridge, but more often preferred palace games of increasing eccentricity. One such was the "carpet of mirth," a rug decorated with colored circles associated with the planets, on which Humayun would require his courtiers to take up position. Each nobleman would then have to stand, sit or lie, depending on a throw of the dice. Astrology guided the emperor's life, determining his schedule of work and pleasure, and even the color of his clothes.

Given such mercurial neglect of the steely concerns of rule, it is perhaps surprising—especially in a nascent state—that Humayun remained emperor for ten years before he was overthrown. In this time, he had on occasion roused himself to deal with restive regions (notably his campaign in Gujarat), but dreamy lethargy often undid his gains. His impatience with things pragmatic sapped the Mughal regime of the dynamism required to fend off active rivals; bereft of a vigorous commander in chief, the army became ill disciplined and unreliable. Regional leaders plotted their own paths to power, stepping in to fill an evident lacuna in leadership. One such was Sher Khan, an Afghan adventurer who had made himself master of Bihar and Bengal. Maintaining control under the nominal suzerainty of the Mughals, in practice he ruled much as he pleased until he judged the time to be right to assert his grand ambition of replacing the invading dynasty with his own. The reckoning came on May 17, 1540, at the battle of Kanauj, near Agra, where the army of Sher Khan destroyed a much larger Mughal force. Barefoot and turbanless, Humayun escaped from the battlefield a mere fraction of the ruler who had taken the field that morning. Just as his father had been years before, Humayun was now a vagabond prince. The Mughal dynasty seemed to be at an end.

For a while, Humayun sought safety in Sind, out of the reach of Sher Khan. By the summer of 1543, however, this sanctuary was proving unproductive and little aid was forthcoming to promote a restoration of Mughal fortunes. The small royal party decided to quit India and journeyed to Afghanistan—incidentally through the Bolan Pass—where Humayun's brother Kamran still ruled. Far from offering asylum to the fallen king, however, Kamran saw Humayun as a threat and made preparations to arrest him; in desperation, Humayun appealed to Shah Tahmasp of Iran, to whose lands he rushed as a refugee in early 1544.

The Shah was more welcoming. As a young ruler of the relatively new Safavid dynasty, he may perhaps have felt sympathy for the hapless Humayun, and no doubt also saw advantage in helping him. The ceremonies and banquets that greeted the Mughal expatriate were a lavish demonstration of the power and wealth of Safavid Iran, and Humayun reveled in such luxurious treatment. Tahmasp also had more robust assistance to bestow: he offered Humayun the use of an army to effect his restoration, in return for the cession of Kandahar, which was at that time in the hands of Kamran. For such generous help, and for his splendid welcome, Humayun gave Shah Tahmasp his most valuable possession, one of the few treasures that had remained with him when he was forced to leave India: the Koh-i-Noor. Thus in 1544 it looked as if Mughal fortunes were about to be recovered, but Humayun was in no rush to take advantage of the assistance on offer. He was enjoying his stay in Iran so much that he delayed for over a year, touring its sights on an extended holiday. Finally, after strong hints from his hosts, Humayun and his Iranian army marched into Afghanistan in the summer of 1545 to begin the first stage of his restoration.

His goal was to conquer Afghanistan and use it to gather his strength before tackling the bigger prize of India itself. He also needed to acquire Kandahar in order to make it over to Shah Tahmasp. Gaining control of Afghanistan meant war with his brothers—Askari as well as Kamran—and this conflict filled a decade. For ten years of vicious struggle, Humayun contested the control of Kabul, the city changing hands almost every fighting season, until he was eventually victorious. Kamran was seized and blinded to end the clash, and Humayun could turn back to India. By this time, Sher Khan was long dead, and—though his rule had been vigorous and efficient—his foundation did not long outlast him. In contrast to the extended contest that Humayun had to fight to gain Afghanistan, the return to India was easily done; in late 1554 he was free of Afghan troubles and set out to cross the mountainous frontier into the Subcontinent. His progress was barely contested, there being little centralized resistance, and in July 1555—fifteen years after he had been forced from the city by Sher Khan— Humayun reoccupied Delhi. After years as a refugee king, clinging to hopes of rule in the midst of hazard and misadventure, Humayun was emperor once again and the Mughal dynasty was restored. They would reign for three centuries more until their rule was ended by the British Raj in 1858.

The restoration of the Mughal Empire was the political effect of Humayun's Iranian journey, but there was an artistic consequence too: it led to the emergence of the Mughal school of painting. This tradition flourished in the years following the royal flight to Iran. Not only was it of Iranian inspiration; it was led by Iranian master painters, brought from their homeland by Humayun and his successors. Stories of great deeds from history and legend are captured with precision and vivid color throughout Mughal manuscripts, along with scenes from court and from daily life in the Mughal realm; the *Baburnama* was a source of inspiration above all others. Religious proscriptions on representation are ignored entirely and likenesses are painted with close and often humorous detail. Such pictures give an excellent view of court life and the Mughal elite.

A powerful element of the Mughal willingness to welcome itinerant artisans from Iran and the Persianized lands of Central Asia lay in their profound nostalgia for their old homeland. Even later Mughal emperors and princes who had never seen Samarkand or Ferghana, nor even crossed the Hindu Kush, longed for these places of ancestral memory, prizing such daydreams above their real kingdom. With his Indian conquests only recently won, Babur considered giving it all up to plunge back into Central Asian affairs, having received word of ructions in the Uzbek realm that might just offer him the chance of a return to the land of Timur. The first thought of Humayun upon discovering a Safavid army at his disposal was to use it to return his family to power in Samarkand. It was only through the failure of these ambitions that the Mughals found themselves restored to the Subcontinent. Accidental emperors of India they were, and somewhat reluctant too.

As the Mughal emperors looked back across the northwest frontier of their Indian empire, the Khyber Pass became a viewfinder of desire. It was the symbolic entrance to the places from which they felt exiled. Akbar— the son and successor of Humayun, who had died in early 1556 in a narcotic tumble down a staircase—built the first paved road through the Khyber Pass. Born in Sind in 1542, Akbar could (in contrast to his father and grandfather) properly be considered "*Indian*," but still he paid attention to the northwest and the way to Samarkand. He made no attempt to conquer lands in Central Asia, but it may well be that his road indicated future ambitions in this direction. Father Monserrate, one of the Jesuit missionaries who spent time at the court of Akbar, hoping to convert the emperor to Christianity, mentions the road building. On the northwest frontier with his army in 1581, Akbar sent one of his sons into the Khyber, accompanied by the Jesuit, who recorded that:

> On the day after the King's departure, the prince began to advance and in two days' time came to a difficult, steep and narrow pass over a very high range, which is called by the natives Caybar . . . The army crossed this pass but with the greatest difficulty. Care had to be taken to pave the road, though in a hasty manner. Even this had taxed to the utmost the skill of gangs of sappers and workmen.

In 1605, Akbar was succeeded by his son Jahangir ("Conqueror of the World") who continued the Mughal obsession with Central Asia but effected no scheme for seizing his ancestral homeland. Shah Jahan ("King of the World") succeeded Jahangir in 1627 and determined to recover Balkh to use it as a base from which to advance into Central Asia. After two false starts and many delays, Shah Jahan eventually succeeded in occupying the city in 1646, and held it for over a year. The adventure ended in humiliation, however, when his army was forced from Balkh, and from northern Afghanistan, in 1647.

Shah Jahan's Central Asian fixation was not only military but artistic too. After his beloved wife Mumtaz Mahal died in 1631 while giving birth to her fourteenth child, Shah Jahan was moved to construct around her resting place the most famous building in India: the Taj Mahal in Agra. This graceful structure of domes and minarets, in a white marble that hints at translucence, was inspired by what was, for a Mughal, a natural source of stimulus: the Gur-i-Amir, the tomb of Timur in Samarkand. That this model for the Taj Mahal had itself been based upon the Jama Masjid of Delhi and built by the Indian craftsmen taken captive by Timur shows the fertile traffic of inspiration through the Khyber Pass.

Aurangzeb, who succeeded Shah Jahan in 1666, was unsympathetic to his father in many things, but nonetheless maintained the Mughal tradition of making plans to conquer Central Asia. He also sent funds regularly for the upkeep of the Gur-i-Amir. His desire to continue the grand project of marching into Samarkand may indeed have been genuine—despite experience as a commander in the disastrous venture of 1646—but in practice Aurangzeb devoted his energies to campaigning in the Deccan, extending Mughal rule almost to the fingertip of India through many years of war.

In addition to his military success, the other notable characteristic of Aurangzeb and his reign was religious intolerance. Because of these two attributes, Aurangzeb can fairly be considered both the last of the great Mughal emperors and a cause of the empire's decline. His predecessors had been liberal in their religion—indeed Akbar was keenly syncretic and invented his own creed to synthesize all the faiths of his empire—but Aurangzeb's prejudice stimulated revolt among his non-Muslim subjects. He also ended the easy access to Mughal India previously enjoyed by itinerant Iranians: as Shia Muslims, they were no longer welcome in his strictly Sunni sphere. India was closed to the talents of adventurous incomers, and the art and literature of the Subcontinent suffered. Aurangzeb added much territory to his kingdom, but provided for its later disintegration through his bigotry: when he died in 1707, the difficulties in his empire were already mounting into a centrifugal impulse that would become a long, slow death for the Mughal realm.

One of these separatist energies, and one which the intolerance of Aurangzeb did much to militate, was manifest in the Sikh community of the Punjab. Guru Nanak had died in 1539, leaving the Sikhs with a profound basis of philosophy but little in the way of organization: theirs was still an inward faith that placed no value on outward expression. As such, it had no ritual or priesthood. This began to change as the community grew and as those who had lived in the time of Nanak died out. Under Guru Amar Das, the third guru, practices were adopted that were directly contradictory to the teachings of Nanak: a well was employed as a place of pilgrimage and special festival days were instituted. These new rituals were a pragmatic response to the organizational needs of a growing community. Further, under Guru Arjan, the fifth of the Sikh gurus, the *Adi Granth*— the Sikh scriptures—were compiled, despite the declaration of Nanak that holy books had no value.

The developing Sikh establishment brought them to the notice of the Mughal authorities in the Punjab. Guru Arjan was arrested and died in a Mughal prison in 1606, setting the Sikhs on a more armed and militant path under Guru Hargobind, his successor. More than anything else, however, it was the execution in 1675 of the ninth guru, Tegh Bahadur— on the orders of Aurangzeb himself—that militarized the Sikh community and set them in determined opposition to the Mughal rulers. The great Gobind Singh became the tenth and last guru and did more than any other to organize the Sikhs into an armed and powerful alternative state: his means for this revolution was the foundation of the *Khalsa* (meaning "pure")—the Sikh Brotherhood that served as an army and administration combined. Besides a fresh commitment to the tenets of the faith, membership of the Khalsa required the adoption of new disciplines, including prohibitions on meat slaughtered in the Muslim fashion, tobacco, and sexual relations with Muslim women. New and distinctive badges of Sikh identity were introduced, known as the Five Ks: uncut hair (*kesh*), a comb (*kanga*), a steel bangle (*kara*), a sword (*kirpan*) and breeches (*kaccha*) that did not cover the knees; perhaps surprisingly, these symbols did not include the turban that makes Sikhs so recognizable in the modern world. All male members of the Khalsa were to add *Singh* (lion) to their name, and all female members were to add *Kaur* (princess). Bound together by shared suffering and symbols, the Sikhs were welded into a powerful and martial force.

The establishment of the Khalsa in 1699 marks the beginning of a century of tumult in the Punjab, culminating in the birth of an avowedly Sikh kingdom on the wreckage of Mughal rule. The Khalsa led this separatist resistance movement and came to face opposition not just from the Mughals but from invading outsiders over the decades after its foundation. The path to Sikh dominance of their homeland was tortuous. When Guru Gobind Singh died in 1708 without an heir—the office of guru had become hereditary—there was no obvious successor, Banda Bahadur (Banda "the Brave") was the likeliest to take his place, but his succession was disputed. While the issue was still unsettled, Banda brought the Sikhs into revolt, and stirred the Punjab into such a condition of turbulence that the Mughals were eliminated from the province, and the Sikhs seemed to have achieved a rapid triumph. The Empire struck back, however, and captured Banda himself: his brutal execution in 1716 both restored the Mughals to power in the Punjab and settled the question of the succession to Gobind Singh; thereafter, the status of guru was not to be invested in a person, but rather in the Khalsa as a body and in the Sikh scriptures—a diffused spiritual leadership that at least provided for flexibility in a time of upset.

Banda's execution was followed by determined Mughal persecution of the Sikhs. The Khalsa remained as a troublesome obstacle to Mughal comfort in the Punjab and continued to contest for power over the following years. It was, however, invasion from without that provided the greatest shock to the rule of the Mughals, both in the Punjab and in the rest of the Empire: Nadir Shah of Iran swept into India in a grand raid in 1739. Of Turkish stock, and once briefly a slave of Uzbek raiders, Nadir made himself a renowned brigand chief in northwest Iran through his military skill and expansive personality. His martial abilities were such that he was raised to be the senior general of the last, waning Safavid Shahs; when the dynasty declined beyond rescue amid Afghan invasion, Nadir himself took the throne in 1736. Immediately, he set about recovering Iranian fortunes, making war on the western frontiers to shore up his flank before advancing into Afghanistan to chastize the invaders and to reassert authority over the south of the country. In Kandahar, Nadir became aware of the weakness of the Mughal hold over Kabul and of the troubled state of affairs in the Punjab. Determining to take advantage, Nadir found excuse for a dispute that allowed him to march into Kabul, taking the city against little resistance in June 1738. In the autumn, he set out to invade India.

Although the Mughal administration of the Punjab had deteriorated, beset as it was by continued Sikh assaults, an army was assembled against the expected invasion, and marched into the Khyber Pass; 20,000 soldiers took up positions to close the Pass at Ali Masjid. Faced with an army blocking his way and manning prepared defensive positions, Nadir Shah responded with some bold generalship: declining to engage the enemy in the impossibly narrow Ali Masjid gap, he set out on November 14 to march a force through the difficult mountains outside the Khyber Pass itself, seeking to outflank the Mughal positions and assault them in the rear. Although it required passage through exceptionally tough terrain, this hazardous maneuver was successful. It allowed Nadir to fall unexpectedly upon the enemy in the less protected flanks and rear of their prepared positions in the Khyber; although the fighting was fierce, the Mughal force was defeated. Nadir brought the rest of his army—numbering perhaps as many as 80,000 men—through the Pass itself, and took Peshawar without further opposition a few days later.

Having entered the Punjab, Nadir found little to prevent him advancing, and he captured Lahore in January 1739. The depredations of Nadir and his army added to an already desperate situation in the province, and ruin and lawlessness were rife. No government claimed the authority to dispense justice and order, and the troops of the invader seized all they could. A battle against the ineffectual Mughal emperor, Muhammad Shah, was fought and won at Karnal in February, after which Nadir saw the way clear to press forward on Delhi. Placing the emperor under arrest, and breaking an agreement to return through the Khyber Pass for an indemnity of five million rupees, Nadir ordered the entry into Delhi.

Nadir Shah arrived in Delhi on March 9, 1739, and, like Timur, he left destruction and slaughter in his wake. On the day after the capture of the city, a rumor passed around the bazaars and streets that Nadir had been murdered by a recalcitrant royal lady. This provoked sporadic attacks by the townspeople on the invading soldiers, and individual assaults grew into a full rising. By the evening of March 10, several thousand of Nadir's men are said to have been killed. The king sent in his army to contain the rioters, but by the morning of March 11, he had lost patience: determining in which wards of the city the nuisance had started, Nadir ordered a general massacre. His soldiers fell upon the condemned wards, killing the men regardless of age, dragging the women and children into slavery and burning the houses. The slaughter ran unchecked until the early afternoon, when Muhammad Shah pleaded with his captor to end the killing. When Nadir Shah ordered his troops to halt, thousands of the people of Delhi lay dead: accounts range from 8,000 to the no-doubt exaggerated figure of 400,000. The suffering of the population did not end with the halt to the massacre—the bodies lay unburied for days, spreading disease and filling the city with the stench of decaying flesh. Even when the people were allowed out to buy food, they found little available, as the countryside for miles around had been stripped bare by the invading army.

The invaders remained in Delhi for a few weeks before setting off to return to Afghanistan in early May, leaving a devastated city and a broken Mughal emperor behind them. Nadir annexed Afghanistan and all lands west of the Indus, putting the Khyber Pass back into Iranian hands for the first time since the Sasanian dynasty more than a thousand years before. Besides the lands that he seized from the enfeebled Mughal realm, Nadir—again following the example of Timur—took home craftsmen, including masons, blacksmiths and carpenters. It is impossible to assess the precise value of the booty that Nadir acquired from his raid on Delhi—some authorities put it as high as 700,000,000 rupees—but without question it was an astounding amount, and included hoards of valuable jewelry and luxurious clothing, 300 elephants, 10,000 horses and 10,000 camels. Most especially of all, the haul included the two most valuable treasures in the world: the Koh-i-Noor diamond and the Peacock Throne.

The fabulous diamond had found its way back from Iran into the possession of the Mughals under Shah Jahan. This is entirely appropriate, for Shah Jahan—besides being the richest king in the world—was a great lover of gems and precious stones, a passion he celebrated by commissioning the Peacock Throne. Made of gold and designed to display the splendor of the Mughal dynasty, the throne was over six feet wide and sixteen feet tall, everywhere covered in rubies, garnets, diamonds, pearls and emeralds. The canopy—encrusted with rubies—was supported by twelve pillars of emeralds, each topped with a tree covered in jewels of all kinds, and a pair of peacocks set with gems that gives the throne its name. It took seven years to construct, and Shah Jahan first seated himself upon it in 1634. Estimates of its cost vary, but one expert observer at the time placed its value at over 100,000,000 rupees. Nadir Shah returned across the Khyber Pass in 1739 with what was surely the most precious cargo ever to pass between its narrow walls.

The Sikhs had not the strength to oppose Nadir Shah in an open fight, but they harassed his return journey through the Punjab, attacking his baggage trains and plundering where they could. Neither were they able to prevent a restoration of Mughal power in the Punjab: although greatly weakened by the expensively brutal visitation of Nadir Shah, the Mughal officers of the province recovered a form of administration, to limp on in power for a few more years. This period is remembered by the Sikhs as a time of special distress and depredation. After the invasion of Nadir, the province lay devastated but had no respite from the angry intentions of outsiders.

One such threat came again from the Khyber Pass: Ahmad Shah Abdali, known also by his adopted name of Durrani—"the pearl." A Pathan tribal leader from the west of Afghanistan, Abdali had been a general in the army of Nadir during the Iranian invasion, and had emerged as the king of nascent Afghanistan after the assassination of Nadir Shah by his own soldiers in 1747. Having witnessed the huge profit to be had in Indian adventures, Ahmad Shah Abdali led his forces through the Khyber Pass no fewer than nine times during his reign. Fighting both Mughals and Sikhs, Abdali was never quite able to place a firm rule over the province, but repeated his attempts at enormous cost to the Punjab. By the early 1750s, the assaults of the Afghans and the truculent opposition of the Sikhs brought Mughal power in the Punjab to a close, never to be restored. Along with a presence in northwest India, the Koh-i-Noor also came into the possession of Ahmad Shah Abdali during the dispersal of the treasury of Nadir, again marking a shift of influence in the frontier region. It was in these years that the modern state of Afghanistan began to take shape.

Afghan invasions and Sikh resistance were not the only threats to Mughal rule. The Marathas too were on the rise and intruded to complicate affairs in the Punjab. A martial Hindu people of the Deccan who had fought long wars against Aurangzeb's conquest, the Marathas had since his death continued upon a rising trajectory of power, spreading north from their home territories. By the middle years of the eighteenth century, the Marathas were for a time able to occupy Delhi—the Mughal ruler being reduced to nominal imperium only—and turned their ambitions to the Punjab. Even with the Mughals removed from contention, the province faced a tripartite struggle for power as Afghan, Sikh and Maratha sought supremacy. The climax of this phase of the turbulent century came in 1761 when the Sikhs stood aside on the battlefield of Panipat, to let Ahmad Shah Abdali and the Marathas fight for their hopes of power. Each destroyed the ambitions of the other, and the Sikhs seized the advantage of the destruction.

Although Abdali launched three more invasions through the Khyber Pass, the Sikhs were gaining steadily, and the last Afghan incursion in 1766 was ineffective in recovering rule, despite the occupation of Lahore. Abdali withdrew to Afghanistan in disappointment, never to return to India, but maintained his hold over the strategic mountain border and the Khyber Pass. With Afghan invasions neutralized, Mughal power long ended, and the hopes of the Maratha interlopers over, the Punjab was finally in the hands of Sikhs alone. However, success against outsiders did not bring an end to the years of tumult: lacking a personified guru or other dominant figure to provide unity, Sikh turned upon Sikh. By this time, the Sikhs had become organized into regiments or warrior bands known as *misls*; as they secured mastery over the province, the Punjab was divided between the eleven *misls*, each one becoming a local administration. Without an external threat to keep them united, the *misls* succumbed to territorial disputes and began to fight each other, further perpetuating the misery of the Punjab. For three decades, the internecine destruction continued.

The turbulent century from 1699 was essential not only to the eventual achievement of Sikh power in the Punjab, but also to the formation of Sikh identity. In these unsettled years of hardship, military virtues were placed to the fore—embodied in the Khalsa—and the Sikh community became distinguished by its discipline and strength of conviction. The military and social dynamism of this period spilled over into other areas of life and inspired a growth in devotional literature and a consequent vitality in religious discussions within the community; becoming especially widespread were the *Janam Sakhis*, hagiographical accounts of the life of Guru Nanak. These popular works came to reflect influences of the time, including reflections on the disorderly nature of life in the Punjab and inspirations from other religions. Whereas the teachings of Guru Nanak himself had been little affected by Islam, containing only a smattering of ideas strained through the filter of the traditions in which he grew up, the *Janam Sakhis* contained abundant Sufi influence. Reflecting perhaps the deeper roots that Islam had grown in the Punjab since the time of Nanak, this strain in the *Janam Sakhis* has led to a frequent but erroneous claim that Sikhism represents an attempt to reconcile Hinduism and Islam through a conscious synthesis. This is untrue: Guru Nanak had seen both of the two religions as essentially wrong, rather than as essentially right and needing only correction and reconciliation. Although the *Janam Sakhis* do contain borrowings from Islam—principally in stories of miracles and so on—they do not depart from Nanak in this principle. One of the most famous, the *B40 Janam Sakhi*—so named from its shelf mark in the old India Office Library in London and now held in the British Library—declares that there is neither Hindu nor Muslim: both faiths must be rejected in favor of the creed of Nanak, rather than being absorbed as errant but essentially correct deviations from the truth. The Sufi influences that were absorbed into Sikh thinking during this period must be seen therefore as a natural and modest evolution in the faith rather than a departure from the thought of Nanak.

Such developments continued through the period of infighting, and although violent division remained between the *misls*, by the end of the eighteenth century the Sikh community had acquired a clearly defined faith and a strong sense of purpose. Manifesting the common conviction that the Sikhs were natural rulers of the Punjab, and offering a powerful figure around whom they could come together, was Ranjit Singh, a *misl* commander who would unite the warring Sikhs and establish a kingdom.

Ranjit Singh was born in 1780 and lost an eye to smallpox at a very early age, a disease that also left his face ravaged by scars. His father was the leader of the Shukerchakia *misl* and died when Ranjit was just twelve, leaving the boy—already highly experienced in war—to assume command. The abilities of the young leader rapidly became evident as his success on the field of both battle and politics allowed him gradually to attach the fragmented *misls* to him. Several years of steady achievement culminated in his capture of Lahore in 1799, and Ranjit was acclaimed as king; although the divisions between Sikhs were not yet ended, this marks the foundation of a united Sikh kingdom, and the symbolic end to the century of discord. Some resistance from disgruntled *misl* leaders continued— requiring fresh fighting—until, in 1808, Ranjit Singh was proclaimed Maharajah—"Great King"—and the Sikhs of the Punjab were finally joined together in an avowedly Sikh kingdom. It had been a long time in the making, many years having passed since opposition to Mughal rule began and since the foundation of the Khalsa, but at last the conviction of rule had been realized and the Sikhs were supreme in their homeland.

The establishment of unrivaled rule in the Punjab did not, however, provide for the removal of all threats: the Afghans were still in charge of the frontier and regularly took the opportunity to raid Sikh territory. In these early years of the nineteenth century, Afghanistan was torn apart with civil war as the multitudinous grandsons of Ahmad Shah Abdali fought each other for the throne. The kingdom descended into a period of vicious scheming in which princes were killed or blinded by their own brothers and no depravity was unexplored in the pursuit of the crown. Some of these royal pretenders sought succor from Ranjit, he being the new regional power most possessed of the capacity to assist their ambitions; one such supplicant was Shah Shujah, for a time king in Kabul before being deposed by Dost Muhammad. Ranjit agreed to ensure the safety of Shah Shujah, who then went into comfortable exile in British territory; the price of his rescue was the Koh-i-Noor. One of the great symbols of power in northern India was now in Sikh hands.

The other, however, was not: the Khyber Pass remained in Afghan territory, despite regular outbreaks of fighting between the Sikhs and their neighbors. In these first decades of the century, Peshawar changed hands several times, and the Sikh armies had some successes, but while the critical points of the frontier were out of their control, security would be elusive. It was not until late in the reign of Ranjit Singh that an attempt was made to fortify a border outside Peshawar in the hope of ending costly Afghan incursions. In 1836, the powerful Sikh general Hari Singh took charge of revitalizing the frontier protections and built a fort at Jamrud, just outside Peshawar on the Khyber road. The rounded, pinkish castle that stands there today is of later British construction, but the value of a fortification at the site is clear, commanding as it does the approach to the mouth of the Khyber Pass.

Immediately upon its completion, Jamrud Fort became an alarm that set the Afghans on a path to war. The King of Kabul, Dost Muhammad, understood the fortifying of the frontier to mean that the Sikhs were planning an invasion of his territory and the capture of the Khyber Pass. Accordingly, he levied his forces—declaring a jihad against the infidel Sikhs—and advanced through the Khyber Pass in the spring of 1837, placing Jamrud Fort under siege on April 23. Although the Sikh forces in the fort were under strength, and Hari Singh lay ill in Peshawar, stout resistance prevented the Afghan army taking the fort, even after heavy artillery bombardment; around 1,000 Sikhs held off an Afghan force of perhaps 25,000. Such an imbalance in numbers, however, made the Sikh position dangerous, as the Afghan army cut off all supplies of food and water and continued their shelling of the fort. The situation began to look hopeless. Sikh commanders inside the besieged stronghold met and decided that their only chance was to get a message to Hari Singh in Peshawar and trust in his bringing reinforcements to their aid. A volunteer was sought for the hazardous mission of taking a dispatch through the siege lines, and it was a woman, Harsharan Kaur, who came forward. Accepting the risk of her death, Harsharan made her prayers, disguised herself as a dog, and set out in the middle of the night, walking on all fours, picking her way carefully through the Afghan encampments.

Against the odds, she was successful, and arrived in Peshawar several hours later: Hari Singh immediately ordered the cannon shot that would tell the besieged that rescue was on the way, and raised himself from his sickbed to set out to lift the siege. With his forces, Hari Singh advanced on Jamrud and heavy fighting took place outside the fort; eventually, the Afghan army began to lose ground and the Sikhs gained the advantage. Forced to raise the siege, the Afghans retreated the short distance into the Khyber. Once inside the Pass, the natural defensive excellence of the rocky cliffs provided refuge and respite for the retreating army, and hard fighting followed: for some time, both the Sikh and Afghan forces were static, none making headway amid such terrain. Eventually—despite the death of Hari Singh during this fighting—the Afghan forces withdrew and the Khyber Pass was finally in Sikh hands.

With their frontier now fixed upon the natural mountain border of the Subcontinent, the Sikhs had secured their kingdom and reached their apogee under Maharajah Ranjit Singh. Through long years of chaos— introduced in part by invasions through the Khyber Pass—Sikh rule had come to triumph, a native Indian state emerging from internal decay and outside invasion, just as the Mauryan Empire had done more than two thousand years before. This success was, however, long in coming but short in life: Ranjit Singh had taken the Sikhs to their most glorious days, but his kingdom would not long outlast him. Just a few years after his death in 1839, Sikh rule in the Punjab was threatened by the rising new power in India: the British Raj.

CHAPTER TEN

The British Raj

British soldiers fighting in Afghanistan: The Illustrated London News, *1880*

When you're wounded and left on Afghanistan's plains
An' the women come out to cut up what remains
Jest roll to your rifle and blow out your brains
An' go to your Gawd like a soldier
The Young British Soldier, RUDYARD KIPLING, 1892

Carved into memorial stones and mounted in clusters in the rocks, the insignia of each of the many regiments that manned this furthest outpost of the British Empire sit above the road in the Khyber Pass (see color plate 12). On my own foray into the Khyber, I saw the badges of the Gordon Highlanders, the Dorset Regiment, the South Wales Borderers, the Royal Sussex Regiment and many others. Since 1947, the British insignia have been supplemented by those of their Pakistani successors: stars and crescents have joined the plumes, horns and castles. All these regimental badges—British and Pakistani—are well maintained. Regular coats of paint keep alive old memories, and the attention they evidently receive makes them seem even more poignant. As I looked upon them, I thought of the British soldiers who had come to fight and die at the edge of empire, of the Scottish highlanders who had been taken thousands of miles from their own mountains to guard those of another continent.

To understand how British soldiers came to die in the Khyber we must go back far beyond the days commemorated by these memorial stones, to the closing years of Tudor England. On the last day of 1600, Queen Elizabeth signed a royal charter to bring into being the trading concern that would grow into an Asian empire: the Honorable East India Company. Blessed with a monopoly of English—and, later, British—commerce with India and the eastern world, its merchants set out to establish trade with lands that were long months of sailing from their headquarters in Leadenhall Street in the City of London. In this era, several European countries were working to extend their reach into the world beyond their home waters, and it was in competition with Portuguese, French and Dutch rivals that English traders strove to master the supply of the luxuries of Asia—spices, perfumes, textiles and tea. In the course of these commercial efforts, the East India Company established trading posts—principally Bombay on the west coast of the Indian Subcontinent, and Calcutta and Madras on the east—from which its influence spread inland through the decades as it grew in wealth and power. Eventually, more than two centuries after its foundation, the East India Company—the Hon. EIC, or "John Company" to its employees—had evolved into a most curious entity: a trading corporation, driven by the pursuit of profit, that had become the ruler of India and that governed its population of millions.

As a commercial undertaking run by a Court of Directors that was ever anxious to avoid needless expense, the East India Company undertook governmental administration with reluctance, and only when it was considered an unavoidable necessity in order to protect its business interests. Guided by this principle, the responsibilities of government were evaded for many decades, even while the Company acquired an army to guard its trading stations and to enforce the numerous trade treaties negotiated with local rulers. Military power and the necessary practice of diplomacy drew the Company into regional politics, however, lending weight to friends where it was profitable to do so amid the fresh states and principalities forming out of the remains of the declining Mughal Empire during the eighteenth century. Its army—largely Indian soldiers commanded by British officers—was on occasion deployed on behalf of such allies, essentially as mercenaries. The Company never forgot its commercial aims.

It was just such an involvement in local power plays that brought the avoidance of rule by the Company to an end. In the early 1750s, business rivalries had amplified into war when the British and French allied with opposing sides in a succession struggle in the Carnatic, a region on the east coast of the Subcontinent, modern Karnataka. It was through his bold march from Madras to capture Arcot, the Carnatic capital, in 1751 and his relief of a British force besieged at Trichinopoli, that Robert Clive—Clive of India—came to prominence. After returning to England in 1753, where he was celebrated as a universal hero, Clive went back to India in 1755 as a lieutenant-colonel and governor of a Company station in Bengal, Fort St. David. The outbreak of the Seven Years War in 1756 caused European politics to intrude upon trade in the east: with Britain and France again at war, India became a proxy battlefield for distant squabbles. Siraj-ad-Daulah, the Nawab of Bengal, allied himself to France and attacked and seized the British trading post at Calcutta, imprisoning 146 British captives in the legendary Black Hole of Calcutta, from which only twenty-three emerged alive. In response, Clive sallied out of Fort St. David with a diminutive army and defeated the Nawab in battle outside Calcutta. Clive's next victory at the battle of Plassey in June 1757 left Bengal at the disposal of the British.

In 1760, with the Seven Years War continuing, Clive was forced by ill-health to return to England for rest, and he was also granted a peerage. By the time of his return in 1765, the war was over and the status of Bengal remained unsettled. It was through Clive's decision to take formal political power in Bengal into Company hands, rather than govern through a puppet nawab, that British rule in India—the British Raj—properly began. It is for this reason that Robert Clive can be considered the founder of the British Indian Empire.

In the next several decades, British influence and rule spread over the Subcontinent. Calcutta, Madras and Bombay, the principal trading posts, became administrative centers of growing power and were given an official identity as "presidencies," overseen by a governor general in Calcutta. The lands ruled by each of the presidencies were gradually extended until they stretched across India from coast to coast, forming continuous arcs of Company territory. As this expansion progressed during the late eighteenth century, the British government increased its control over the Company, though it remained a commercial endeavor: new territories were—in theory—only taken under Company rule if business reasons so dictated.

The Company continued to avoid the expensive responsibilities of government where possible, and developed a battery of techniques of informal control to ensure that its power was recognized even where it did not rule. The calculated use of force against bordering states, careful grants of subsidies to friends and intricate treaties with Indian rulers allowed British influence to be exerted without the military conquest that promised to disrupt trade. One important device was the use of the last Mughal emperors to cover Company actions with a veil of ancient authority. By the early nineteenth century, the Mughal dynasty was entirely reduced in its power: it held purchase only over Delhi itself and was dependent upon subsidies from the British. Nonetheless, it still possessed an imperial lineage and grand titles, status symbols that the Company employed to its advantage on occasion by taking care to issue decrees and collect revenue in the name of the Mughal emperor. By such brazen pretences, the parvenu traders attached to themselves the aura of a once magnificent dynasty. The glories of an ancient set of interlopers were seized by a new.

An arrangement that had particular value throughout India was the use of treaties with individual princely states in which the Company took over all outward aspects of politics—trade, war and foreign relations—while leaving the domestic management of the territory to the prince, assisted by a British Resident at court. The Indian ruler thus had his position guaranteed by the rising power, and the British secured a compliant ally with little expenditure. At the height of its power in the late nineteenth century, one third of the British Raj was composed of such princely states.

The Residents who handled British affairs in these allied territories were generally drawn from what developed into an elite cadre of officers from the Political Department of the Company. Known broadly as "politicals," they were, typically, ambitious young army officers who had acquired sufficient knowledge of local languages to secure a prized and potentially lucrative position as an assistant in the Department. When posted to a princely state, they would acquire great responsibility early in their career, taking charge of Company relations with the host kingdom and conducting diplomacy with neighboring principalities as required. As the conduits of intelligence, they could wield significant influence over the formulation of policy. In those princely states in the front line of the advancing British frontier, this monopoly on information could be dangerous: when combined with the ambition of many young politicals, it often led to expensive departures from the standard Company refusal to acquire territory except where commercially advantageous. Committed by their position to argue the importance of their area in British strategic calculations, and generally keen to place themselves in the heat of affairs, politicals tended to agitate for annexation and advance, sometimes more for the advantage of their own careers than for the benefit of the Company. Often dynamic and forceful characters, and deeply knowledgeable about the language and culture of India, the politicals were crucial to the changing shape of the British Raj and came to the fore especially in the 1830s and 1840s when the North West Frontier was being shaped. The men of these years—Alexander Burnes, James Abbot and John Nicholson first among them—formed the great generation of the political officer.

With these politicals often in the vanguard, the Company extended its control with businesslike efficiency, through diplomacy, negotiation and the suborning of allies. All such means were, of course, backed by the steady threat of military action. By the turn of the nineteenth century, the British Raj could field an army of over 150,000 men, combining native regiments raised from Company territories with British units hired from the Government for use in India. When it was deemed necessary, war was pursued enthusiastically: major conflicts were undertaken against, among others, Tipu Sultan of Mysore in 1799 and—under the command of Arthur Wellesley, later Duke of Wellington—against the Marathas in the early years of the nineteenth century.

As British territory continued to grow, frontier problems and treaty relationships with Indian rulers became commensurately more complex and anxiety about the security of Company territory grew accordingly. Aided by the politicals, such nervousness in the official sphere began to form into a "frontier logic" that argued for expansion into bordering regions in order to protect existing British possessions, quickly followed by fresh arguments to expand into the new border areas to ensure the safety of the recently acquired lands. This mechanism led to continuing advances, and by 1818 the Company was unarguably the paramount power in India. British territories—ruled either directly by Company civil servants or indirectly through allied princes—stretched across India from the Gangetic plains in the north to the southern tip of the Subcontinent, and from Bengal in the east to the Sutlej river in the west. This river formed the border between the Raj and its only potential rival for power in India: the Punjab of Ranjit Singh.

At the turn of the nineteenth century, the British knew little about the Punjab since their gradual advance across the Subcontinent had not yet brought the Sikhs close enough to make them a factor in Company calculations. They had not appreciated the growing strength of Ranjit Singh and the threat that he could pose to the developing British power in northern India. With the extension of the British frontier to the Jumna river in 1803, however, the Punjab suddenly became an area of concern: Ranjit Singh was striking southeast just as the Company was striking northwest. Between Ranjit and the British—in the lands bounded by the Sutlej and Jumna rivers—stood a number of independent Sikh chiefs who had as yet avoided absorption into the consolidating kingdom of Ranjit Singh. Sitting between two expansionary empires, the independent Sikhs became the unwilling focus of tension between them.

In 1805 a treaty was agreed by Ranjit and the British that settled some matters arising from their new proximity but left the issue of the independent Sikhs unresolved. Aware of the likelihood that the British would seek to curtail his freedom of action on his eastern frontier, Ranjit sought to accelerate his efforts in this direction in an attempt to seize as much advantage as he could before the opportunity was curtailed by war or diplomacy. He launched two campaigning seasons against the Sikh chiefs beyond the Sutlej in 1806 and 1807, and made gains that alarmed the Company. In response, the governor general in Calcutta sent a diplomatic mission to Lahore in the summer of 1808—under Charles Metcalfe, a rising young officer of the Political Department—charged with gaining the friendship of Ranjit Singh and his agreement to assist the British if they should come under attack from an outside invader. The problem of the independent Sikhs was to be quietly forgotten, but if Ranjit forced the matter, Metcalfe was empowered to grant him a free hand in the area. The essential aim of the Company at the time was to ensure that Ranjit Singh remained a friendly neighbor.

The suspicious—almost hostile—response of Ranjit to these overtures hardened the Company's attitude to the Sikhs. Ranjit—newly raised to the status of Maharajah of the Punjab—was, however, reluctant to accept any treaty obligations that limited his frontiers. Accordingly, he sought to evade Metcalfe and set off across the Sutlej for the campaigning season in September 1808, leaving the political to trail after him. Faced with a refusal to come to terms, and judging that Ranjit would be unlikely to accept the role of quiet ally, the Company changed its approach: Metcalfe was issued revised instructions that transformed him from a meek supplicant into a threatening herald of British ire. Having decided that the territory of the independent Sikh chiefs could not be allowed to fall into the hands of

Ranjit Singh, the Company declared that they were under British protection. Metcalfe now chased Ranjit around his kingdom repeating the British demands whenever he gained a royal audience; to add steel to his diplomacy, a Company force was ordered to advance toward the Sutlej. By early 1809, Ranjit had become thoroughly alarmed, and now felt that he needed a treaty with the British to secure his own position.

The Treaty of Amritsar of April 1809 settled matters between the British and the Punjab, and established an alliance that was to last for over three decades. Under its terms, Ranjit agreed to abandon his claims over the Sutlej Sikhs and accepted their new status as British protectees; he further agreed to maintain only limited forces in his own possessions beyond the Sutlej river. In return, the British would raise no objection to expansion of the Sikh kingdom in any other direction. It was thus the 1809 Treaty that determined the manner of the growth of Ranjit's kingdom over the subsequent years: to the north into the Himalayan hill states, to the west against the Afghans in Peshawar and to the south against the independent Muslim states of Sind and Baluchistan; never to the south-east against British territory.

A decade after the treaty with the Maharajah, the British had consolidated their paramount hold over India; with the majority of the Subcontinent suborned to its will through war or diplomacy, and a continuous and stable defensive frontier now resting on the Sutlej, the strategic thinking of the Company came to focus on threats from outside India itself. Such fears were not entirely new: officials naturally had been very aware of the repeated Afghan invasions of the Punjab during the eighteenth century and had also feared—until the defeat of Napoleon—that the French might invade overland in alliance with Iran or Afghanistan, or work to provoke rebellion among those Indian rulers allied by treaty to the British. Uneasiness about internal disturbance never disappeared, but the supreme anxiety became the possibility of invasion across the mountains of the northwest, following the pattern of irruptions that had troubled India throughout its history. When the French threat receded, it was soon replaced by another source of constant alarm: as Russia conquered south into the Caucasus Mountains and Central Asia, a distant threat seemed to be coalescing. The continuing growth of the Russian Empire in the middle years of the nineteenth century gave rise to what would become celebrated as the "Great Game": the anxious Anglo-Russian struggle for influence in the Central Asian lands that lay between the advancing Russian border and the North West Frontier of the British Raj. Whether a Russian invasion of India was a real danger is highly debatable, but fear of it often seems to have been used by politicals and other officials to justify their own schemes. Nonetheless, the Russian threat became the significant feature of Indian strategic discourse throughout the nineteenth century and the driving motive behind many feats of adventure and espionage by energetic politicals.

The Punjab became an essential part of such calculations. Reluctant alliance with the British in 1809 had given it the status of a buffer state, a benign territory that insulated British lands from potential enemies further afield. As a consequence, as long as the alliance with Ranjit held, the British welcomed the expansion of his kingdom and the strengthening of his military power. His defenses had become proxy British defenses, and the North West Frontier of British India was protected by the Sikh soldiers of the Maharajah.

Indeed, not all of the soldiers of Ranjit were Sikhs: Muslims and Hindus from the Punjab were well represented in his army, and other groups, such as Gurkhas from the Himalayas, were recruited as the Sikh kingdom expanded. Neither were all the men of the Maharajah even from India: keen to develop a modern army capable of adding to his lands and—if it came to it—resisting the British, Ranjit Singh employed numerous European mercenaries and adventurers. The final defeat of Napoleon at Waterloo in 1815 meant that many thousands of soldiers were released from service in Europe and became available for hire. Ranjit took advantage and hired perhaps as many as 200 European soldiers, from generals to artillery gunners. These men helped to transform the Sikh army—already fearsome and professional—into a modern force during the years of peace with Britain: by the 1830s, it had become an effective army drilled and dressed in European fashion. French and Italian generals, including Allard, Ventura and Court, were at the forefront of this effort. Most famous among them was General Paulo Avitabile, the eccentric and ruthless Italian governor of Peshawar who became renowned for his enthusiasm for hanging wrongdoers, whether proven or only suspected. Observers from the time speak of large gibbets at all the gates of the city, each kept well stocked with ten or twenty fresh corpses. Peshawar under Avitabile was a relatively quiet city.

While most of Ranjit's foreign officers were unemployed refugees from Napoleon's army, they included a small number of British adventurers. One was Colonel Leslie, a shadowy figure (neither the title Colonel nor the name Leslie were genuine) who was for a time the warden of the Khyber Pass in the 1830s. From his headquarters at Ali Masjid Fort, Colonel Leslie (also known at times as Rattray) levied tolls on passing caravans and delighted in damming the stream through the Khyber Pass that supplied Jamrud Fort with water, demanding payment to restore the flow. It appears that Colonel Leslie converted to Islam and took the name Fida Muhammad Khan, an opportunistic move that disgusted the surrounding tribesmen. He was described, with evident distaste, by Captain John Wood, a British political at work in the Khyber region in 1837:

> An ill-conditioned, dissolute-looking Englishman, slipshod, turbaned and robed in a sort of Afghan deshabille—having more the look of a dissipated priest than a military man.

The presence of Captain Wood in the Khyber was not accidental: he was an assistant to Alexander Burnes, the celebrated political and the driving force of British policy toward Afghanistan at the time. A talented, ambitious and boastful Scot, Burnes advocated the bold extension of British influence in the country, and indeed further afield in Central Asia. When he arrived in Kabul in September 1837, he began sending out his junior politicals around the region, aiming to turn Afghanistan into the hub of a new Central Asian political system that Britain—and thus Burnes himself—would control. Concerned by the prospect of Russian or Iranian influence in Afghanistan, Burnes wanted to create a grand network of active British political agents who could forestall any hostile intentions toward British interests. One such concern had arisen when the Afghans had fought the Sikhs earlier in the year: an Afghan threat to the Sikh kingdom also threatened British India. Arguments for interference in Afghanistan were thus strengthened, and it was the growing dominance of Burnes and his supporters that set the British on a course to war in Afghanistan within the year.

In the meantime, Burnes and his politicals were busy, conducting diplomacy with fractious Afghan leaders and gathering information to prepare the way for an aggressive new policy. It was during this period that one of the earliest British maps of the Khyber Pass was produced: Lieutenant Robert Leech of the Bombay Engineers, a fat and amiable assistant of Burnes, made his *Reconnoitering Survey of the Khyber Pass from Jumrood to Dhaka* in 1837 (see color plate 13). A simple plan of the mountain contours that rise about the Pass, Leech's map charts the entire length of the Khyber from Jamrud to Dakka and highlights the critical importance of Ali Masjid for controlling the Pass. Significantly, the map was copied for printing and distribution in March 1842 in the aftermath of the greatest military disaster ever to befall the British: the retreat from Kabul.

The war that precipitated this calamity came about through the divergent strategies of British officials. In Kabul in late 1837, Burnes was continuing to advocate active intervention beyond the Punjab through a strong alliance with the Afghan king, Dost Muhammad. He argued that this friendship should be cemented by granting him Peshawar at the expense of the Sikhs. In December 1837, a Russian envoy named Vitkevich arrived in Kabul with his own set of proposals for the Afghans, a development that caused Burnes great anxiety. Although it could not be known what Vitkevich sought from Dost Muhammad, Burnes was certainly prepared to believe the worst and multiplied his passionate appeals to his seniors in India for action in Afghanistan. However, the governor general, Lord Auckland, would not accept that the Russian presence in Kabul was a serious threat and was in no mind to undertake what Burnes demanded. At the turn of 1838, Auckland informed Burnes that his strategy would not be adopted, and nothing would be offered to Dost Muhammad: he could see no danger from Russia or Iran, and felt that little value would be found in an alliance with Kabul.

In just a few months, this seemingly firm decision was reversed entirely: the indecisive Auckland was beset with appeals from officials in India urging grand schemes beyond the Punjab while London remained unhelpfully quiet. Burnes, of course, played a strident part in this campaign. He took advantage of his control of the flow of intelligence from the country to engineer a version of events that best suited his project.

What is more, he had an ally in William Macnaghten, chief political secretary to the governor general himself, who had his own reasons for advocating a bold policy. An intelligent man who was sadly (and, it would later prove, fatally) unsuited to diplomacy, it appears that Macnaghten was nagged into ambition by his wife. An aggressive official policy might serve to burnish his personal aspirations, including the grant of a baronetcy.

These advocates of a forward policy were assisted in the spring of 1838 by Dost Muhammad himself. After several months of unproductive discussions with Burnes (who had been playing his weak hand for all he could), in April the king made a great show of a public audience with Vitkevich, who had been kept on the margins in Kabul while talks with the British drifted on. It seemed that the Afghans had made their choice, albeit reluctantly; feeling vindicated in his warnings of the Russian threat in Afghanistan, Burnes abandoned his hopes of alliance and left the city. In the resulting flurry of politicking in the highest ranks of the British Indian government, a forward policy in Afghanistan was at last decided, with a crucial and expensive difference: having lost the chance of an alliance with Dost Muhammad, the British would replace him with their own King of Kabul. To this end, Shah Shujah was dragged from his comfortable exile in British India and prepared for a return to power. An army was slowly assembled for the invasion of Afghanistan.

Having finally decided that intervention was necessary, Auckland planned to pass the burden of the military action to Ranjit Singh and his powerful army, offering a subsidy and the promise of some Afghan territory in return. A Sikh force accompanied by British officers would advance into Afghanistan through the Khyber Pass and install Shah Shujah on the throne in Kabul. Macnaghten was placed in charge of securing Ranjit's agreement to this plan but was entirely outwitted by the Maharajah. The outcome of their negotiations was that the British would supply the great majority of the necessary army, while the Sikhs would contribute a token force for which they were to receive a generous payment. Furthermore, Ranjit forbade the use of the Khyber route into Afghanistan, being alarmed at the thought of a British army passing through his kingdom. So, instead of a Sikh army taking the direct Khyber road to Kabul, a British army would have to travel the long road through the Bolan Pass, all the way remaining outside Sikh lands. Access to this southerly route required the British force to journey through the dry and bandit-ridden territories of Sind and Baluchistan. Here, at least, British diplomacy did not fail, and agreement for passage and provision was successfully forced upon the *amirs* of these regions.

In the later months of 1838 and into the following year, an invasion force was drawn together from the Company armies in Bengal and Bombay. In April 1839, by sea passages and long marches, this "Army of the Indus," as it was known, assembled at Quetta, a town in Baluchistan lying to the south of the Afghan border. The invasion of Afghanistan began with a march on Kandahar, which was taken on April 25 with little resistance. Here the army paused for two months before continuing north, advancing on Ghazni and taking it by storm in July. Shortly afterward, on August 7, Kabul was captured and Shah Shujah was proclaimed king; Dost Muhammad had already fled the city. The ease of victory appeared to vindicate the adventurous scheme, and Macnaghten took up his post as resident in Kabul.

For a time, it seemed that the endeavor was indeed successful, and Macnaghten was awarded his coveted baronetcy, ruling Afghanistan as Sir William. There were, however, hints of future trouble. The unpopularity of Shah Shujah came as something of a revelation to the British, who had planned to install their friendly king and then withdraw immediately to avoid the cost of maintaining a Company army on active service abroad. With the new king finding little support among his own countrymen, however, he was entirely dependent upon the British, and the Company army would have to stay.

Keeping a British force in Afghanistan multiplied the importance of the direct Khyber road between Kabul and India, since official dispatches, reinforcements and supplies could not efficiently be sent around the lengthy southern route through the Bolan Pass and Kandahar. The Pathan tribes in the Khyber Pass and in eastern Afghanistan had, however, refused to cooperate with the invaders and had resisted the passage of the Sikh contingent at the opening of the war: the Khyber Pass had to be forced, at some cost. Such resistance promised to become a troublesome burden on a much-needed road, but the British solved the problem by paying the Pathan leaders an enormous subsidy of £8,000 in order to keep the Khyber and the road to Kabul open. It was during this time that one of the most

Afghan tribesmen in battle: The Illustrated London News, *1879*

curious of all passages through the Khyber took place: in 1841, the 27th British Native Infantry escorted some 600 women from Shah Shujah's harem all the way from Peshawar to Kabul. Shepherding these royal wives and concubines past opportunistic tribesmen and through arduous terrain was—to say the least—a delicate exercise in applied diplomacy.

The British maintained their increasingly fragile presence in Kabul for over two years, and had their hopes raised in late 1840 when Dost Muhammad surrendered himself after a failed rebellion. He was taken into exile in India. Besides such minor successes, however, the British position was steadily becoming an embarrassment as the unpopularity of Shah Shujah grew and as the expense to the Company mounted. In an effort to trim costs during the autumn of 1841, Macnaghten halved the size of his army by sending a brigade home to India. He also halved the subsidy payments to the Pathan chiefs. This move was a dreadful mistake: the unhappy Pathans responded by denying passage to British soldiers, messengers and supplies. With the Sikhs unable to secure the Khyber, the position in Afghanistan, already uneasy, became precarious. In an effort to display a lasting commitment to the country, and to keep the soldiers happy through the long months of garrison duty, the British had brought their wives and families to Kabul: altogether, with soldiers, wives and camp followers, the British presence in the city numbered some 16,000 persons. With the Pathans closing the road against them, the invaders were now trapped inside Afghanistan.

From this time on, the British in Kabul rapidly became a focus for discontent, and in November 1841 this resentment burst on to the streets of the city. The British Residency was attacked by a mob of townsmen and several British officials were killed, Alexander Burnes among them. Sir William Macnaghten and General Elphinstone, the old and ailing commander of the British forces in Kabul, failed to make a resolute effort to put down the rebellion and it grew into a wholesale revolt. The rising rapidly found a promising leader in a son of Dost Muhammad, named Muhammad Akbar, who had raced to Kabul from his hiding place in the mountains as soon as he heard the news. Before long, the entire British contingent was pressed into their cantonment on the edge of the city: they were now under siege. Since defense works had not been built, the camp could not be defended against a serious assault and a political solution was essential. Macnaghten made an attempt to play off Muhammad Akbar against the other leaders of the rising but once again his diplomacy failed. Riding out to parley with Muhammad Akbar late in December, Macnaghten succeeded only in being shot dead. With the position now desperate, the Afghans allowed the British to vacate Kabul and to begin the journey to India via Jalalabad and the Khyber Pass. They did not, however, give any guarantees for safe passage or protection.

The march out of Kabul began on January 6, 1842. With the Afghan tribes intent on blocking their progress, the prospects looked grim as the long convoy set off at the height of the vicious Afghan winter. The catastrophe was total. On January 13, a wounded and exhausted Dr. Brydon staggered into the British camp at Jalalabad on a horse that was barely alive, bringing news of calamity. He was almost the sole member of the column of 16,000 soldiers, families and camp followers to reach safety at Jalalabad, and had been allowed to escape alive only to report the disaster to his countrymen. The Army of the Indus had been comprehensively destroyed as they struggled through the snowy passes, decimated by sniping Afghan tribesmen and the frozen weather. As the convoy gained distance from Kabul, it began to lose any semblance of order or discipline, and stragglers fell behind, only to be picked off with ease. Over the next few days, the column broke up into isolated fragments that became even more vulnerable targets for the Afghans. From the hills about the road the tribesmen used their *jezails*—long-barreled and accurate muskets—to ruthless effect, cutting down soldiers and wives without fear of retaliation. Alongside the jezail, the *talwar*—the powerful curved sword of the region—became especially feared among the British.

At Gandamak, a number of men of the 44th Foot—one of the few regiments of European soldiers in the Army of the Indus—gathered on a small hill to make their last stand, an action that has become the abiding image of the retreat from Kabul. Perhaps fifty bedraggled and weary soldiers stood together, back-to-back on their modest hilltop in their famous British red coats, facing countless tribesmen. Wrapped in furs and blankets against the fierce cold, the soldiers in shakos and officers in flat undress caps, the 44th offered their final resistance. To protect the regimental color to the last, Captain Souter wound it around his waist, leaving both arms free for fighting to the end. Armed with only a few bayoneted muskets, little ammunition and the swords of their officers, these men warded off repeated assaults by Afghan tribesmen until gradually they were killed, falling among their dead comrades one by one.

More than anything, it is the retreat from Kabul that has formed the lasting idea of Afghanistan in the British imagination. It became renowned as a wild and deadly place, populated by savage tribesmen, and from which few intruders emerge alive. The poetry of Rudyard Kipling—himself born in India—made a powerful contribution to this view: in his poem *The Young British Soldier*, written in a later generation but reflecting an image of Afghanistan that arose from the slaughter of the Army of the Indus, he expressed the seeming inevitability of death on the plains of Afghanistan. Moreover, in this extract from *Arithmetic on the Frontier*, Kipling speaks of the accurate strike of a jezail bullet as an almost unavoidable fate for a British officer on the frontier:

> A scrimmage in a Border Station—
> A canter down some dark defile—
> Two thousand pounds of education
> Drops to a ten-rupee jezail—
> The Crammer's boast, the Squadron's pride,
> Shot like a rabbit in a ride!
>
> No proposition Euclid wrote,
> No formulae the textbooks know,
> Will turn the bullet from your coat,
> Or ward the tulwar's downward blow
> Strike hard who cares—shoot straight who can –
> The odds are on the cheaper man.

Literature was the response of another age; the immediate reaction to news of the disaster was the assembling of a fresh force—the Army of Retribution—at Peshawar, ready for an advance through the Khyber Pass; little thought was given this time to Sikh sensibilities as British regiments marched through the Punjab to join General Pollock, the commander charged with securing revenge. Forced by the winter snows to delay the new invasion, it was not until May 1842 that the Army of Retribution set out, fought its way through the Khyber Pass armed with copies of Lieutenant Leech's map and relieved the British garrison at Jalalabad. Together with the troops still at Kandahar, two British armies now stood on Afghan soil, but for revenge they needed to take Kabul. Accordingly, while General Pollock advanced on the city from Jalalabad, General Nott marched from Kandahar, and the two armies reached Kabul only two days apart in September. The city fell to them with little resistance.

From the recaptured city, columns were dispatched to attack and ravage the areas that had caused the British the most problems months before; villages were destroyed and the male inhabitants shot or bayoneted where they were found. The righteous anger of revenge spurred the British and Indian soldiers to a summer of terrible acts of violence: murder, rape and looting were common. In Kabul itself, it was decided to leave a lasting mark of British retribution by destroying the ancient bazaar, a roofed commercial quarter that had hosted many generations of merchants from across Afghanistan, India and Central Asia. Army engineers blew up the structure with gunpowder and two days later, on October 12, the Army of Retribution withdrew from a smoking and pillaged Kabul. Retracing their steps was, however, something of a second retreat for this invasion force: passing along roads strewn with the bodies of their comrades slain a few months before, and harried continually by the snipers of the same tribesmen, this journey was a long way from the triumphal return of a victorious army.

Besides the cruel recovery of some prestige for British arms, a curious piece of salvage was brought back to India: what were said to be the gates of Somnath, torn from the great temple by Mahmud of Ghazni over eight centuries before. The new governor general, Lord Ellenborough, decided to make a great show of returning this booty to India and ordered their removal from the tomb of the conqueror at Ghazni. Despite firm evidence that the stone pieces could not possibly be the ancient gates, Ellenborough insisted, having conceived a plan for a strange attempt at public relations: the gates would be paraded around India before being restored to the temple of Somnath to demonstrate to the Hindu population that Britain was a protector of their interests and a worthy ruler of their country. To widespread ridicule among the British, and a generally baffled reception from townspeople everywhere, the gates were toured around India, escorted by the recently promoted Major Robert Leech, enjoying a welcome rest from duty on the frontier. Since the temple at Somnath had long fallen into ruin, the gates could not be returned there and so were quietly laid to rest in Agra, a bathetic end to a comically misconceived attempt to exploit symbols for political ends.

Not long after the Army of Retribution completed its passage through the Khyber back into India, Dost Muhammad journeyed along it into Afghanistan. Shah Shujah had been assassinated by Afghan rivals in the spring of 1842 and the British could see no purpose in preventing Dost Muhammad from returning to recover his throne. The entire Afghan strategy had failed. With Dost Muhammad reigning in Kabul once again, the forward policy of Burnes and Macnaghten had succeeded only in ending many lives, disgruntling the Afghans and damaging Britain's reputation. Added to the instability in the Punjab that had followed the death of Ranjit Singh in June 1839, the collapse of the Afghan scheme left British India with a very uncertain frontier. The next few years saw a significant reorganization of British policy and dramatic changes in the borders of Company territory.

The first of these transformations was the annexation in 1843 of Sind, the independent territory that had allowed the Army of the Indus to pass through on its way to invade Afghanistan. Coming immediately after the failings in Afghanistan, many observers felt that this action made Britain seem like a bully who, having been kicked in the street, returns home to beat his wife. There was no justification for this action except Britain's changing strategic needs. Attitudes to the Punjab were changing too. The death of Ranjit Singh had introduced a period of murderous rivalry between his competing heirs until finally his youngest son, the infant Dalip Singh, became Maharajah in 1844. The instability caused by the years of fratricide, and the uncertainties attached to the rule of a boy-king, made the Punjab a much less attractive ally. The Sikh army gained an important role in politics and, deprived of its commanding leader, became a major source of disorder. Tensions arose with the British across the border as the Punjab became anarchic; official opinion began to drift toward a military solution to the unstable confusion on the frontier.

In the event, it was the Sikh army that provoked a confrontation: in December 1845 they crossed the Sutlej river into British territory and advanced upon the Company forces. The resulting First Sikh War was a quick one: two inconclusive battles were fought on the British side of the Sutlej before the decisive engagement at Sobraon in February 1846 allowed the British army to cross the river and force the Sikhs into peace negotiations. The settlement that followed, left the Punjab as an independent state but gave significant powers to a new British resident at the court in Lahore and considerable influence to a network of political officers under his charge. For a time, the politicals were to the fore in the Punjab, and two uneasy years passed in which the Sikh army and British politicals chafed against each other. In April 1848 this tension burst into a rebellion against British influence in which two politicals were murdered and which developed into the Second Sikh War. Through the summer, the situation in the Punjab grew worse as the rebels gained adherents while the British waited for the hot weather to pass. In the last two months of the year, two indecisive engagements were fought, before a near disaster for the British at Chilianwala in January 1849, followed finally by a conclusive British victory at the battle of Gujarat in February. The Afghans had also entered the war after the Sikhs offered them Peshawar as an incentive; the closing movement of the war saw a British force advancing on the city to chase its new occupiers back into the Khyber Pass. Peshawar had suddenly increased in strategic importance, and Britain would not countenance its returning to Afghanistan.

The consequence of the Second Sikh War was annexation of the Punjab to the British Raj. The Company frontier was advanced to within a rifle shot of the great mountain barrier between India and Afghanistan; the furthest outpost of British rule in India stood just beyond Peshawar, at Jamrud Fort. The Land of Five Rivers was in British hands and the empire of the Sikhs—slow in its rise and brief in its glory—was ended. Along with signing away his rich kingdom, Maharajah Dalip Singh was required to surrender the Koh-i-Noor.

For the next three decades, the Khyber Pass remained in Afghan control while the British guarded Peshawar and the plains. In these years, the British launched numerous minor expeditions against the local tribes, a column of soldiers regularly being sent into the mountain valleys to hunt down malefactors or burn a village in retaliation for petty theft or disturbances. No armies, however, passed through the Khyber—the peace with Afghanistan held. This frontier quietude became of crucial importance during the Great Mutiny that broke out among the Indian soldiers of the Company army in 1857. This was an unparalleled challenge to British rule in India that looked likely to bring the Raj to an end and that certainly exposed its vulnerability to internal rebellion. A simultaneous invasion from outside would have multiplied the difficulties faced by the small and beleaguered British forces, and many feared at the time that the Afghans would descend the Khyber Pass to recover Peshawar and seize territory in the Punjab. However, Dost Muhammad, still king in Kabul, stood by his treaty obligations. Eventually, after months of vicious fighting and awful bloodshed on both sides, the Mutiny was put down and British rule forcibly restored. The biggest casualty of the war was the Honorable East India Company itself: after a shock of such magnitude, the government in London decided to end the curious circumstance of a company of merchants ruling an empire, and India became a crown possession. The Mughal dynasty was a casualty also. Having been proclaimed as king by the mutineers in Delhi, the old emperor Bahadur Shah was removed when the British restored their power, becoming the last in a line of emperors that stretched back to Babur. In 1876, Queen Victoria would be given the title of Empress of India—without, of course, ever having set foot in the Subcontinent.

It was not long after the Mutiny that fresh hints of Asian tension with Russia emerged: in the 1860s, the Russians continued to advance through Central Asia. Just as British politicals had done much to extend the British frontier in India, so too did ambitious Russian frontier soldiers and agents do much to advance their own borders; Tashkent and Samarkand—the old heart of the empire of Timur—fell to the Tsar, and the frontier of the Russian Empire reached the Oxus river. Alongside fresh disruption in Afghanistan following the death of Dost Muhammad in 1863, these Russian gains raised suspicions about their intentions toward India.

In the summer of 1878, an uninvited Russian mission entered Afghanistan amid tension between Russia and Britain over affairs in Europe; although Sher Ali, the new Afghan king, pleaded with them to return to Russia, some members of the party remained in Kabul long enough to raise British irritation. In response, Britain insisted that its own mission must be accepted, and a delegation set out under the charge of Sir Neville Chamberlain with a strong escort of soldiers and without waiting for assent from the Afghans; Sher Ali wanted neither Russians nor British in Kabul, and was caught unhappily between two powerful forces. On September 3, 1878, Sir Neville attempted to lead his mission into the Khyber Pass, but they were denied entry by the tribes. Unable to force a passage, and taking affront at the slight to British dignity, the Chamberlain mission returned unsuccessful. This trivial event was the trigger for the Second Afghan War.

Sher Ali was issued a hurried ultimatum: apologize for the insult to British pride and accept a permanent British mission in Kabul, or face war. Finding himself in a delicate situation, Sher Ali decided to accept a British representative in his capital, but by the time his reply was received the deadline had been reached and war was under way. The British had made ready long before: three forces were waiting to advance, and set out to invade Afghanistan on November 21, 1878. One army of 12,000 men under General Stewart struck from the south, reprising the 1839 invasion to capture Kandahar, while General Roberts fought his way along the Kurram valley with a smaller column of 6,500. The principal force, however, set off to advance through the Khyber Pass under the command of General Sam Browne: 15,000 men massed at Jamrud and then marched out to force the Pass.

General Browne and his army were allowed to enter the Khyber and continued forward for several miles: the principal Afghan resistance was to be at Ali Masjid, the strategic center of the Pass. On the heights around Shagai, south of Ali Masjid, the British came under fire and their advance halted. With the Afghan army manning the fort and tribesmen holding the cliffs around it, the invading force was unable to make headway. Forced to deploy his soldiers for a major action, General Browne began the battle of Ali Masjid as an extended artillery duel, his own array of guns blasting against the modest Afghan armament. Surgeon-Major Evatt, an army doctor attached to the Khyber force, was a witness to this action:

> Wilson's elephant battery was in action against Ali Masjid from a level space on the Sherghai heights, and at intervals a shrieking 40-pound Armstrong shell went flying over the intervening valley, and either struck against the stony profile of the fort, or dashed against the masses of living rock behind it, leaving a great white patch where it struck, and a few missing both fort and rock fell behind Ali Masjid in a gorge where a number of Afghan troops were under canvas, and suffered some loss from the fire.

Next, an attempt was made to turn the flank of the Afghan position by sending columns through the mountains. This effort failed after the territory proved intractable and denied passage to those who lacked knowledge of its secret trails and pathways. With the end of the winter day approaching, Browne launched a direct assault on the high peaks that formed the flanks of the Ali Masjid position, but this failed also and the army was in some confusion as night fell. Messengers struggled to find General Browne amid the disorder and over the unknown ground. Despite the failure of the assault, however, the British situation improved with daybreak: the Afghans had withdrawn during the night, having been worn down by the heavy artillery fire on Ali Masjid. When British soldiers approached the abandoned fort, they found a virtual ruin, knocked to pieces by the Armstrong shells; around twenty artillery pieces lay among the wreckage.

With the opposition withdrawn from Ali Masjid, the British could continue on their way. Cavalry were sent forward to ensure that the passage to Landi Kotal was clear, and the army moved ahead once again. One voice urging rapid progress was Major Louis Cavagnari, the political officer accompanying General Browne, an intelligent and brave man with a delicate air and carefully waxed moustache. As the man responsible for the achievement of the policy goals of the invasion—rather than just a military victory—Cavagnari was keen to press on to allow a quick settlement with the Afghan king: the approaching winter would increase the difficulty of maintaining an invasion force in the country and raised the specter of the 1842 catastrophe. Browne and Cavagnari arrived at Jalalabad by the end of the year, but too late to reach a political conclusion.

Several months of frustration passed until the spring weather promised a return to action; negotiation was desired, however, by both Cavagnari and Yakub Khan, the new Afghan king (Sher Ali having died during the winter). They met for talks at Gandamak in May 1879, Cavagnari in his medals and spiked pith helmet and Yakub Khan in his splendid white uniform of European style, replete with golden epaulettes (see color plate 14). The resulting treaty seemed for a while to bring the war to an end: Britain was to gain control over the foreign relations of Afghanistan and would be allowed a permanent British mission in Kabul; Afghanistan would be paid a subsidy of £60,000 per annum by the British government. In addition, some border territory would be ceded to Britain, including the entire length of the Khyber Pass. It was thus through the Treaty of Gandamak that Major

Cavagnari secured the Khyber for Britain, taking the frontier of the British Raj to its furthest extent; following upon Zoroastrians, polytheists, Vedic Brahmins, Buddhists, Hindus, Muslims and Sikhs, the great gateway to India was in Christian hands.

Having negotiated the treaty, Cavagnari was to be the first new resident in Kabul, and he took up his post, freshly knighted as Sir Louis, in July 1879. With the crisis apparently resolved, General Browne withdrew his army through the Khyber Pass and General Stewart departed from Kandahar. However, the Second Afghan War was to become a reprise of the First: in September of 1879, with the main British forces safely back in India, the British Residency in Kabul was attacked by a mob of disgruntled Afghan soldiers and Cavagnari was killed as he led a counterattack against the assailants. Shortly afterward, the Residency was in flames and all the staff inside were killed. Although this action was not ordered by the king, his attempts to quell the disturbance had been so ineffectual as to be negligent and the British saw every justification for resuming hostilities. General Roberts and his contingent in the Kurram valley were the only British forces remaining in Afghanistan, and they fought their way to Kabul, seizing the city on October 12, despite pleas for peace from Yakub Khan. Vengeance was sought for the murder of Cavagnari, and Roberts— a diminutive and aggressive man—hanged anyone who was found to have any connection with the attack on the Residency: by the account of Roberts himself this was eighty-seven men, but was considerably more according to other British officers. Occupying the city during the winter, Roberts had to fight some desperate battles against the tribesmen who rallied against his force. However, British artillery and volley fire at the battle of Sherpore, just outside Kabul, in December 1879 allowed the British force to remain in place through the winter. General Stewart arrived in Kabul with his army, by way of Kandahar, in May 1880.

The war ended soon afterward. Abdur Rahman, an Afghan prince with solid Russian connections, was—somewhat surprisingly, given their motive for war—accepted by the British as king in place of Yakub Khan. General Roberts then marched south to avenge a British defeat near Kandahar before following the other British troops out of the country in September 1880. Although it seemed that British aggression had engineered precisely the end it had sought to avoid—namely an Afghan king friendly toward

Russia—Abdur Rahman proved to be a model patriot and a strong ruler, unintimidated by Russian pressure. With this new king in place, the Treaty of Gandamak continued in force: Britain conducted Afghan foreign affairs and remained the new master of the Khyber Pass.

Master only in a sense, of course: on the map, the Khyber Pass had become a part of the British Empire, but control on the ground was dependent on relations with the Pathan tribes who lived there and who could close the roads whenever they chose. Britain could man forts and guard posts throughout the length of the Pass, but the key to keeping it open was daily diplomacy with tribal leaders: subsidy, appointments, rewards and the threat of war were the means by which Pathan chiefs were persuaded to cooperate with the new regime and to keep the roads open. The raising of military forces from among the tribes—such as the Khyber Rifles, recruited largely from the Afridi Pathans of the area—was also used as a means of binding the local population to the British. Given the complexity of alignments among the Pathan tribes and subtribes, and their tendency to erupt into fighting for trivial reasons, such efforts at keeping the peace on the frontier often failed. On these occasions, a punitive expedition might be launched into tribal territory to burn villages, seize livestock and arrest truculent tribesmen until the *Pax Britannica* was restored. Between the Treaty of Gandamak in 1879 and 1900, twenty-one such operations were launched: the North West Frontier was the liveliest border region in the world. The worst outbreak of tribal disturbances in the Khyber came in 1897, when the British even had to abandon Ali Masjid. Military control was not restored until the following year.

These were the days that formed the British view of the North West Frontier: the soldier guardians of India manning their mountain posts in the searing heat of summer or cruel cold of winter, clad now in khaki, the famous red coat having been abandoned as too great an aid to the Pathan sharpshooter. In fighting clothes the color of dust, men from across the British Isles and the Subcontinent of India stood watch on the frontier, camouflaged against the dun hillsides, patrolling the creeks and valleys of the Khyber mountains. The Gordon Highlanders fought in the actions of 1897–8, scrambling up rocky slopes in kilts of dark green tartan below khaki tunics and wide pith helmets, Lee Enfield rifles slung across their shoulders, long tartan socks and bright white gaiters wrapping their legs and feet. This is the lasting picture that is celebrated with affectionate humor in *Carry On Up the Khyber*: the Highlander on the mountain border, struggling against the rugged surroundings and hostile tribes, making his spirited best out of a precarious situation, a slim line of defense protecting the British Raj.

The vulnerabilities of the frontier were again exposed in the spring of 1919 when Afghanistan launched an invasion of India—more for reasons of internal politics than considered strategy—and the Third Afghan War began. Although a British force at Landi Kotal served to block the principal invasion, fighting continued for some time in the Khyber itself and the surrounding mountain areas. The action on the ground was indecisive, and it was an innovation that propelled the war to an end: British aircraft bombed Kabul. This new technology had a particular value in the North West Frontier as it allowed the British freedom of movement and attack normally denied them by the difficult mountain territory. It also let them strike Kabul without the time and expense of mounting an invasion. Assisted by aircraft, therefore, the war came to an end in the summer of 1919 with little tangible result on the ground, although Afghanistan recovered control of her own foreign policy and in return surrendered the annual subsidy from Britain.

One lasting result of the Third Afghan War was the Khyber Railway. Military men had for many years desired a rail link to the furthest point of the frontier, and the difficulties of supplying and reinforcing British forces operating inside the Pass in 1919 turned minds once again toward a railway to the Afghan border. For a generation it had been considered impossible to force a passage through the broken mountains and sheer cliffs, but a masterful survey by Lieutenant-Colonel Gordon Hearn—later Sir Gordon—demolished this myth and construction began in 1920. The railway had been extended to Jamrud in 1901; that the final thirty miles to the Afghan frontier took six years to lay speaks of the tremendous difficulties facing the engineers. Three miles of tunnels and almost a hundred bridges and culverts were required; three million cubic yards of rock had to be shifted, much of it with dynamite; steep gradients and daring twists were wrestled out of the rock. By April 1926, the final section was opened. Although it was never continued into Afghanistan, the railway strengthened Britain's hold on the crucial mountain route.

It was during the 1920s that the British presence in the Pass was augmented by the construction of Shagai Fort, a large, low bastion of brown and red brick built on the heights south of Ali Masjid. Sitting in an open stretch of the Khyber, Shagai Fort was designed to increase the British manpower stationed in the Pass rather than close its narrowest parts; the fort at Ali Masjid remained garrisoned for the latter purpose. Sprawling across the floor of the Khyber and overlooking the road, Shagai Fort is manned in the modern day by the Punjab Regiment of Pakistan. Thus with the railway and the new fort in place, the British hold on the Khyber Pass was tightened in the 1920s.

It was not much longer, however, until British rule of the North West Frontier came to an end, not through outside invasion through the Khyber Pass but through withdrawal from India when the British Raj was wound up in 1947. Throughout the twentieth century, Indian participation in the government of the Subcontinent had been increased, each wave of reforms raising the status and responsibility of Indian officials until they amounted to an alternative government waiting for the opportunity to rule their own land. Opposition to the British had been growing too, inspired by Mohandas Gandhi and Jawaharlal Nehru, and hardened by outrages such as the Amritsar shootings in 1919, in which over 300 protesters were shot dead. The demands of World War II—in which the Indian army, over two million men strong, served with distinction—were a drain on British power around the world, and increased the likelihood of independence for India. It came shortly afterward: with pressure for a British exit from India growing, and amid worsening conflict between Hindus and Muslims, the British sped up their timetable for departure and the Raj came to an end in August 1947. Dividing the Subcontinent between the two principal religious groups, the British left and the Khyber Pass became the territory of the new Muslim state of Pakistan.

CHAPTER ELEVEN

Pakistan

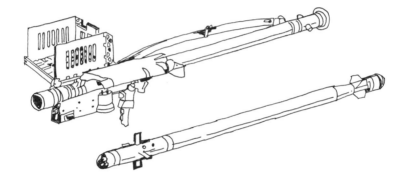

The Stinger missile

Roam the earth and see what was the end of those who came before you.

THE KORAN, 30:42

In the gun town of Darra Adam Khel, deep inside the Tribal Areas and outside the remit of Pakistani law, perfect replicas of modern weapons are crafted by hand in dozens of basic workshops. This tradition of gun making dates back to the British days, and the plentiful supply of cheap firearms from Darra has long helped the region to maintain its reputation as a wild frontier.

The main street is a simple line of scruffy flat-roofed buildings with shops that open on to the road. It felt like a distinctly masculine place: I could see no bright blue burqas, and a sullen sense of foreboding replaced the usual bustle of a market town. Bursts of gunfire rang out intermittently. Nobody—apart from me—seemed at all concerned about such shooting, and I soon learnt that it was simply buyers testing their purchases by firing into the air. It took me some time to get used to, however, and bursts of adrenalin kept running through me when gunshots flashed just meters away. A khasadar of the local force took charge of my (illegal) visit after we negotiated a suitable payment over numerous cups of tea. Several thousand rupees having changed hands, he escorted me to see the first of the simple workshops that are found all over town.

Sitting cross-legged on the bare concrete floor of a dim room, a white-bearded tribesman worked at a vice secured to a big block of wood before him (see color plate 15). He was filing a piece of steel that was locked between its jaws, and I could see that it would soon become an automatic pistol. Wearing a blue denim jacket over his shalwar kameez, he was surrounded by ordinary tools—hacksaws, hammers, measuring tape—and was using them with great precision. The gentle rasping sound of his tool was continually interrupted as he stopped to check his work with a ruler. Craftsmen in Darra work by taking apart a weapon of any kind, replicating every piece hundreds of times over and then assembling them into virtually perfect copies of the originals. This technique allows them to reproduce almost any available firearm, and I saw hundreds of AK 47s, Beretta shotguns, Heckler & Koch submachine guns, Mauser pistols and even old Lee Enfield rifles, all indistinguishable from those made in advanced factories in Russia, Italy or Germany. Over a century of collective experience has made the artisans of Darra experts in their work.

In another workshop, a bespectacled craftsman with a professorial air showed me the most sophisticated piece of machinery that I saw in Darra—a freestanding electric drill, a giant green apparatus with levers and winding wheels, apparently decades old but superbly maintained. He bustled around it proudly, firing it up and demonstrating its use by pulling a lever to drill a hole in a useless offcut. Every other workshop, however, relied upon hand tools, big vices and expert labor for what can be delicate tasks with some risk attached. I saw one young man assembling cartridges, pouring gunpowder into the empty shells and then gently knocking in the bullets with a hammer, a hazardous and painstaking process that is undone easily: while it took this man perhaps a minute to put together each cartridge, an AK 47 fires them at over ten rounds per second.

Scattered among the factories were numerous gun shops, each one displaying racks of weapons lined up neatly in great quantities. In one shop, over a hundred automatic pistols were hung from nails by their trigger guards. In another I saw row upon row of AK 47s—easily the favored product in Darra—and long lines of pump-action shotguns. Some shops were devoted to selling ammunition, and the cartons of cartridges were piled high in garish displays that made them seem like boxes of sweets. This deceptive quality only added to the unsettling experience, for the range and quantity of merchandise was a frightening sight: I saw enough modern weapons and ammunition to equip a small army, and it was all for sale to the first buyer. What is more, the area is almost entirely outside government control.

After my tour of the workshops and arsenals, we went to the edge of town to test the merchandise. As we walked, a dozen or so children joined us, drawn by the rare sight of a foreigner. Most of them were boys, but the group included two or three girls, young enough to go unveiled, and I learnt that they were all Afghan refugees, still unable to return home. Darra seemed an unlikely place to host refugees, and the children were clearly living in serious poverty. Besides the obvious financial hardship, however, the most shocking aspect of these boys was their easy familiarity with firearms and their eagerness to have them. They clustered around with great excitement as I took up position in front of the cliff face that was to be my target.

I began with a locally made replica of a Beretta pump-action shotgun. Next I tried a Mauser pistol, one of the many hundreds that I had seen displayed so neatly in the gun shops. Finally I fired the firearm that has become iconic of so many struggles around the world, good and bad: the AK 47. The khasadar handed it to me, and then passed across a full magazine of ammunition. I jammed the magazine into the weapon, pulled back the cocking handle and set the selector to automatic fire. Keeping the stock tight into my shoulder, I released a burst of fire into the cliff as the little boys scrabbled around to pick up the hot, spent cartridges that were being ejected on to the rocky ground. I slipped the selector to single fire and squeezed off a few lone rounds before returning to full automatic and emptying the magazine into the rocks. The glee on the children's faces was palpable, and they dashed about merrily, pushing each other and shouting happily.

My one-man live-firing exercise was over, and the boys clamored around, jostling for the chance of holding one of the now empty weapons. The khasadar passed them over without hesitation, and the boys adopted martial poses, calling for me to take their photograph, striving to look as warlike as their few years would allow; the girls stood aside shyly. As we walked back into town, the boys marched along like rowdy soldiers and puffed their chests as much as they could. Back in town, they handed the weapons over sadly. This enthusiasm for lethal firearms struck me as troubling, but it did not escape me that I was exactly the same. I had, after all, come miles out of my way just to loose off a few dozen rounds into a cliff face.

I took two lessons away from Darra. The first was the great power of the Pathan tribes, manifest in their easy access to modern weapons and the relative impotence of the government in the Tribal Areas. The second was more disturbing. The children of the region are growing up in a gun culture, surrounded by an atmosphere of continual, violent tension. There is small chance of their escaping that life when guns represent both status and wealth in a hazardous and poor environment. I can see no alternative emerging to replace them in the immediate future.

The Tribal Areas, of course, represent Pakistan only at its most extreme: although it shares many of the problems of developing countries everywhere, only in this region do guns count for so much and the government for so little. That being so, however, Pakistan—meaning "Land of the Pure"—itself came into existence amid great violence. On August 15, 1947, this new Islamic country was created from the Muslim regions of the British Raj. Partition, as it is known, was a reluctant political response to the escalating bloodshed between Hindus and Muslims as the departure of the British approached, and the emergence of India and Pakistan (along with Burma and Sri Lanka) was accompanied by dreadful birth agonies. Bengal in the east and the Punjab in the west—two of the principal provinces of British India, both mixed in the religious affiliation of their populations—were each split between Pakistan and India, prompting extensive and hurried migration as Hindus, Muslims and Sikhs sought to cross the partition lines into their preferred nation. Attacks on refugees were widespread and many died: perhaps a million people were killed and over six million crossed the new borders. Memories of those days of violence continue to inflame relations between Pakistan and India today.

The territory that is now Pakistan originally comprised the northwest provinces of the Subcontinent—Baluchistan, Sind, the North West Frontier Province and part of the divided Punjab—allied to the Muslim rump of Bengal far to the east. Thus the two parts of the state were separated by hundreds of miles of India, an uneasy circumstance that lasted until the eastern province became the independent state of Bangladesh in 1971 amid war with India. This territorial separation was not, however, the source of the most damaging Indo-Pakistani tension. That dubious honor is reserved for Kashmir, a beautiful mountain princely state under the British Raj that has become the cause of an unending dispute between the two powers and has lain divided between them ever since the last British soldiers left Bombay. Of the three wars that the adversaries have fought, two have been over Kashmir, and Indian and Pakistani soldiers still face each other today across the Line of Control that marks the de facto border in the province.

With the rivalry with India occupying Pakistan's attention since independence, the character of the North West Frontier changed: no invading army has marched through the Khyber Pass in the era of Pakistani control. In the years following the British exit, the line of partition, the border between the largely Muslim Pakistan and the largely Hindu India, replaced the ancient mountains as the front line of tension. The anxious relationship continues today, amplified by the mutual possession of nuclear weapons but lessened by occasional diplomatic thaws.

This is not to suggest that the North West Frontier is no longer important: it was propelled once again to prominence in December 1979 when the Soviet Union invaded Afghanistan in support of a faltering communist government in Kabul. All over the country, tribesmen, villagers and soldiers rose up to face the invaders. These Mujahideen fought with whatever weapons they had against the colossal power of the Soviet Union: Lee Enfield rifles dating from World War I were carried into battle against Russians armed with modern tanks and helicopters. This conflict rapidly gave the Khyber region a new identity as a Cold War frontier: with the Russians waging war in Afghanistan, the United States of America saw the opportunity to oppose its competitor and began supporting the Mujahideen resistance from Pakistan. Afghanistan thus became a proxy battleground for the superpowers and the North West Frontier provided the essential routes of espionage and supply. In collaboration with Pakistani Inter Services Intelligence, the Central Intelligence Agency of the United States worked to channel guns and money across the ancient frontier.

The harsh mountains of Afghanistan combined with the fighting traditions of the inhabitants to prevent the Soviet Union from dominating the countryside: despite their profound technological advantage, the Russians were unable to quash the Mujahideen and endured numerous ambushes and guerrilla attacks. The Afghans suffered greater losses, however, and had not the means to effect a victory against an invader so well supplied with men and the matériel of modern warfare. Although the Mujahideen seized some weapons from their communist enemies, they were still at a significant disadvantage, even after supplies of weapons and equipment began to trickle across the border with Pakistan. The greatest difficulty faced by the Afghan resistance was the crushing air power that the Russians could bring to bear: Soviet helicopter gunships—the Mi 24 Hind first among them—were able to launch shocking assaults on Mujahideen camps and to deliver murderous volleys on villages friendly to the resistance; operations could be mounted under air cover and convoys moved with protection, making ambush costly. The poorly armed Afghans had no answer to the Hinds. Thus the early years of the 1980s saw something of a stalemate develop in Afghanistan: the communist government continued to rule in the cities, but the Mujahideen commanded much of the countryside, and little headway could be made by either side. In 1985, as many as 118,000 Russian soldiers were fighting in the country but could not destroy the Mujahideen in their mountain hideouts. Meanwhile, the Afghan resistance was impotent against the Hind gunships.

Into this deadlocked situation stepped a remarkable figure: a roguish Congressman from Texas, Charlie Wilson. Tall, handsome and with a noticeable fondness for surrounding himself with glamorous models and beauty queens, Wilson cut a dash in Washington with his Texan charm, booming voice and propensity for scandal. He was also, however, one of the most powerful men in Congress through his membership of the Appropriations Committee—the body responsible for directing the spending of the enormous budget of the United States government—and particularly its subcommittees on Foreign Operations and on Defense. He was thus well placed to influence affairs when he became converted to the cause of the Mujahideen: in the summer of 1980, when Wilson first took an interest in the Afghan war, the CIA was funding the resistance with an annual budget of just $5m; when the war ended with the Soviet withdrawal from Afghanistan in 1989, the CIA Afghan spending was running at hundreds of millions of dollars a year, making it the largest covert operation in history. Although many people were involved in escalating the American commitment to the Mujahideen, Charlie Wilson combined a personal determination to beat the Russians in Afghanistan with the power to give the Mujahideen the means of victory.

Wilson supplied more than just money to the Afghan cause: undoubtedly his greatest contribution was in championing the pressing Mujahideen

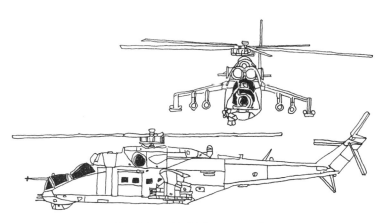

The Mi 24 Hind helicopter gunship

need for a defense against Soviet air power. While the Hinds continued to take such a toll on resistance fighters—and their villages and families—the stalemate would continue, at terrible cost to the Afghan people. Convinced that allowing the Mujahideen to take on the Hinds would change the war, Wilson sought to arm them with a weapon capable of bringing down a helicopter gunship. With his allies in the CIA, he worked to supply suitable anti-aircraft cannon or missiles, but with little success at first.

Wilson fought this campaign largely on the battlefields of Congressional committee chambers and meeting rooms in CIA headquarters, but as a dynamic man in the cowboy-adventurer mold, he was drawn to the actual field of battle. Causing great alarm among American and Pakistani security personnel, he began making regular visits to Peshawar, from where the CIA was running its operation. Not content even with this proximity to the war, Charlie Wilson wanted to be closer to the action. Consequently, it was in the spring of 1983 that the Texan Congressman visited the Khyber Pass with his companion Carol Shannon, a belly dancer posing—for the benefit of their conservative Pakistani hosts—as a member of his staff. Looking down on the border from the Khyber Rifles post at Michni, Wilson could see Soviet artillery shells exploding inside Afghanistan, the sound of gun-fire drifting faintly up the Torkham gap to where they stood. It was a tantalizing glimpse of a battle that he was desperate to escalate, and senior officers of the Pakistani army were on hand to discuss the war and their own military needs.

After this inspiring visit into the Khyber, the Wilson campaign still had some time to run until he reached his goal. The transformational success came in 1986, when the Mujahideen were supplied with the most sophisticated piece of anti-aircraft technology in the U.S. arsenal: the Stinger shoulder-launched surface-to-air missile. The decision to provide Stingers to the Afghans breached the previous guidelines under which this war had been fought: anxious to avoid diplomatic retaliation from the Soviet Union, the Americans had refused to allow any firm evidence of their involvement to be left on the battlefield. Pakistan, moreover, was worried about Russian military action across the North West Frontier, should Pakistani assistance to the Mujahideen and the CIA become too obvious or too successful. With the very best of American technology being placed in Mujahideen hands, however, involvement could no longer be denied: Stinger missiles manufactured in California were carried on mules across the mountains of the North West Frontier in the summer of 1986.

The change in the balance of power on the ground was dramatic. On September 26, four Hind gunships were flying in formation in Nangarhar province when they came under attack by Mujahideen armed with the new Stingers. Three were shot down. From this point on, Russian aircraft losses soared and the military situation was changed entirely: Soviet helicopters were forced to fly very high or very low and fast, directly affecting their combat value. Whereas Russian soldiers had previously advanced into battle in armored personnel carriers under air cover, they now had to throw out wide screens on foot for the same convoys, making them vulnerable to Mujahideen attacks. Morale among Russian soldiers began to falter as combat losses multiplied.

In Afghanistan the Stinger achieved an impressive kill rate of sixty-eight percent, but its psychological value was probably as great as its combat effectiveness: shorn of their ability to strike with impunity, the Russians lost the appearance of invincibility. Mujahideen confidence rose alongside the Soviet death rate, and they gained victories in increasing numbers. The invaders began to lose the war. Finally, in February 1989, the last Russian soldier retreated across the border in a damaging blow to the prestige of the Soviet regime; later in the same year the Berlin Wall came down and the Soviet Union deteriorated into oblivion shortly afterward. As the moving spirit behind the arming of the Mujahideen, Charlie Wilson can be said to have played an essential role in the winning of the Cold War.

With the Russians out of Afghanistan, the American commitment to the country disappeared. The communist government in Kabul struggled on without Russian military backing until 1992, when the various Mujahideen factions reached the city; in the absence of this common communist enemy, the resistance—already formed into rival groups—split apart and fought each other. Rebels no longer, they were now struggling for power over the country. It was into this unhappy situation that the Taliban burst. An extremist group of clerics, the Taliban successfully used their ruthless brand of Islam to gain and militate enough support to allow them to explode out of Kandahar in the autumn of 1994 and go on to conquer much of the country. After capturing Kabul in September 1996, the Taliban soon ruled most of Afghanistan, though parts of the northeast were still held by a Mujahideen grouping known as the Northern Alliance and other small pockets of resistance were scattered around the country.

It was under the Taliban regime that Afghanistan became a center of terrorism: Osama bin Laden—formerly trained and supported by the Americans when he fought against the Russians—and his Al Qaida organisation established training camps in the country to prepare Islamic fundamentalists for attacks on American and other western targets; many of the Mujahideen who had been armed and enthused by the United States as useful proxies in the Cold War now turned on their former patron. After Al Qaida bomb attacks on the U.S. embassies in Kenya and Tanzania in August 1998, the United States launched cruise missile attacks on suspected terrorist camps in Afghanistan; it was not, however, until after the September 11 outrages in 2001 that the United States once again became seriously engaged in the country. Swinging behind the anti-Taliban Northern Alliance and supporting them with air assaults on enemy forces, the Americans ensured that the Taliban regime was brought down: Kabul was captured by the Northern Alliance in November 2001, and a new government has been installed. Under President Hamid Karzai, this administration is seeking to reunite and rebuild the country after its long period of war and civil strife. It is an exceptionally difficult task, given the damaged national infrastructure, the millions of landmines that lie strewn around the countryside, and the vast amounts of arms and ammunition still in the hands of tribesmen and in the private armies of warlords.

The most significant problem remaining after the fall of the extremist regime, however, is the ongoing guerrilla fighting against Taliban remnants and Al Qaida militants: special forces from the United States and allied powers continue to sweep the mountains of Afghanistan for this residual opposition, engaging their motivated enemy wherever they can be found. However, the rugged landscape of the Afghan countryside provides plentiful hideouts and refuges—as it has for centuries—and the American forces are finding it difficult to finally quash the mountain resistance, just as the Russians struggled before them; the campaign will continue for some time. Two areas in which these guerrilla actions have taken place are close to the Khyber Pass: the Tora Bora cave complex to the west of the Khyber and the Waziristan tribal district of Pakistan to the south, in which the Pakistani army has been fighting against Al Qaida militants. The identity of the North West Frontier has changed again. Today, it is a battleground of the war on terror, as outrages in New York and Nairobi redound thousands of miles away in this ancient zone of invasion and exchange.

Epilogue

The eastern exit from within the Khyber Pass

Peshawar cantonment at dawn, when the cold morning air is not yet touched by the smog of exhaust fumes, seems like the cleanest city in Pakistan. I stood outside my hotel in the half-light, waiting for my driver. This was my last day in the country and, having absorbed everything I could about the invasions and migrations through the Khyber, I was setting off to make my own passage through the great mountain pass. If all went according to plan, I would see dawn in Peshawar and nightfall in Kabul.

Soon I saw headlights coming toward me. A car slowed then stopped and Shafi jumped out, ready to drive me through the Khyber Pass to the Afghan border. Rubbing his hands against the cold and wearing a sheepskin coat over his shalwar kameez, he hailed me a brisk good morning and bustled around, ensuring that I was safely inside his car with my rucksack. A sprightly tribesman in his sixties, Shafi was old enough, as he told me happily more than once, to remember the British days in India. He wore his Chitrali hat at an especially jaunty angle and grey bristle peppered his chin.

We drove to the Khyber Political Agency at the edge of town to collect an armed guard. Many khasadars (tribal police) sat around the courtyard completing their morning preparations, cleaning their firearms or having breakfast; one of them was detailed to accompany us and climbed into the backseat of the car with his AK 47, looking alert despite the early hour. With our protection in place, we set off on the Khyber road heading west out of Peshawar. The town was warming up as the sun began to appear, and I saw early risers in the streets, clad for the cold weather. The ubiquitous auto-rickshaws were gathering in packs also, but not yet finding much custom. Shafi chattered gaily beside me in florid English as we passed the university and then Smugglers' Bazaar. Assuming that I had not been tempted into breaking the law by going there, he told me that it was a wonderful market where all the best modern things could be bought—watches, clothes, electrical goods—"but not guns or hashish, oh no Sahib, nothing like that . . . ." A little further on there was a huge refugee camp of dispossessed Afghans, brown mud huts stretching across many acres of otherwise undeveloped land. As the refugees return home in increasing numbers, the homes they leave behind are destroyed by the government, and thus great swathes of the camp lay flattened, as if a war zone. Crude wooden items, worked by the refugees, were offered for sale by the roadside—besides benches and tables, a large number of coffins was displayed to passing traffic.

This sight—a symbol of death against a scene of conflict—turned my mind to what lay beyond the Khyber, to my idea of Afghanistan. The Westerner learns from the media that the country is a land of severe religion, acute violence and daily hardship, and I wondered about the safety of my plan to drive to Kabul: remnants of the Taliban remained active in the east of the country, especially around the border with Pakistan, and several foreigners had recently been kidnapped and killed. Incidents of this sort were not uncommon, and intermittent fighting continued between U.S. forces and Al Qaida or Taliban militants. There was thus some risk in traveling through the area, but it was a calculated one: I expected to travel only during daylight and would be in Kabul before dusk; I had been assured that the principal road from the border crossing to the capital was reasonably safe. Moreover, this journey had acquired an importance for me that transcended risk: this was the realization of a personal ambition that I had long cherished. I had immersed myself in the Khyber crossings of the great conquerors and the civilizations they had dragged in their wake; now I was emulating them in my own tiny way, a passage meaningless to history but very meaningful to me. Kabul was my goal and I needed to get there to complete my adventure.

As we passed Jamrud Fort, I saw once again the inviting gap in the mountains that forms the mouth of the Khyber Pass, lit by the rising sun behind us. Stretched across the mile of road ahead, I could see many Pakistani soldiers—more than a hundred—tramping toward the breach.

Perhaps they were setting off to comb the tortuous mountains that surround the Khyber, searching for Al Qaida militants or the recalcitrant tribesmen who assist them. The Tribal Areas are difficult territory for such operations and the government of Pakistan has found it no easier to exert its will there than did the British and the many other rulers before them.

We overtook the final soldiers and the great mountain gates were before us, looming over the road on both sides, then suddenly we were inside the Pass. Shafi gunned the engine into the first of the rising curves of road, and I stared about us trying to capture a picture of everything at once: the sunlight—now full—on the dusty rocks, the clear blue sky behind the sharp ridges above, the first of the many forts looking down on the road. Soon we came to Shagai Fort, its red brick walls bright against the faded earth and stone. Nothing could be seen of its inhabitants; I imagined them to be at a morning parade or inspection, but we did not slow to find out: this time, I was not in the Khyber as a sightseer but as a traveler and I had another driver waiting for me over the border inside Afghanistan.

We drove onward as quickly as Shafi's car would take us, and as the traffic would allow. The road was busy with trucks at this early morning hour: those driving into Afghanistan set off promptly to ensure that their journeys are completed before dusk. The roads of eastern Afghanistan are an uncertain place at the best of times; after nightfall they become very dangerous, preyed upon by the few remaining Taliban fighters or tribesmen loyal to Al Qaida. There was a clear sense of urgency on the road, a cheerful determination to press on and accept no delay. The big trucks, however, old and polluting vehicles that seemed to have been kept in service by vigorous and creative repairs over decades, were holding us back, and Shafi was frustrated at our slow speed.

Overtaking a shuddering truck, we zoomed into the Ali Masjid gap, Shafi's car made insignificant by the mountains around us. With the cliff faces just a few feet away as we passed through, and the slow traffic hampering the road, I thought again about the enormous armies that had squeezed their way through this constriction. Given the hazards involved in marching an army along such a route, it is remarkable that so many successful invasions, both of India and of Afghanistan, have been dependent upon it.

The regimental insignia dotted the rocks above the road as we wound along. These reminders of British rule of the Khyber seemed even more alive, perhaps because I was making my own journey through the Pass, perhaps because Shafi served as a living connection to the days of the Raj. When he was a boy, the soldiers commemorated by these memorial stones might have marched this very road. As the Pass opened out after Ali Masjid, we saw a reminder of a much older history: the Buddhist stupa. Beneath it, in the shadows along the side of the road, a line of soldiers strode, bearing their firearms aggressively. It was an incongruous tableau of ancient pacifism and modern firepower.

We drew near to Landi Kotal, clustered more densely with soldiers. Army jeeps passed us, machine guns mounted above: we were close to the border and the uneasiness was mounting. Shortly beyond the scruffy town we passed the Khyber Rifles post at Michni, and set off down the road that I had previously only looked upon: the final mile to the Afghan border. In a wide arc across the northern slope of the Khyber Pass, we descended toward Torkham, the little town that I had seen before only as a faraway jumble of tiny buildings at the base of the great mountain rising above it. Now, close up, the roadside was jammed with people and their piles of baggage. I could see strange combinations of belongings assembled together into neatly bound packages—a caged parrot lashed to what looked like a microwave oven—ready for hoisting aboard a truck or on to the roof of a bus.

I said good-bye to Shafi and the khasadar with much shaking of hands and then crossed the border easily: I was proud to find that I had passed as an Afghan, no doubt assisted by my unkempt beard, unwashed shalwar kameez and overall weather-beaten scruffiness. I was soon met by Wassi, my driver for the journey to Kabul, a prosperous Afghan with sleek cheeks and a modest moustache. I climbed into his jeep, excited to be in Afghanistan at last, and we set off for Kabul.

I had been inside Afghanistan for just a few minutes when we passed a tribesman strolling along the roadside with an RPG 7 slung over his shoulder—a powerful rocket-propelled grenade launcher that could destroy Wassi's expensive vehicle with a single round, and us along with it. This Russian weapon is a hangover from the Soviet invasion of 1979, and that such firepower should be carried so casually left me in no doubt that Afghanistan could be a violent place. I soon saw evidence of what such weapons could achieve in the hands of determined Mujahideen: a burnt-out Russian tank by the side of the road. The gun turret had come to rest pointing on to the road, and though the tank was long empty, it was unsettling nonetheless. I saw several such charred and corroding remains on the journey to Kabul, left where they were destroyed several years ago.

For much of the drive, the road followed the Kabul river, a wide and shallow slick of muddy water that can be used as an alternative route into India: Alexander the Great dragged part of his army along the banks of this river in 327 BC, striking north into the valleys that join it. Apart from a bad stretch where it became just a dusty track, the road was in fine repair and we made good time. There was virtually no other traffic, and we passed just a handful of vehicles in a full day of driving, having long ago overhauled the sluggish trucks. The empty road and sparse mountains—free of any sign of life—made Afghanistan seem entirely abandoned. Where were the people? What had happened to the countryside? The cause of this emptiness was war: over a quarter of a century of invasion and civil war has not yet come to an end, despite the presence of many foreign soldiers attempting to impose peace and security in the country. Many international agencies are also assisting reconstruction, but there is still much to do until Afghanistan becomes a stable and functioning state. Foreign armies and aid workers will be in Afghanistan for some time to come.

Out here in the countryside, however, neither could be seen; only the occasional lonely post of the Afghan army guarded the route to the capital—a machine gun mounted on a rock above the road, or an individual soldier sitting by a hut. This impression of neglect and devastation became overwhelming when we drove across the Shomali Plain, a once-populous area that suffered especially during the war against the Soviets. I saw the ruins of several villages, virtually destroyed in the fighting and abandoned years ago.

Only as we approached Kabul did the foreign soldiers begin to make an appearance, then suddenly come to dominate. We drove past some vast bases occupied by American and NATO forces, strongly fortified with concrete blocks. Armored vehicles and well-armed jeeps sped about, carrying these men in comfort as if the streets of the city were too dangerous to walk through. By the time we reached the center of Kabul, the outside presence prevailed. Big white U.N. vehicles dashed about with a show of importance, the tinted windows hiding the occupants and lending them an air of mystery. The number and variety of foreign officials made

Kabul feel like a restless place, as if something important was happening and nobody was allowed to relax.

Although Kabul was crowded with foreign soldiers, it was still vulnerable to guerrilla attacks by the Taliban, and during my time in the city several rockets were fired upon it randomly. Their goal was to spread panic and fear rather than to destroy specific targets: the chance that a rocket could explode anywhere at any time created an atmosphere of tension that was met with an impressive defiance. The city center was lively with markets and money changers, both doing an active trade and both showing determination to make the most of the opportunity to rebuild their city. There is a great deal to do. Much of west Kabul was destroyed completely in the Mujahideen infighting in the early 1990s and still lies in ruins. I saw acres of shattered buildings, the rubble strewn about where it fell a decade before and barely a whole building for hundreds of meters.

Amid the damaged and destroyed buildings, Kabul is full of curious juxtapositions resulting from the recent conflicts, odd conjunctions of Communism and Islam. A traffic policeman, dressed in a big Russian greatcoat and a military cap with an improbably large peak, stands next to a tribesman who looks like the epitome of the Mujahideen veteran, scarred and bearded and with a Chitrali hat pulled low over his forehead. An unveiled girl in tight jeans strides through a crowd of women in enveloping burqas.

This meeting of old and new was characteristic of Kabul, and I saw tradition at its most vivid at a game of *buzkashi*, played on a rough pitch near the center of the city (see color plate 16). Buzkashi—meaning literally "dead goat"—is reminiscent of polo, but more violent and with fewer rules. It is played by two teams of horsemen, but in place of the ball and mallets of polo, they use the headless carcass of a goat or calf: the game is begun with the decapitation of the unfortunate animal, and then the players seek to score goals by maneuvering the bleeding body to one of two goals placed at the ends of the pitch, leaning out of the saddle to grasp it with their hands. Another difference is the size of the teams: whereas in polo each side comprises just four horsemen, in buzkashi the teams are huge and barely regulated, and I counted over fifty horsemen on the field. For much of the time, this mass of horses and riders formed an immobile mass around the dusty, limp carcass. Horses were locked together as their riders yelled and thrashed around with their whips, lashing their own horse, those of others, and even opposing players themselves as they fought to get close to the corpse. This was not a game for the polite or timid. Then, suddenly, a rider would break free of the pack, carcass in hand, and race off toward the goal amid a flurry of shouts and hoofbeats. The scrum would dissolve into a pursuing string of riders, urging their mounts onward with desperate frustration.

Several players of one team wore long coats in deep burgundy, each with a large white circle on the back. Most players, however, were dressed haphazardly in their daily clothes, and it was thus impossible for an on-looker to tell who was on which team; I was unsure even if the players themselves could be certain amid the confusion. The crowd—including several members of the Afghan government surrounded by numerous bodyguards, and many off-duty foreign soldiers—looked on with slightly baffled curiosity, becoming really interested only when a horseman achieved a breakout and stirred the pack into action.

Looking back on this unusual scene, the similarities between the game of buzkashi and Afghan politics are clear to me: the hidden violence that flares up into sudden outbreaks of bloodshed, the uncertainty about who is on which side and the difficulty of knowing what is happening, all seem very like the past twenty-five years of war and crisis in Afghanistan. Moreover, the country has been neglected by the outside world until it spills out into the worst violence, just as the spectators in Kabul took interest in the game only when a rider cut his way out of the pack and dashed for the goal with the bleeding carcass. The peacekeepers and aid workers watching the game at its liveliest moments represent the international community, turning its sporadic attention to Afghanistan only when the uproar is at its height.

Suddenly, the exciting but confusing game was interrupted: a large black Mercedes limousine appeared on the rough pitch and drove right across the middle toward the main stand. The windows of the car were tinted and thus the occupant remained mysterious as it picked its way across the broken ground; the crowd hushed in anticipation. The car pulled up in front of the main stand, the door opened, and a murmur of excitement passed through the crowd: it was General Dostum, the power-ful militia commander. An ethnic Uzbek from the north of Afghanistan,

Dostum rules a large part of the northern region from his headquarters at Mazar-i-Sharif, and has been intimately involved in every stage of politics and war in the country over the last quarter of a century. He has proved adept at surviving the many minefields of Afghanistan, real and political, and was an essential ally of the Americans in ousting the Taliban in 2001. A big man, powerfully built, he mounted the V.I.P. stand and shook hands with a number of ministers and officials, before sitting down next to Marshal Fahim, the Northern Alliance commander and—at the time— defense minister.

Some time later I was fortunate to be invited to meet General Dostum with a B.B.C. reporter, and found him to be—despite a fearsome reputation—amiable and welcoming. With a thick shock of greying hair, a heavy moustache and densely thatched eyebrows, he had a round face and the eyes of a Turco-Mongol. Though I imagined that he could be quick to anger, he smiled broadly as he shook our hands. Through an interpreter, we chatted about buzkashi, and Dostum—something of an expert player himself—criticized the standard of the game that we were watching, inviting us to go up to Mazar-i-Sharif to see *proper* buzkashi.

The immense respect that Dostum commanded from his aides and officials struck me forcibly. He seemed to me to be treated like a conqueror of old; given the power that he holds in the north of Afghanistan, in a previous age he would indeed have become a king. Just as Genghis Khan and Timur did before him, Dostum raised himself to this position from modest beginnings, governing through force of charisma and of arms; in the twenty-first century, however, kings are not made as they once were, and no royal title has been added to his name.

Days after my meeting with General Dostum, I boarded a flight at Kabul airport and returned home to London. Having entered Afghanistan through the Khyber Pass, I was able simply to fly out of the country: in the age of flight, the mountain road has lost its essential importance. From 1919, when the British could bomb Kabul without marching an invasion force through the Khyber, the traditional purpose of the great Pass has been superseded by technology: in its recent campaign, the United States airlifted an entire army into Afghanistan rather than march it through the slim defiles that have been followed by generations of invaders. The stra- tegic focus of the North West Frontier has shifted from the critical line of advance through the Khyber Pass to a diffuse and nebulous zone of guerrilla warfare. Rather than contest a passage through the Pass, modern armies fight in all dimensions: jet fighters rove the mountains for militants, helicopters land soldiers wherever they please. The Khyber Pass remains militarized and is still defended as no other frontier in the world; the Khyber Rifles man their posts and continue to guard the Pass from the whitewashed fort atop Ali Masjid, but the enemy of the day does not threaten a grand invasion. No distant army from Persia or Central Asia, or from as far away as Greece or Mongolia, gathers to force an entrance into the Subcontinent as in previous eras. The age of invasions through the Khyber Pass is over.

It has, however, left its mark in every facet of life in modern South Asia. Pakistan itself, as a Muslim country, could not have come into being without Mahmud of Ghazni's invasions through the Khyber Pass. His were thus some of the most consequential of all passages of the gateway to India, infusing another of the great world religions into a land of faiths, already seeded centuries before by the Vedic precursor to Hinduism, Zoroastrianism and the polytheism of the Greeks. The traffic was in both directions; India was no mere collector of religion: the export of Buddhism—probably along the Khyber Pass—has had a profound impact on China, Japan and other Eastern countries, and upon spiritual exploration around the world in the modern day.

Aryan migrants brought religious inspiration to India in the very earliest times, entering the Subcontinent from Central Asia, most likely through the Khyber Pass. Their Vedic texts and epics provided a sophisticated foundation for spiritual reflection, a rich and plentiful cultural source out of which grew Hinduism, Buddhism and Jainism. Their language evolved also, from Sanskrit into the Hindi and Urdu of modern India and Pakistan. This early infusion was followed by many others: the passage of peoples has been the notable characteristic of the Khyber. The Persians of the Achaemenian Empire were followed by the Greeks who destroyed them; no doubt the Scythian blood of Central Asia remains on the Khyber today in the Pathans; the Kushan and White Hun nomads swept off the steppe into the wealthy lands of India, echoing their Aryan forebears; many generations of Turkic elites came to rule as Ghaznavids or Sultans of Delhi; the Mughals entered India to found a great empire.

The Khyber Pass provided the means for all these invaders to enter the Subcontinent to colonize and rule.

The impact of Khyber passages can be felt far away, as when British soldiers marched through the Pass to protect the profits of a faraway trading company in the city of London. Even in ancient ages, remote consequences could follow upon a Khyber crossing, such as the treaty in 305 BC in which Seleucus acquired the elephants that helped him settle the affairs of competing states far to the west, or when Jerusalem fell in 1244 to the wandering Khwarizmian soldiers of Jalal al-Din, finally dispossessed of his kingdom by Genghis Khan's march through the Khyber. In the modern age, it is strange to reflect that the Cold War was won in part across the North West Frontier, the Stinger missiles supplied by the United States defeating the Russian invaders of Afghanistan, a damaging blow against the Soviet Union that echoed around the globe. That a Texan congressman stood in the Khyber Pass with his belly-dancing companion in 1983, plotting the downfall of communist Russia, reminds us of the complexity of the world and its history. Many such curiosities emerge from the story of the Khyber: Greek kings ruling on the Ganges over a century after Alexander the Great, converting to Buddhism and infusing their own traditions into India; or the Hazara descendants of the iconoclastic Mongols of Genghis Khan protecting the great Buddhas of Bamiyan until their destruction by the Taliban in 2001, centuries after their ancestors had themselves devastated its Buddhist community; or Scottish Highlanders being drafted from their own mountains to guard the Khyber Pass for the British Raj.

Globalization is nothing new. It is not restricted to the big corporations and international markets of the current day. Before the advent of Islam and before even the birth of Christ, the Khyber Pass provided the conduit for a passage of ideas and influences that we might recognize today as globalization. Although the tempo was vastly slower, the process of mixing and blending was the same over the past twenty-five centuries as in the modern world. The common linguistic and cultural area created by the widespread use of Persian parallels the current dominance of the English language in business and diplomacy; just as a modern British company might have a German chief executive, a government department in Mughal India might be headed by an Iranian official. Migration, comprising conquering kings, soldiers and officials, but also artists and artisans, priests and missionaries, poets and philosophers, was widespread. Capital, too, flowed between continents, and whether it was earned in trade or seized as booty, it was analogous to the modern movement of monies and wealth around the globe. The syncretism at the base of all spiritual and religious exploration from the earliest times has some parallels to modern multiculturalism and inclusiveness. The global exercise of power is no more a feature of the twenty-first century than of earlier times: although the army of Alexander, or the Mongols of Genghis Khan, traveled at a fraction of the speed of an American cruise missile, they were no less effective at exerting force halfway around the world.

Throughout its diverse and concentrated history, the Khyber Pass has provided the essential thoroughfare for armies and the civilizations that followed in their wake. It has been at the center of political change and cultural fertilization for over two thousand years. If we know anything, it is that empires rise and fall, and we can only wonder what influences and inspirations may travel through the mountains in the twenty-first century to continue the story of the Khyber Pass.

Bibliographic Essay

Researching and writing a story that covers 2,500 years and several major civilizations requires some adroit handling of the available sources and some hard decisions about what to cover and what to leave out. There are considerable difficulties in reconstructing ancient periods, and these problems are compounded when dealing with nomadic cultures that often left no written material and a scattered archaeological record that is open to a variety of interpretations. Moreover, the constraints of a word count means that long periods must sometimes be dealt with in a few lines or even words, to the undoubted dissatisfaction of some.

Caveats of this sort have largely been left out of the text in the name of readability. In the hope of assisting interested readers in pursuing abbreviated periods or controversies that I have glossed over, suggested reading is detailed below. The emphasis here is on works that are readily available outside of an academic library, but I have also included some more obscure texts where they are particularly valuable in evidencing points that I have made. Not all works consulted in my research are listed here.

GENERAL WORKS

An excellent Indian history in one volume is Romila Thapar's *The Penguin History of Early India: from the Origins to 1300 AD* (London, 2003), which is highly recommended. For greater depth, and for material on the modern age, the *New Cambridge History of India* (various volumes, series editors C. A. Bayly, G. Johnson and J. F. Richards) is an authoritative source. The magisterial *Cambridge History of Iran* (seven volumes, 1968–1991, series editor H. Bailey) is an invaluable resource for Iranian history from the earliest times to the modern day. *Iran*, the journal of the British Institute of Persian Studies, contains many useful articles.

For an introduction to the people of the North West Frontier, *The Pathans: 550 BC–AD 1957* (London, 1962) by the distinguished British diplomat Olaf Caroe remains valuable; a detailed examination of the structure of Pathan society can be found in *Social Institutions and Leadership Organisation in Afridi Tribes of the Khyber Agency: a Micro-Level Sociological Study* by Noor Shahi Din (Peshawar, 1989). Interesting material on the Indo-Aryan debate, including a counter to the conventional argument, is available in *The People of South Asia: the Biological Anthropology of India, Pakistan and Nepal* edited by John Lukacs (New York/London, 1984). Although dated, Arnold Toynbee's *A Study of History* (Oxford, 1934–'61) provides many stimulating ideas about nomadic state formation and their role in history across centuries.

CHAPTER ONE—THE FIRST PERSIANS

Iran by Roman Ghirshman (English translation London, 1954) provides a very useful look at Iranian history from the archaeological perspective and *The Persians* by Alessandro Bausani (Florence, 1962) is an excellent single-volume account of Iran from the Achaemenians to the modern era. For translations of the inscriptions at Bisitun and Persepolis, see *The Persian Empire from Cyrus II to Artaxerxes I* by Maria Brosius (London, 2000). A particularly stimulating look at cultural exchange between Iran and India can be found in *Iranianism: Iranian Culture and its impact on the world from Achaemenian times* by Suniti Kumar Chatterji (Calcutta, 1972). *Zoroastrians: Their Religious Beliefs and Practices* by Mary Boyce (new edition London, 2001) is an excellent account of the faith and its history. *The Greek and Persian Wars 500–323 BC* by Jack Cassin-Scott (Oxford, 1977) and *The Scythians 700–300 BC* by E. V. Chernenko (Oxford, 1983) are recommended for material on the visual record. The Aubrey de Sélincourt translation of *The Histories* by Herodotus is available in a revised edition by John Marincola (London, 2003).

CHAPTER TWO—ALEXANDER THE GREAT

Conquest and Empire: the reign of Alexander the Great by A. B. Bosworth (Cambridge, 1988) and *Alexander the Great: the Hunt for a New Past* by Paul Cartledge (London, 2004) are both highly accessible and authoritative. *The Army of Alexander the Great* by Nick Sekunda (Oxford, 1984) is valuable for the military dress and arms of the period. *The History of Alexander* by Quintus Curtius Rufus is available in a translation by John Yardley (London, 1984) and *The History of the Peloponnesian Wars* by Thucydides in a translation by Rex Warner (London, 1954). The quotations are from Curtius 10.3.13 and 9.2.26, respectively.

CHAPTER THREE—THE MAURYAN EMPIRE

Chandragupta Maurya by P. L. Bhargava (revised edition, New Delhi, 1996) is a valuable biography. *Studies in Kautilya* by M. V. Krishna Rao (Delhi, 1958) provides useful material on Chanakya and his political philosophy, and the George Bull translation of Machiavelli's *The Prince* (London, 1961) is recommended. The quotations are from chapters XVIII and XIV, respectively. *Asoka and the Decline of the Mauryas* by Romila Thapar (revised edition Oxford, 1997) is essential reading for the period and includes translations of the rock edicts. *The Later Mauryas* by Hector Alahakoon (New Delhi, 1980) provides some interesting additional material. The *Dhammapada* is available in a translation by Juan Mascaro (London, 1973). The quotations are from verses 270 and 103.

CHAPTER FOUR—GREEKS AND NOMADS

The Rise and Fall of the Graeco-Bactrian Kingdom by H. Sidky (Jaipur, 1999) is recommended. Despite its age, *The Early Empires of Central Asia: a study of the Scythians and the Huns and the part they played in world history* by William McGovern (Chapel Hill, 1939) remains a valuable source for a neglected region and era. *The Art and Archaeology of Ancient Persia: New Light on the Parthian and Sasanian Empires*, edited by V. Curtis, R. Hillenbrand and J. M. Rogers (London, 1998) is useful on the Parthian influence on the Bactrian Greeks. For important detail on the numismatics of the period, see volume 5 of *Indo-Greek and Indo-Scythian Coinage (Establishment of the Scythians in Afghanistan and Pakistan: the Parthians, the dynasties of Otannes and Vonones, the conquests of Maues circa 130 to 40 BC)* by Michael Mitchiner (London, 1975). *Rome's Enemies (3): Parthians & Sassanid Persians* by Peter Wilcox (Oxford, 1986) is excellent for material on the physical remains of dress and arms. A highly readable prose translation of *The Mahabharata* by R. K. Narayan (London, 1978) is recommended and *The Complete Odes and Epodes* of Horace is translated by W. G. Shepherd (London, 1983). The *Milindapanha* can be found in an English translation by T. W. R. Davids (Oxford, 1890). The quotation is on page 6.

CHAPTER FIVE—THE KUSHANS

India in the Age of Kanishka by Manoj Thakur (Delhi, 1998) is a good introduction to the era and contains a useful summary of the controversy surrounding the dating of Kanishka. *Kushan Studies in the USSR: Papers presented to the UNESCO Conference on History, Archaeology and Culture of Central Asia in the Kushan Period* (Dushanbe, 1968) contains important material by various authors on the archaeological record and the role of the Kushans as transmitters of Buddhism to China. *New Light on Ancient Afghanistan: the Decipherment of Bactrian* by Professor Nicholas Sims-Williams (London, 1997) is a very interesting pamphlet and includes valuable material on the Rabatak inscription. For discussion of Buddhist literary remains from the period, see *Ancient Buddhist Scrolls from Gandhara: the British Library Kharoshthi Fragments* by Richard Salomon (London, 1999).

CHAPTER SIX—SASANIAN PERSIANS AND WHITE HUNS

Bausani and Ghirshman, as listed under chapter 1, are excellent for this period also. The *Art and Archaeology of Ancient Persia*, mentioned under chapter four, is valuable for the Sasanian view of the Achaemenians and for the interpretation of the Bamiyan mural. *The Early Empires of Central Asia* by McGovern is again of great value for the White Huns. Ammianus Marcellinus is available in a translation by Walter Hamilton called *The*

Later Roman Empire AD 354–378 (Harmondsworth, 1986). The quotations are from books 5.1.3 and 24.6.8, respectively. Procopius' *History of the Wars* and *Secret History* translated by H. B. Dewing are published in seven volumes by the Loeb Classical Library (Cambridge, MA, and London 1914–'40). The quotation is from book 1.3.1.

CHAPTER SEVEN—THE FIRST MUSLIMS

Albert Hourani's *A History of the Arab Peoples* (London, 1991) is recommended for an account of the rise of Islam. Two authoritative works by Clifford Bosworth are essential reading for the Ghaznavid period: *The Ghaznavids: their Empire in Afghanistan and Eastern Iran 994–1040* (Edinburgh, 1963) and *The Later Ghaznavids: Splendor and Decay* (Edinburgh, 1977). *The Delhi Sultanate: a Political and Military History* by Peter Jackson (Cambridge, 1999) is useful for the Ghorids in India, and *Al-Hind: the Making of the Indo-Islamic World* (*Vol 2—The Slave Kings and the Islamic Conquest 11th–13th Centuries*) by André Wink (Leiden, 1997) is an excellent work for the early Muslim polities in India. See *Armies of the Caliphates 862–1098* by David Nicolle (Oxford, 1998) for useful insights into the military material culture of the age. I have used a translation of the Koran by N. J. Dawood (revised edition, London, 1995).

CHAPTER EIGHT—GENGHIS KHAN AND TIMUR

Excellent recent biographies are *Genghis Khan* by John Man (London, 2004) and *Tamerlane: Sword of Islam, Conqueror of the World* by Justin Marozzi (London, 2004). For detail on the nuts and bolts of each empire, see *Flexibility and Limitation in Steppe Formations: the Kerait Khanate and Chingis Khan* by Isenbike Togan (Leiden, 1998) and *The State under Timur: a Study in Empire Building* by Syed Jamaluddin (Delhi, 1995). Jackson and Wink, as listed under chapter seven, are very good for the Sultanate of Delhi and the impact on India of both conquerors. For the visual record, *The Mongols* by Stephen Turnbull (Oxford, 1980) and *The Age of Tamerlane* by David Nicolle (Oxford, 1990) are recommended. *The Secret History of the Mongols* has been translated and adapted by Paul Khan (Boston, 1998). *Tamburlaine the Great* by Christopher Marlowe is available in numerous editions; I have used the Manchester University Press edition of 1998 and the quotations are from Part I, act 3, scene 1 and Part II, act 4, scene 1. The letter of the Master of the Hospitallers, William de Chateauneuf, to Lord de Merlai is from Matthew Paris's *Chronica Majora,* translation by J. A. Giles (vol. 1, London, 1852, page 497).

CHAPTER NINE—MUGHALS AND SIKHS

A recommended single-volume history of the Mughal dynasty is *The Mughal Throne* by Abraham Eraly (London, 2003). The last days of the Sultanate of Delhi are well covered in *Twilight of the Sultanate* by K. S. Lal (Delhi, 1979) and the military aspects of the Mughal era, including the battle of Panipat, in *Armies of the Great Mughals 1526–1707* by R. K. Phul (Delhi, 1978). *Mughal India and Central Asia* by R. C. Foltz (Karachi, 1998) is very valuable for the Mughal attitude toward Central Asia. An authoritative source for Sikh history is the work of Huw McLeod: four classic books are collected together under the title *Sikhs & Sikhism* (Delhi, 1999), which also provided the quotation from the *B40 Janam Sakhi. The Sikh Empire 1708–1849* by P. S. Data (Delhi, 1986) is useful for the politics of Sikh rise and decline. *Nadir Shah in India* by Sir Jadunath Sarkar (Calcutta 1925, reprinted 1973) is helpful for details of his invasion. *Mughul India 1504–1761* by David Nicolle (Oxford, 1993) is good for military dress and armaments of the period. Various editions of the *Baburnama* are in existence, and I have used the version edited by Wheeler Thackston (Oxford, 1996). *The Commentary of Father Monserrate* is available in a translation by J. S. Hoyland (Oxford, 1922).

CHAPTER TEN—THE BRITISH RAJ

For the story of the political officers who conducted British policy on the North West Frontier, see Charles Allen's excellent *Soldier Sahibs* (London, 2000), including an account of the death of Alexander Nicholson. A magisterial overview of British strategy toward the frontier region can be found in *Strategies of British India: Britain, Iran and Afghanistan, 1798–1850* by Malcolm Yapp (Oxford, 1980). A substantial number of British soldiers and officials left personal accounts of their experience on the frontier and in the Afghan wars, including *General Gilbert's Raid to the Khyber* by R. W. Bingham (Calcutta, 1850); *The Death March through the Khyber Pass in the Afghan Campaign 1878–79* by Surgeon-Major G. J. H. Evatt (Calcutta, 1891); and *The Pathan Borderland: a consecutive account of the people on and beyond the Indian frontier from Chitral to Dera Ismail Khan* by C. M. D. Enriquez (2nd edition, Calcutta, 1921), which also provided the quotation by Captain Wood about Colonel Leslie. *Queen Victoria's Enemies vs India* by Ian Knight (Oxford, 1990) and *North West Frontier 1837–1947* by Robert Wilkinson-Latham (Oxford, 1977) are valuable for military dress of the period. For detail of the Khyber railway, see *Couplings to the Khyber: the Story of the North Western Railway* by P. S. A. Berridge (Newton Abbot, 1969) and *Permanent Way Through the Khyber* by Victor Bayley (1934). The poems of Rudyard Kipling, including *The Young British Soldier* and *Arithmetic on the Frontier*, are available in various editions, for example the Wordsworth Poetry Library *The Collected Poems of Rudyard Kipling* (Ware, 1994).

CHAPTER ELEVEN—PAKISTAN

For the story of U.S. assistance to the Mujahideen in the 1980s, see *Charlie Wilson's War* by George Crile (New York, 2003). *Ghost Wars* by Steve Coll (London, 2004) is an admirably full account of the CIA involvement in Afghanistan up to September 11, 2001. *The Fateful Pebble: Afghanistan's Role in the Fall of the Soviet Empire* by Anthony Arnold (California, 1993) and *Parallels: the Soldier's Knowledge and the Oral History of Contemporary Warfare* by J. Hansen, S. Owen and M. Madden (New York, 1992) are both valuable on the Russian experience in Afghanistan. Once again, I have a quoted from the translation of the Koran by N. J. Dawood (revised edition, London, 1995).

Index

Numbers in *italics* refer to illustrations